The illustrated
Children's
Bible

The illustrated
Children's
Bible

By David Christie-Murray

Illustrated by
Ken Petts, Neville Dear, and Norma Burgin

Grosset & Dunlap
A FILMWAYS COMPANY
Publishers • New York

Original edition published under the title of
THE ILLUSTRATED CHILDREN'S BIBLE
by The Hamlyn Publishing Group Limited

The text and some of
the illustrations reproduced in this
book were first published in 1974 in the paperback
Hamlyn Bible for Children.

© Copyright The Hamlyn Publishing Group Limited 1976
ISBN: 0-448-14293-7 (Trade Edition)

Library of Congress Catalog Card Number: 77-73187
PRINTED AND BOUND IN THE UNITED STATES OF AMERICA

Contents

Introduction

The Bible is not one book but a library of sixty-six, written throughout a period of over a thousand years. Several hundred years can be added to this thousand, for many of the stories in these books were old and handed down by word of mouth long before they were written. Just as you would expect a book written today to be very different in language and ideas from one of King Alfred's time, so the later books are different from the early ones.

The sixty-six books have been collected into one because there is a thread which runs through them all. The Bible begins with a story of the creation of the world and all things living. Then, from the peoples of the earth, God chose a single family, that of Abraham, his son, Isaac, and his grandson, Jacob. This family grew into the twelve tribes out of which the nations of Israel and Judah were formed. Their two kingdoms were tiny – together they were about the size of Wales, and, too weak to survive for long against the great empires which grew up round them, they lived as free nations for only a few hundred years.

Slowly, painfully, and with many slips back into worshipping false gods, they came to know truths about God hidden from the rest of the world. They made many mistakes and did many foolish and evil things; but they learned in the end that there is only one true God, who created everything that is – the Lord and Master of the whole universe.

They discovered that God is good and wants those who love and follow him to show their love by obeying him and living the best lives they can. They came to hope that one day there would appear on earth the Messiah of God who would bring God's rule to the world. They expected an earthly king, a great conqueror who would lead them to victory over all the other nations. So, when Jesus told them that he had come to bring the Kingdom of God to them, but that it was not a kingdom of this world, not even the closest of his friends understood him until after he had died and risen from the dead.

But, without knowing it, the Israelites of the Old Testament prepared the way for the Christians of the New: and if we were to read only the New Testament, as is sometimes suggested, we should lose more than half the story of the way God revealed himself to the world. For he had to do this little by little as men grew less savage and more able to understand him. They had to learn that peace is better than war and that God who loves all his creatures is better than a tribal god who leads his worshippers in battle against men led by other tribal gods.

The stories in this book are only a selection of

those to be found in the whole Bible. Most of them could not have been left out, but some of them could have been replaced by others. The stories here were chosen partly because they are complete in themselves, partly because one leads on to the next. That is why they should be read the first time in order: for in this way it can be seen that God works in history, and man learns more about him as the centuries go by. Favourite stories can then be read as many times over as you please.

Are the stories true? This is a difficult question to answer with a simple 'yes' or 'no'. Some of the stories that Jesus told, such as *The Good Samaritan* and *The Prodigal Son,* could have happened. But Jesus told them as stories, and whether they happened or not is not the important thing about them. What is important is that they teach how man should behave to his fellow men and how God deals with man. There are stories in the Old Testament that are like them. Some people think that they happened, others do not. But, like Jesus' stories, the really important thing about them is the truth they tell. If you read these stories after asking God in prayer to show you what they mean and then look for the meaning, you will learn about God and his ways of dealing with men, and you will discover in them the kind of truth that matters.

The name 'Jehovah' is an English spelling of a name of God so holy that no Jew would ever have allowed it to pass his lips. It has been used in many Old Testament stories here to distinguish the God of Israel from the gods of other nations.

Sometimes young readers of Bible stories are puzzled by phrases such as 'God said to Moses'. How did God speak to people and why does he not speak to them now? The answer is that God spoke then as he does still. He guided men in their thoughts and feelings and the decisions they had to make. Sometimes they knew by instinct that God wanted them to take a certain course of action. Sometimes they realized long afterwards that God had been guiding them without their knowing it and described their experience by saying, 'God said to me'. The only differences between them and us are that they lived in an age when the earth was full of mysteries which they did not understand and which seemed to them to be the work of spirits both good and bad; and in the silence of the desert distances and the loneliness of mountain and moorland, God was so close to them that they listened for his still small voice and heard it clearly speaking within themselves.

God can speak to us today exactly as he spoke to the men and women of the Bible: but to hear his voice we have to learn to listen.

The Creation

Genesis 1

This is the story of how the universe was made.

When God began to create the universe, there was nothing to be seen. Darkness covered an endless waste of waters but the Spirit of God hovered over the deep.

God said, 'Let there be light.' He saw that the light was good, and separated it from the darkness, calling the light Day and the darkness Night. Evening came, followed by morning, making one day.

Then God said, 'Let a heaven appear above the earth, to divide the waters above it from those below.' This happened on the second day.

On the third day God said, 'Let the waters below the heaven be gathered into one place, so that dry land may appear.' And it happened so. God called the dry land Earth and the gathered waters he called Sea. He saw that this part of his work was also good.

Then God said, 'Let plants bearing seeds, and trees which grow fruit with seed in them grow out of the earth.' And this was so. Once more God saw that his work was good; once more evening and morning came, making a third day.

On the fourth day of creation God said, 'Let there be lights in the heaven. Let them mark out the days, the seasons and the years. Let them shine in the sky to give the earth light.' God made two great lights, the greater light to rule the day and the lesser light, together with the stars, to rule the night. So the sun and moon and stars were made and set in heaven,

and by their movements, day and night, and light and darkness were established on the earth. God saw that these, too, were good, and evening and morning brought the fourth day to an end.

Then God said, 'Let the waters swarm with shoals of living creatures, and let the sky under the vault of heaven be filled with birds.' God made great sea-monsters and every kind of living creature that moves in the oceans and rivers, and filled the skies with every sort of bird. God blessed these first living creatures which he had made and said to them, 'Let the fish increase and fill the waters of the world. Let the birds increase on land.' Again evening came and morning, and the fifth day passed.

On the last day of creation God said, 'Let the earth produce every kind of living creature: cattle, reptiles and wild beasts,' and the earth did so. Finally, God made man. 'Let man be made in the likeness of God,' he said. 'Let him be master of the fish in the sea, the birds in the air, and every animal and every reptile on the earth.'

When God had made man, he blessed him, saying, 'Be fruitful and increase. Fill the earth and be master of it and all the creatures in it. I have given you for food every plant on the earth that bears seed and all the trees that give fruit. To the birds and animals, too, I have given all green plants for food.'

It happened exactly as God said. He looked round on everything he had made and saw that it was very good.

On the seventh day God ceased from his work of creation. Because of this he blessed the day and made it a holy day of rest, a time when men might end their labours.

The Garden of Eden

When God had made man, he planted a garden in the land of Eden far away to the east, which was full of trees beautiful to see and bearing delicious fruit. Among them, in the centre of the garden, grew two very special trees. One was the Tree of Eternal Life, and the other was the Tree of the Knowledge of Good and Evil. If a man were to eat the fruit of the second tree, he would learn that good and evil existed and would long for ever-increasing knowledge, in spite of all the problems and difficulties that would arise.

God put Adam (which is the Hebrew name for Man) in the garden to look after it. He said to him, 'You may eat the fruit of every tree in the garden except that of the Tree of Knowledge, for on the day that you eat its fruit you will become mortal, and so will one day die.'

Then God brought all the wild animals and birds he had made to Adam for him to name, but for the man himself no partner had yet been found. God caused Adam to fall into a deep sleep. While he slept, God took one of his ribs, closed the flesh over the wound, and shaped the rib into a woman. Then he gave her to Adam, so that he should not be alone.

Adam called the woman Eve, a word which means Life, because she was the mother of all mankind.

Among the creatures God made, none was more cunning than the serpent. He asked the woman, 'Is it true that God has forbidden you to eat some of the fruit in the garden?'

Eve answered, 'We can eat any fruit except that from the tree in the centre of the garden. If we eat that, we shall die.'

'Of course you will not die!' said the snake. 'God has told you not to eat it because he knows that as soon as you eat that fruit, you will become like him, knowing both good and evil.'

Eve looked at the fruit and saw that it would be good to eat. She looked again, and the more she gazed, the more luscious the fruit appeared. She did not want to disobey God, but the temptation was too much for her. She

picked some fruit and ate it, and gave some to Adam, and he ate it, too.

The first result of eating the fruit was that they knew that they had done wrong. At last they understood what disobeying God meant. They became ashamed of their naked bodies and tried to cover them with clothes made from fig-leaves.

When God came to walk in the garden in the cool of the evening, they hid from him. 'Where are you?' God called to them.

Adam answered, 'I heard you walking in the garden. I was afraid because I was naked, and so I hid myself.'

'Who told you you were naked?' God asked. 'Have you eaten the fruit I forbade you to eat?'

Adam blamed Eve. 'The woman you gave me for a companion gave me the fruit, and I ate it!'

Then God said to Eve, 'What is it that you have done?'

Eve blamed the serpent. 'The serpent tricked me, and I ate the fruit,' she said.

Then God punished each of the three. To the serpent he said, 'You shall be more accursed than any other creature. You shall crawl on your belly and eat dust all your life, and men and snakes will be enemies for ever.'

To Eve he said, 'I will make child-bearing painful for you, yet you will long for your husband, and he shall be your master.'

To Adam he said, 'Because you listened to Eve and ate from the tree which I forbade you to touch, the ground will be accursed for your sake. You shall sweat, and labour, and suffer all your life in order to make your living from it, and you shall struggle unendingly against thorns and thistles to grow your food. In the end you shall die, and turn back into the dust from which you were made.'

Then God made clothes out of animals' skins for Adam and Eve, and he drove them out of the garden, in case they should eat the fruit of the Tree of Life and live for ever in their misery. The way into the garden was barred by angels with swords, the blades of which were like flames of fire, whirling and flashing in every direction.

So it was that man lost Paradise.

Cain and Abel

Genesis 4–6

It was believed that in the days when men first appeared upon the earth, they lived to a far greater age than we do now. Adam was nine hundred and thirty years old when he died and his descendants all lived to well over eight hundred years. So it was possible for Adam and Eve to have had many hundreds of descendants before they died, although we are told the names of only three of their sons.

The eldest was called Cain. He was the first baby ever to appear on earth, and when he was born, Eve, his mother, said, 'With the help of the Lord I have brought a man into being.' Later she had another son whom she called Abel. In the course of time, Cain grew up and became a farmer; his brother Abel chose the life of a shepherd.

A day came when they both brought presents to God. Cain brought some of the corn and fruit which he had grown, and Abel some of the first-born lambs from his flock. God received Abel and his gift with favour, but he did not acknowledge Cain and his present. We are not told exactly why this was, though we can guess that Cain had done something to displease God. For when he was angry and downcast after his gift had been rejected, God said to him, 'Why are you so angry? If you do well you will be accepted. But if not, sin is like a demon crouching at the door, eager to be at you, and it will master you.' But Cain took no

notice of the warning. He was sullen and resentful against God and jealous of his brother, and he waited for an opportunity to harm him.

His chance came one day when they were alone together in the open country. Then Cain attacked Abel without warning, and killed him, thinking that no one had seen him. But God knew what he had done and said to him, 'Where is your brother Abel?'

'How do I know?' replied Cain. 'Am I my brother's keeper?'

But God said, 'What have you done? Your brother's blood is crying out to me from the ground. That ground will no longer give you corn and fruit when you try to cultivate it. You will be accursed and banished from it, and condemned to be a wanderer through the world.'

Cain cried out in despair, 'My punishment is more than I can bear! You are driving me from the land I know and banishing me from your presence. I am to be a wanderer abroad, and anyone who meets me can kill me.'

But God put a mark on Cain to prevent his being killed. Cain then left God's presence and wandered far to the east, to settle in the land of Nod, which means Wandering.

But Eve had other children to make up for the two sons she had lost by murder and through banishment. We know the name of only one – Seth, which means Granted. He was the first to be born after Abel's death, and Eve said, 'God has granted me another son in place of Abel whom Cain slew,' and she was comforted.

The Great Flood
Genesis 6–9

As the descendants of Adam and Eve increased in number, so that where there had been tens there were now thousands, the terrible results of man's knowledge of good and evil began to be felt. Evil seemed much more exciting than good; and there was sadness in the heart of God who had made a universe that was wholly good when he saw men continually finding new ways to be wicked. He was sorry that he had made man, and he decided that he would wipe the human race and all living creatures off the face of the earth by bringing a great flood upon it.

But there was a man called Noah, who was the only one among all mankind who tried to live his life as God wanted.

God decided to spare him and his family, and said to him, 'The earth is full of wickedness and violence, and I have resolved to put an end to all that live upon it. Only you and

your wife and your three sons, Shem, Ham and Japheth, and their wives shall be saved. Build for yourself an ark, a great ship of gopher wood, three hundred cubits long, fifty cubits broad, and thirty cubits high. Make windows in it and a door in its side, and build it with three decks, each divided into compartments.

'When the time comes, you are to take into the ark one pair, male and female, of every beast, reptile and bird, except for those which are fit for human food, which are called clean; of every one of these you are to take seven pairs, together with enough food for them all. For I am going to send a flood of water over the whole earth, to destroy everything that lives, except you and the creatures that are with you in the ark.'

Noah and his sons did as God commanded them, and began to build the great ship. How the men who lived round about must have laughed at them for working so hard and so long at a task which was apparently useless! But at last, after many months, the huge

vessel was finished; and seven days before God brought the flood upon the earth he warned Noah to take his family into the ark and load it with all the creatures he had collected. At the end of the seven days, God shut Noah into the ark just as it began to rain.

Never had such rain been seen upon the earth. It was like great waterfalls pouring out of sluice-gates in heaven. The waters of the oceans also rose, perhaps through volcanic action beneath the seabed, and colossal tidal waves overflowed the land, drowning and destroying everything in their path. Day after day after day it rained, until there was nothing to be seen as far as the horizon on every side but the ark, floating alone in a waste of water that buried even the mountain tops. Only Noah and his family and the living creatures with him survived.

After many days the rain stopped. The sea-bed sank slowly back, draining the water from the land. God sent a great wind to help dry the earth, and five months after the flood began,

God instructed Noah to build the ark from gopher wood, generally thought to be cypress, probably *Cupressus sempervirens*, the Mediterranean Cypress.

the waters started to subside. At last Noah felt the ark grate on solid ground as it lurched and settled on Mount Ararat in the land of Armenia.

But he did not yet dare try to disembark. Only the tops of the mountains had appeared above the water as yet. After waiting a while, he sent out a raven to see if it could find anywhere to settle. It did not return, and a week later Noah sent out a dove. The bird flew back on the same day, for there was nowhere for it to rest dryfoot, and Noah knew that he had still to be patient.

For another week he waited, then again sent out the dove. All day it was away; but when evening came it returned with a freshly-plucked olive leaf in its beak. So Noah realized that small trees were showing above the surface of the water. Seven more days he waited and again sent out the dove. This time it did not return, and Noah knew that it was time to leave the ark. He opened the hatch, pushed away its covering and looked out. As far as he could see in every direction, the ground was dry.

Then God said to Noah, 'Leave the ship with your family and let out all the creatures so that they swarm on the earth and increase.'

God blessed Noah and his sons with almost the same blessing that he had given Adam.

'Be fruitful and multiply and refill the world with people. All living creatures will fear and dread you and you shall have power over them. They shall be your food, as once I gave plants to feed you.'

The first thing Noah did on leaving the ark was to thank God by sacrificing to him some of the clean birds and animals of which he had taken seven pairs into the ark. God accepted the sacrifice and said, 'Although man's mind is always inclined to wickedness, I shall never again curse the ground nor destroy every living creature in a flood. As a sign that I shall keep my promise, I shall set my rainbow in the clouds when I send them over the sky, to remind me of the lasting agreement that I have made with every living creature upon the earth.'

Noah lived long enough after the flood to see his descendants peopling the earth with the ancestors of all the nations which lived in the lands known to the writers of the Bible. Among them was the father of the nation of Israel, Abram, a direct descendant of Shem, who was born fifty years before Noah died, in a city called Ur of the Chaldees.

19

God's Promise to Abram

Genesis 12

With the story of Noah we leave the history of all mankind and begin that of God's Chosen People, Israel, of whom Abram was the founder and father. For some time, Abram with his wife, Sarai, his father, Terah, and his nephew, Lot, lived at Ur. It is thought today that there was a change of religion in the city, so that Terah and his family, remaining faithful to their God, were forced to leave it. For several months they travelled northwards to a city called Harran, where God – they felt – was worshipped in the right manner. But even Harran was not to be Abram's final home.

'Leave your country, family and friends,' God said to him, 'and go to a land that I shall show you. I will bless you and make a great nation of your descendants.'

So Abram said goodbye to those with whom he had lived all his life, and went away with his flocks and herds and servants, taking only Sarai and Lot of his own family with him. The nomad tribe moved westwards, seeking pasture for the cattle, and God guided their wanderings till they came to the land of Canaan. There God revealed to Abram that this was the country which he would one day give to his descendants.

Several times more in the years that followed, God repeated his promise. The first occasion was just after Abram and Lot had agreed to part, because their herds were too numerous to share the same pasture.

'Look in every direction,' God said to Abram. 'I will give all the land that you can see to you and your descendants for ever. They shall be as numerous as the dust of the earth. Travel through the length and breadth of the land, for I have given it all to you!'

Later on, God appeared to Abram in a dream, saying, 'I shall bless you and reward you richly.'

Sarai was too old to have children, and Abram was unhappy, because if a man did not have a son to carry on the family, it was regarded in those days as one of the saddest fates that could befall him.

But to reassure him, God told Abram to look at the stars, and said, 'Count them if you can. Such shall be the number of your descendants.'

'How can I be sure that what you promise will happen?' asked Abram. 'And how can I

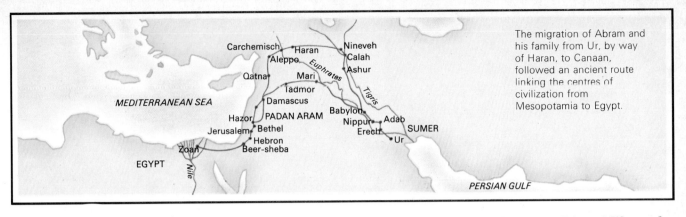

The migration of Abram and his family from Ur, by way of Haran, to Canaan, followed an ancient route linking the centres of civilization from Mesopotamia to Egypt.

know that my children's children will possess this land you have promised me?'

God told him what to do. 'Take animals and birds for sacrifice,' he said. 'Kill them: cut the animals in two and place the halves and the birds opposite each other. Then wait.

Abram did so, and kept watch over the sacrifice, driving off the birds of prey, until the sun went down. Eventually he fell into a trance. Suddenly he felt a great terror in the darkness. Then he heard the voice of God.

'Your descendants shall dwell in a land not their own, slaves to a hostile people for four hundred years. Then shall they escape and return to this land which I shall give them – a land which stretches from the River Nile to the River Euphrates. You yourself shall live to a ripe old age.'

The voice ceased. In the darkness, a smoking brazier and a blazing torch, symbols of the presence of God, passed between the pieces of the animals, and Abram knew that God had made a solemn agreement to keep his promises. For in those days, when two men made an agreement, they killed and cut animals in two as Abram had done, and made their promise after walking between the lines and meeting each other. The meaning of the ritual was, 'If I break this agreement, may I be killed like these animals.'

Abraham and Isaac
Genesis 18

Some time after the making of the covenant, God changed Abram's name to Abraham, and Sarai's to Sarah. Abraham's new name meant Father of a multitude, and that of Sarah, Princess. He spoke to Abraham again through three messengers, who told him Sarah would give birth to a son the following spring, although she was long past the age of child-bearing. Sarah overheard their message and laughed, but they reproached her, saying that nothing was too hard for God to bring about.

When the spring came, Sarah did indeed give birth to a baby boy. She called him Isaac, which means Laughter, for she said, 'God has given me good reason to be happy, and all who hear of it will rejoice with me.' Abraham had already had a son by another wife, Sarah's

Egyptian handmaid, Hagar; for when Sarah had borne no children, she had urged her husband to marry another wife, as was allowed in those days. The second wife was regarded as inferior to the first, and if the first wife had had no children, she could, by ancient custom, regard the children of the second wife as her own. Hagar's son was called Ishmael.

At last the day came when Abraham decided to celebrate the fact that Isaac was no longer a baby but a little boy. Until Isaac's birth, Ishmael had been Abraham's heir. But now all hope of succeeding him had gone, and in his anger Ishmael mocked his little brother. Sarah, seeing him taunt Isaac, demanded that Abraham send Hagar and Ishmael away for ever. Abraham did so the next morning; and though the mother and son came very near death in the desert, God saved them. Ishmael grew up to be the ancestor of the Arabs, as Isaac was the founder of the Israelites.

Although Abraham's faith had been tested

by having to wait many years for the birth of a son, God decided to test him once again.

'Take your son, Isaac, to a hill I shall show you,' he said, 'and there offer him as a sacrifice.'

Obediently, Abraham set off the next morning, taking firewood for the sacrifice loaded on his ass, and accompanied by Isaac and two servants. For three days they travelled, until Abraham saw in the distance the place chosen by God. Leaving the servants behind, he and Isaac climbed the hill, carrying the wood, the fire, and the knife for the sacrifice.

'Father,' said Isaac, puzzled, 'we have fire and wood, but where is the lamb for the sacrifice?'

'My son,' Abraham replied, 'God will provide himself with a lamb.' The two went on until they reached the spot which Abraham knew instinctively was to be the place of sacrifice. In agony of heart and mind, the father built an altar from the stones lying around, arranged the wood on the altar, bound his son hand and foot, and lifted him on to the wood. The Bible says nothing about the grief of the father and the fear of the boy as he realized that he was to be the victim, but it is easy to imagine how terrible it must have been.

Then Abraham stretched out his hand for the knife with which to slay his son. He raised it high. He tensed himself for the downward stroke, when suddenly a voice called his name from the sky.

Abraham understood that an angel of God was speaking to him.

'Do not harm the lad! God now knows that you worship him sincerely since you have not grudged him your only son.'

Abraham looked up, and saw a movement out of the corner of his eye. It was a ram caught in a thicket by its horns. He took the animal and sacrificed it in Isaac's place, and he named the hill Jehovah-jireh, which means 'The Lord will provide.'

Isaac and Rebecca
Genesis 24

Many years had passed. Isaac was nearly forty years old. Sarah, his mother, was dead. Abraham, more prosperous than ever, was now extremely old. The time had come for him to see that Isaac married in order to carry on the family that was to become the great nation promised by God.

He was determined that Isaac should not marry a Canaanite woman, but instead a girl who worshipped the true God. So he called his steward, his most trusted servant, and ordered him to go to Harran and choose a girl from Abraham's own family to be Isaac's wife.

So the steward set out on his lengthy journey, reaching Harran one evening at the time when the women went to draw water at a well.

'Oh, God,' he prayed, 'when the women come to draw water, guide me to the girl you have chosen for Isaac's wife, to whom I shall say, "Please lower your pitcher that I may drink." If she replies, "Drink, and let me also give your camels water," then I shall know that she is the girl you want Isaac to marry.'

Scarcely had he finished praying, when a beautiful girl came to the spring bearing a

Both nose-rings and ear-rings were worn by men and women as decoration in the Middle Bronze Age. The weight of a ring was approximately six grammes.

pitcher on her shoulder. So sure was he that she was the girl whom God had chosen, that he hurried to meet her. He asked her for water, and she immediately replied with the answer he had prayed for. When his camels had finished drinking, he gave her golden bracelets and a golden nose-ring (which is to this day a betrothal present in Arabia), asking her who she was. When she replied that she was the daughter of Bethuel, Abraham's nephew, the servant praised God for leading him straight to his master's own family.

Rebecca, bewildered by what had happened, ran back to her family and told them of Abraham's messenger. Her brother, Laban, hastened to welcome him and brought him home, with his camels and companions. Food was set before him, but the steward said, 'I will eat nothing till I have given you my message.' He then told how Abraham had prospered, how Sarah had borne Isaac in her old age, how Abraham had sent him to find a wife for his heir from his own family, and how God had guided him to speak to Rebecca.

'This could only come from God!' exclaimed Bethuel and Laban. 'Take Rebecca back with you, and let her be Isaac's wife.'

Abraham's steward again praised God and gave costly gifts to Rebecca and her family. That night he rested. When he rose next morning he said, 'I must return at once to my master with Rebecca.'

'Let the girl remain with us for a week or ten days in order to prepare herself for her new life,' her family pleaded. 'Then she can go.'

'Do not delay me,' said the man. 'God has given me success and I must return.'

'We will ask Rebecca,' they replied, 'and do as she says.'

But Rebecca was eager to go at once to the new life for which she had been chosen. Her family blessed her, saying, 'Be the mother of many, and may your descendants conquer all their enemies!' Then Rebecca and her nurse mounted their camels and followed the man into the desert.

The marriage was happy. Isaac loved Rebecca, and Abraham died content, knowing that all God's promises to him were being fulfilled.

Esau and Jacob
Genesis 27

In due time Rebecca bore Isaac twin sons. The first born was covered with hair, so he was called Esau which means 'hairy', and his brother was called Jacob. Esau became a skilful hunter, who pleased his father by keeping him supplied with venison. Jacob, who was his mother's favourite child, grew to be a quiet man who preferred to stay at home.

Since Esau was the elder, he owned the birthright. This was very important in those days. It not only meant that he was heir to all his father's possessions, but also that he was considered to be the master of his brother.

One day Esau came in from hunting, hungry and tired. He asked Jacob to give him a bowlful of some lentil soup which he was cooking.

'I will only give you some of my soup,' said Jacob, 'if you promise to let me have your birthright.'

'I am dying of hunger – what use is my birthright to me?' said Esau, and he stretched out his hand for the bowl.

Jacob jerked the bowl away. 'Not till you swear to give me the birthright,' he said. So Esau swore a solemn oath that Jacob should have it. This showed how little he valued his great privilege. Then Jacob gave him bread and soup in exchange.

Years passed, and Isaac, old and blind, knew that he had not long to live. So he asked Esau to go hunting and prepare him a feast of venison. When he had eaten it, he would bless him.

Blessings and curses were regarded then as more than just simple wishes or words. It was believed that any good or bad wish would be fulfilled. If a father blessed his son, saying, 'Be lord over your brothers,' the son would in fact become his brothers' master.

Rebecca overheard Isaac promising Esau his blessing, and hurried to Jacob, her favourite son.

'Quick,' she said. 'Kill two young goats from the flock and bring them to me, and I will make them into a dish for your father. Take it to him, pretend to be Esau, and he will give you the blessing in your brother's place.'

'But if Father touches me,' Jacob answered, 'he will know that I am not Esau, and he will curse me instead of blessing me, because I have deceived him.'

'Leave that to me,' said his mother. 'Only do as I tell you.'

When the meal was ready, Rebecca dressed Jacob in Esau's clothes, and fastened the goats' skins over Jacob's smooth hands and neck. Then he went in to Isaac, taking the food.

'Father,' he said, 'here is your venison.'

'Who are you, my son?' asked the old man.

'I am Esau,' replied Jacob. 'I have done as you asked. Eat, then give me your blessing.'

'How quickly you caught the animal!' said Isaac, surprised.

'God brought it to me,' the cunning Jacob answered.

But Isaac was suspicious. 'Come close and let me touch you,' he said, 'to make sure that you really are my son, Esau.'

Jacob went to him and Isaac felt his hands. 'You sound like Jacob,' he said, 'but these are Esau's hands. Are you really Esau?'

'I am,' Jacob said. Then he gave his father the venison.

'Come near, my son, and kiss me,' said Isaac when he had eaten. As they embraced, Isaac could feel and smell Esau's clothes. Then he blessed Jacob.

'The smell of my son is like the smell of countryside blessed by God. May God give you dew from heaven and rich soil in your fields, and corn and wine in plenty. Tribes and nations shall serve you, and you shall be lord over your brothers. Cursed be those that curse you; blessed be those that bless you!'

Scarcely had Jacob left Isaac, than Esau returned from his hunting and brought in the meal he had prepared for his father. 'Eat, Father,' he said, 'and give me your blessing.'

'Who are you?' asked Isaac, confused.

'I am your elder son, Esau.'

At his words, Isaac trembled violently. 'Who then has already given me venison? I blessed him! Yes, and blest he shall be!'

Esau gave a loud and bitter cry. 'Bless me, too, Father,' he wailed.

'I cannot, for your brother has had your blessing,' said Isaac.

Esau wept bitterly. 'Twice he has cheated me: first out of my birthright, now out of my blessing. Have you no blessing at all left for me, Father?'

'I have made him lord over you. I have given him corn and wine. What is there left, my son?' replied his father, sorrowfully.

'Had you only one blessing, Father? Bless me, bless me, too!'

Isaac gave him what he could. 'You shall live far from rich soil and from the dew of heaven,' he said. 'You shall live by the sword and serve your brother; but in time you will grow restive and break his hold over you.'

Esau so hated Jacob for the trick he had played that he plotted to murder him when Isaac died. But Rebecca learned of his plan and, calling Jacob, she said, 'Fly to my brother, Laban, in Harran, and stay there until your brother's anger cools. When the time is ripe, I will send for you!' So, with Isaac's agreement, Jacob left; and his parents hoped that there he would be safe from Esau's anger.

The Adventures of Jacob

Genesis 28–33

Jacob fled from Esau's anger as fast as he could. Having journeyed on foot for several days, he arrived at a place where the hills of limestone rock rose above each other in the form of great steps. Perhaps it was the sight of these before he slept which caused him to dream of a great staircase reaching to the sky, with the messengers of God going up and down it to carry out their Master's commands. In Jacob's dream, God stood by him and repeated the promise he had made to Abraham. Jacob, he said, would be the founder of a great nation which would live in the land of Canaan. 'Wherever you go,' God said, 'I shall be with you, and will bring you safely home again.'

Jacob awoke, awe-struck and afraid. 'God is here,' he said, 'and I did not even realize that this was the gate of heaven.' He took the stone on which his head had rested while he dreamed, set it up as a holy pillar and called the place Beth-el, or God's House. After praying to God to protect him, he continued on his way.

Eventually he reached Harran and asked shepherds who were watering their flocks from a well whether they knew Laban. 'Yes,' they said, 'and look – there is Rachel, his daughter, coming to the well with her sheep.'

Jacob helped her to water her flock before he made himself known to her. Then he told her who he was. He kissed her and, overcome with emotion, he was moved to tears.

Just as Rebecca had done a generation earlier, Rachel ran home and told her father; and just as Laban had raced all those years ago to greet Abraham's steward, so now he ran to welcome Jacob.

For a month Jacob worked willingly for Laban, refusing to be paid for his labour. During that time he fell in love with Rachel, who was as beautiful as her elder sister, Leah, was plain. At the month's end Laban said to Jacob, 'Because you are my nephew, that is no reason why you should work for me for nothing; what will your wages be?' Jacob replied, 'I will work for you for seven years if you will give me Rachel to be my wife.'

Laban willingly agreed, and so great was Jacob's love for Rachel that the years passed like days. But when their wedding day came, Laban tricked Jacob. Her face hidden by a thick veil, it was dull-eyed Leah who came to Jacob in the darkness of the night. Not until morning did he discover who she was.

'You have deceived me!' he stormed at his uncle. 'I served you seven years in order to marry Rachel. Why have you done this to me?'

Laban had his answer ready. 'It is against the customs of our country to allow the younger daughter to marry before the older. Complete Leah's week of marriage celebrations. Then marry Rachel and work for me for another seven years.'

Jacob agreed to his uncle's plan, but he loved Rachel and did not feel affection for Leah. Yet Leah bore him four fine sons while Rachel remained childless. At last this led to a quarrel between Rachel and Jacob. 'Give me children,' she shouted, 'or I shall die!'

Jacob was furious. 'Am I God,' he said, 'who has made you childless?'

'Marry my slave-girl, Bilhah!' Rachel cried. 'Her children will count as mine.'

Bilhah bore Jacob two sons, and Leah, fearing that she might have no further children herself, and determined not to be outdone by her sister, gave Jacob her slave-girl, Zilpah, in marriage. Then, to her joy, for she thought that her many sons would endear her to her husband, Leah had two more, as well as a daughter. Only then did Rachel bear Joseph,

29

the first of her two sons. His brother was born later, after Jacob's return to Canaan. These twelve sons of his were the ancestors of the twelve tribes of Israel.

By the time Joseph was born, Jacob had served Laban for twenty years. For the last six he had been paid in sheep and goats, and although Laban had tried to cheat him, Jacob had managed to outwit him and had grown rich. Laban's sons were jealous, and Laban himself became increasingly unfriendly.

One year, therefore, when Laban and his sons were all far away shearing sheep, Jacob fled westwards with his wives and children, together with his flocks and herds. So well did he time his flight that it was three days before Laban heard of it. Setting off at once in pursuit, he caught up with him after seven days' hard riding. But the night before he did so, God warned him in a dream not to harm Jacob.

Although Laban obeyed, there were bitter words between the two men. Each reproached the other for the wrongs he had committed. Laban accused Jacob, saying, 'Everything you have is mine; but let me at least do something for my daughters and grandchildren. Let us make a solemn treaty never to attack one another; and may God keep his eye upon us when we are out of each other's sight.' So they parted in peace, and Jacob prepared to face what he feared might be a far worse enemy – his brother Esau.

To him he sent messengers with words of peace; but they returned with the terrifying news that Esau was already on the march with four hundred men. Jacob divided everything he had into two companies so that if Esau attacked one, the other at least might escape. Then he prayed earnestly to God for help. Finally, he took nearly six hundred of his

choicest animals and divided them into five herds.

'Leave a good distance between the herds,' he told their drovers, 'and as each of you meets Esau, tell him that the animals are a present for him, and that I am following you.' To himself he thought, 'Perhaps these gifts will persuade him to receive me.'

That night a strange adventure befell Jacob. He had withdrawn to a solitary place, wanting to be alone, perhaps to plan what he should say to Esau when they met. Suddenly, in the darkness, he was aware of a man who challenged him to wrestle. From the awe he felt, Jacob knew that this was no ordinary man; and he realized too, that he had no choice but to accept the challenge. They wrestled until dawn broke. Then the mysterious being seeing that he could not overcome Jacob, struck him, dislocating his thigh. Even so, Jacob would not let the man go until he had been blessed by him. The stranger finally agreed to do so, saying, 'Your name, Jacob, will be changed to Israel, Striver-with-God, because you have wrestled with God and man and have prevailed.' Jacob, who had cheated Esau and tricked Laban, had, through God's grace, changed his character with his name and become a worthy founder of God's People.

Nor did God desert him the next day when he met Esau. Far from remembering his old anger, Esau wept with joy to see his brother again and embraced him warmly. There was nothing but kindness between the two, and, after their meeting, they settled in different districts of Canaan and lived in peace. His mother, Rebecca, had died before Jacob's return, but he was reunited with his father, Isaac. So God's promise that Jacob should be brought safely back to Canaan was fulfilled.

The Story of Joseph

Genesis 37–50

When Israel's son, Joseph, was seventeen, he used to accompany his brothers while they were in charge of the sheep and then give his father a bad report of their wild behaviour. Naturally, they hated him for this, and were furiously jealous when Israel gave him a coat with long sleeves which was the sign of being the head of the family. He loved Joseph more than any of his other sons, and regarded him as his heir before them all. Then Joseph had a dream which increased his brothers' loathing of him.

'I dreamed that we were binding sheaves together,' he said, 'when my sheaf stood upright and all your sheaves bowed low before mine.'

Shortly after, he described another of his dreams to his family which caused even his adoring father to reprove him. 'The sun and moon and eleven stars bowed down before me,' Joseph told them.

'Do you really think that I and your mother and your brothers will bow before you?' demanded his father. But all the same he remembered the dream.

Some time later, when all the brothers except Joseph were away grazing their sheep, Israel sent the boy to see if all was well with his other sons. They saw him coming in the distance.

'Here is our chance to put an end to this dreamer and his dreams,' they said. 'Let us kill him, throw his body into a pit and tell our father that a wild beast has devoured him.' But the eldest son, Reuben, urged them not to kill Joseph, but instead to imprison him in a deep, dry water-cistern until they could decide what to do with him. Privately he planned to restore the boy safely to his father.

When Joseph arrived, they attacked him without warning, stripped off his sleeved robe and threw him into the pit. A little later a band of traders passed by, and the brothers saw their chance of combining profit with revenge. They decided to sell Joseph to the merchants as a slave. Reuben was away when this happened, and on his return he found the cistern empty. 'The boy has gone! What am I to do?' he cried out in terrible despair.

But the brothers did as they had originally planned. They took Joseph's coat, tore great rents in it, dipped it into the blood of a goat which they killed, and took it to Israel. He recognized it at once and gave a great cry of anguish. 'It is my son's coat – a wild animal has devoured him!'

Day after day, week after week, he mourned for Joseph and would not be comforted. 'I will sorrow for my son until I die,' he wept.

Meanwhile Joseph had been taken to Egypt and sold to Potiphar, captain of the guard of Pharaoh, King of Egypt. In a short time Potiphar grew to trust him so completely that he put him in charge of his whole household. Potiphar's wife, however, fell in love with Joseph, who was very handsome, and when he refused to have anything to do with her, she took revenge by accusing him falsely of insulting her. Potiphar was enraged, and threw Joseph into the royal prison.

But even there God was with him. Before long, the prison governor made him overseer of the whole prison and everyone in it. Now it happened that among the prisoners under Joseph's care were Pharaoh's chief butler and baker. One morning Joseph found them looking dejected and they told him that they had both had dreams which they could not understand.

'Tell me your dreams,' Joseph said. 'Perhaps God will show me what they mean.'

'I dreamed I saw three bunches of grapes on a vine,' said the butler. 'I picked them, crushed them into Pharaoh's cup and gave it to him.'

'Your dream,' said Joseph, 'means that in three days you will be freed and restored to your former position as Pharaoh's butler. But when this happens, tell Pharaoh about me and help me to get out of this place, for I have done nothing to deserve imprisonment.'

The baker then related his dream. 'I was carrying three baskets of white bread on my head, and birds were eating the food out of the top basket.'

'This dream,' Joseph said reluctantly, 'means that in three days Pharaoh will hang you.'

The dreams came true. But in his joy at being restored, the butler forgot Joseph for

The camel gave nomadic tribes complete control of the trade routes between Asia and Egypt from the earliest times. A riding camel can travel up to 160 kilometres a day and requires very little food or water, since its hump and stomach can store all that it needs for many days.

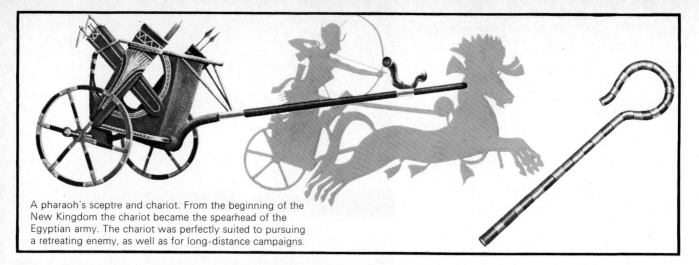

A pharaoh's sceptre and chariot. From the beginning of the New Kingdom the chariot became the spearhead of the Egyptian army. The chariot was perfectly suited to pursuing a retreating enemy, as well as for long-distance campaigns.

nearly two years. Then it so happened that Pharaoh had two dreams which troubled him, and he became all the more anxious as none of his wise men could interpret them. Suddenly the butler remembered Joseph's ability to explain the meaning of dreams and told Pharaoh about the young Hebrew.

Pharaoh immediately sent for Joseph. 'I have heard that you can tell the meaning of dreams,' he said.

'Not I,' replied Joseph, 'but God will answer Pharaoh.'

'I dreamed,' said the King, 'that I was standing by the Nile when seven fat cows came out of the river and started grazing. They were followed by seven others, the thinnest I have ever seen, which ate up the seven fat cows, but were no fatter after eating them than they were before. Then I dreamed another dream. I saw seven ripe ears of corn growing on one stalk which were swallowed up by seven other ears, shrivelled and thin and blighted.'

'These dreams have the same meaning,' said Joseph. 'There will be seven years of wonderful harvests in Egypt. These will be followed by seven years of terrible famine which will destroy all the good of the first seven years.

'Let Pharaoh therefore put a man in charge of the whole country with controllers under him, to collect and store one-fifth of the produce of Egypt during the years of plenty. These stores can then be used during the years of famine.'

Pharaoh said to Joseph, 'What man could be better than you, who have the spirit of God in you? You shall be the man in complete charge of the whole of Egypt. Only I, Pharaoh, on my throne, shall be greater than you.'

So, at a stroke, Joseph became, under Pharaoh, the greatest man in Egypt. During the seven years of plenty he stored grain in quantities so colossal that he stopped trying to measure it. The grain was as plentiful as sand on the sea-shore.

Eventually the famine came. Not only in Egypt but in all the countries round about, the crops failed. From every land long lines of pack-animals travelled to Egypt, their drivers carrying treasure to exchange for the precious corn. From Canaan came ten of Joseph's brothers, sent by their father, Israel, who kept Benjamin, the only other son of Rachel, his beloved wife, at home with him.

More than twenty years had passed since Joseph had been sold into slavery. It was not surprising that his brothers did not recognize the majestic figure in Egyptian dress into whose presence they were shown to buy corn. But they themselves had not greatly changed, and Joseph knew who they were instantly. However, he pretended not to, and spoke harshly to them.

'You are spies,' he said through an interpreter. 'You have come to spy out the weak points in our defences.'

'No, sir,' they protested. 'We have come only to buy food. We are twelve brothers, all sons of one man. One of our brothers disappeared long ago, and the youngest is at home with our father.'

'You shall be put to the proof,' said Joseph. 'I shall imprison all but one of you who will return to bring your brother here. Then we shall see if you are telling the truth.'

He terrified them by imprisoning them for three days. Then he summoned them before him. 'I am a God-fearing man,' he said, 'so I shall keep only one of you imprisoned. The rest will take back food to your households and bring your youngest brother to me. So shall you prove yourselves to be honest men.'

Not knowing that Joseph understood every word they spoke, the brothers said to each other, 'We deserve to be punished for what we did to Joseph.' And Reuben added, 'Did I not tell you not to harm the boy? Now his blood is on our heads, and we must pay for our crime.'

Joseph, deeply moved by what they said, withdrew and wept. Then he returned having decided to play a trick on them. First, he bound Simeon, the second oldest of the brothers, before their eyes. Then he secretly

put every man's money which he had brought to buy corn back into his sack. One of the brothers found the money in his sack on the way back and the others when they arrived home, and they were all terrified and bewildered.

When he heard their story, Israel was bitterly angry with his sons. 'You have robbed me of my children,' he said. 'Joseph has gone, and Simeon has gone. Benjamin shall not go.'

The famine grew worse. When the corn was finally used up which they had brought from Egypt, Israel had to tell his sons to return to Egypt to buy more food.

'We will not go without Benjamin,' they said.

'Why have you treated me so badly?' wailed their father. 'Why did you tell the man you had another brother?'

'He questioned us closely,' they replied. 'How were we to know he would tell us to bring Benjamin to Egypt?'

Israel resisted as long as he could, but at last the need for food forced him to let Benjamin go. His sons took double the amount of silver so that they could give back what had been restored to them, perhaps by accident, as well as presents of precious spices and other produce of Canaan, and set out for Egypt.

When Joseph knew that they had come, he told his steward to prepare a feast for them. The brothers were afraid when they were taken into Joseph's palace, for they thought they were to be punished for stealing the silver. Quickly they told the steward what had happened and that they had brought the money back with them. But he reassured them. 'Set your minds at rest. I did receive the money,' he said. 'God must have put the silver in your sacks.'

The steward then brought Simeon out to them, and they were all overjoyed to be reunited. Then he gave them water to wash with after their long and dusty journey, and food for their asses, and Joseph himself came out and greeted them. When he saw Benjamin, he was so overcome that he had to withdraw to weep. But he washed his face, mastered his feelings, and came out and feasted his brothers.

After the meal, Joseph ordered his steward to give each man as much food as he could carry, and again to put each man's silver into his pack. In Benjamin's he was to hide Joseph's own silver goblet. The next day, shortly after the brothers had set out, the steward was ordered to pursue them and accuse them of stealing the cup.

'My lord, how can you say such things?' they protested. 'Search us. If you find any of us has taken the goblet, that man shall die and we shall all become your slaves.'

The steward searched from the oldest to the youngest. Benjamin's was the last pack to be opened, and there the goblet was found.

In utter despair the brothers returned to the city. They threw themselves on the ground before Joseph who said, 'Did you not realize that a man like myself would use magic to discover your crime? Benjamin shall be my slave. The rest shall go free.'

Judah, the fourth brother in age, pleaded with Joseph. 'If the boy does not return to our father, Israel, he will surely die. Let me stay instead, my lord. I cannot bear to go back and see my father suffer.'

Judah's anguish pierced Joseph to the heart. Ordering all his attendants to leave him, he

cried out, 'I am Joseph!'

His brothers could not speak, so astonished were they, and frightened.

'Do not reproach yourselves that you sold me into slavery,' Joseph continued. 'It was God's doing, for he used me to save men's lives and to make sure that you, too, would survive and become a nation. Return to Israel. Tell him his son Joseph is lord of all Egypt, under Pharaoh. Bring him here with your families and live in the district of Goshen in Egypt where I can look after you and feed you all, for there are still five years of famine to come.'

So they returned and told Israel that Joseph was alive. At first he did not believe them, but when he saw the wagons and gifts that Joseph had sent, he was convinced, and agreed to go to Egypt and see his son before he died.

Before they set out, he sacrificed to God, who afterwards said to him in a dream, 'Fear not to go to Egypt. I will make you a great nation there and bring you back to Canaan.'

So Israel journeyed to Goshen and Joseph met him there. They embraced with tears, the old father saying, 'Now that I have seen you alive, my son, I am ready to die!' But he lived happily seventeen years more; and when he died, his body was taken back to Canaan and buried with Abraham and Isaac. The Israelites stayed for over four hundred years in Egypt, and prospered, growing from a small clan into a mighty nation.

Moses Frees God's People

Exodus 1–12

Centuries passed. The sons of Jacob became a mighty nation – so strong that the Egyptians began to be alarmed by their numbers. So the King made slaves of them, trying to crush their spirit with hard labour. But the Israelites grew still more numerous, until at last Pharaoh ordered all their male children to be killed at birth.

Their mothers hid most of them successfully. But there was one mother who nursed her baby son until she could conceal him no longer. When he was three months old, she decided to put him in a little boat which she floated among the reeds bordering the Nile, telling her daughter to stay a short distance away to make sure nothing happened to him.

One day Pharaoh's daughter went to bathe in the river. She caught sight of the boat and, curious to see what it was, sent slaves to fetch it. As soon as she saw the baby in it, she realized that this was one of the Hebrew children, and because he began to cry, she pitied him and decided to take him and bring him up as her own.

The baby's sister timidly approached the princess and asked her if she would like an Israelite woman to nurse the baby. Pharaoh's daughter agreed, so the girl arranged for their own mother to look after the child until he was old enough to be given the education of an Egyptian prince.

The child was named Moses, but in spite of

his Egyptian upbringing, he never forgot that he was an Israelite. When he was grown up, he saw an Egyptian attacking a Hebrew; he killed the attacker and hid his body in the sand. The next day he tried to stop two Israelites quarrelling. One of them asked Moses, 'Who made you our judge? Will you murder me as you murdered the Egyptian yesterday?' Realizing that his deed was no longer a secret, Moses fled from Egypt to the land of Midian.

There he lived for many years as a shepherd. Then, one day while minding his flock, Moses saw a strange sight in the desert – a burning thornbush which blazed and blazed yet did not burn away. He approached it and was startled to hear a voice coming out of the flames. Terrified, he covered his face.

'I am the God of Abraham, Isaac and Jacob,' said the voice. 'I have heard the cry of my people suffering in Egypt. I am sending you to Pharaoh to rescue them and bring them back to their own land of Canaan.'

'Who am I,' said Moses, 'to go to Pharaoh and lead the Israelites from Egypt?'

'I will be with you,' answered the voice.

'They will ask me your name,' said Moses. 'What shall I call you?'

'Tell them,' said the voice, 'that Jehovah – I AM – has sent you; for that is to be my name for ever.'

'Suppose they do not believe me?' asked Moses.

'Throw down your shepherd's crook,' said the voice. Moses obeyed, and immediately it turned into a snake. The terrified man fled, but the voice commanded him to catch the snake by the tail.

Moses did so, and it became a staff again.

Still Moses hesitated. 'Lord,' he said, 'I am no speaker. I shall not know what to say.'

God's anger blazed against him. 'Who enables men to speak? Is it not I? But your brother, Aaron, who is already on his way to join you, speaks well, and he shall go with you. You shall tell him what I give you to say, and he shall be your spokesman.'

So Moses and Aaron returned to Egypt, gathered together the Israelite chieftains and gave them God's message. They worshipped and gave thanks to Jehovah who had remembered them in their distress, and, encouraged by their welcome, Moses and Aaron went to the King of Egypt.

'Our God has commanded us to travel into the desert to hold a festival in his honour and sacrifice to him,' they told Pharaoh.

'Your God?' Pharaoh said. 'I know nothing about him. I will not let Israel go!'

That day Pharaoh spoke to his slave-drivers. 'Up till now,' he said, 'you have been giving the Israelites straw for making bricks. Now make them gather it for themselves, but demand the same number of bricks from them as before. For they are a lazy people – that is why they are clamouring to sacrifice to their God.'

When the Israelites found it impossible to make as many bricks as before, the Egyptians flogged their leaders, who complained bitterly to Moses. 'You have made us hateful in the eyes of Pharaoh, and have given him an excuse to kill us.'

In despair Moses prayed to God. But God reassured him, saying, 'Now you shall see what I shall do to Pharaoh. He will be forced to let you go. Indeed, he will drive you from his country.'

Moses told the Israelites what God had said, but they would not listen to him, so hard-pressed were they with toil. So once more he and Aaron went into Pharaoh's presence and demanded that he let their people go.

'Do some miracle to prove your God has sent you,' Pharaoh sneered. Aaron threw Moses' staff to the ground, and it became a snake. But Pharaoh's magicians did the same, and although Aaron's snake swallowed up their snakes, Pharaoh did not heed the warning. He still refused to let the people of Israel go.

The next morning, when Pharaoh went down to the Nile to bathe or to worship (for the river was a god to the Egyptians), Moses was there waiting for him.

'Hear God's words,' he thundered. 'Since you have not let his people go to worship him, when I strike the waters of the Nile with my rod and stretch it over your canals, reservoirs and ponds, they shall all turn to blood!'

Moses did so. The fish in the rivers died, the Nile itself stank, and because they could not drink from it, the Egyptians were forced to dig round about the river for water. But Pharaoh's magicians did the same by conjuring, and Pharaoh remained obstinate.

A week later, Moses brought another message from God to Pharaoh. 'If you still refuse to let my people go, the Nile will swarm with myriads of frogs which will crowd into your houses, ooze into your beds, your ovens and your food, and crawl all over your people.'

It happened as Moses said. Every year the Nile produces frogs, but this time the stagnant, blood-red water produced swarms such as had never been known before. So horrible were they that Pharaoh summoned Moses. 'Take away the frogs,' he cried, 'and I will let the people go.'

Moses prayed, and everywhere the frogs died. They were piled up in great heaps which filled the whole country with the stench of decay. Once again Pharaoh changed his mind.

So a third plague visited Egypt. Maggots, bred from the decaying frogs, crawled over man and beast, wriggled into food and drink, and squirmed like a living carpet on the ground. Even Pharaoh's magicians warned him, 'This is God's doing!' But he heeded them no more than he did Moses. Still he refused to let the Israelites go.

Once more, when Pharaoh went to the Nile in the morning, he found Moses and Aaron

The golden throne of Tutankhamun, late Eighteenth Dynasty. The arms are decorated with winged cobras wearing the double crown of Upper and Lower Egypt, and the front legs end in lions' heads. Moses is thought to have lived about 100 years before or after Tutankhamun.

standing in his path. 'Hear the word of God now,' they said. 'Swarms of flies will invade your country. But, that you may know that I, the Lord, am here in the land, making a difference between your people and my people, there shall be no flies in Goshen where the Israelites dwell.'

Immediately, dense swarms of flies infested Egypt. 'Sacrifice to your God,' cried Pharaoh, 'but stay in Egypt to do it.'

'No,' said Moses. 'We should have to sacrifice animals sacred to the Egyptians under their very eyes, and they would stone us for it. We must travel three days into the desert to sacrifice to our God in the way he requires.'

'Then you can go,' said Pharaoh, 'only do not go far, and pray that the flies will leave us.'

But again, when the flies disappeared, Pharaoh hardened his heart and a fifth plague came. A deadly pestilence, carried, perhaps, by the flies, struck all the cows, sheep, horses, asses and camels. But in Goshen not a single animal belonging to the Israelites died. Yet still Pharaoh would not let the people go.

After the cattle, it was the turn of the Egyptians. God commanded Moses and Aaron to take two handfuls of soot from a kiln and toss it into the wind so that it was blown far and wide. This was a sign that everywhere in Egypt the people would be afflicted with boils and blisters breaking out all over their bodies. Perhaps the humans caught their

sickness from the pestilence-striken cattle. Even Pharaoh's magicians were no match for Moses against this plague, for they, too, were covered with boils.

But Pharaoh's heart remained as hard as rock. So again Moses met him early one morning and warned him. 'If you do not let my people Israel go, about this time tomorrow I shall bring such a storm of hail on your land that everything caught out in the open, whether man or beast, shall die.' Many Egyptians who had learned to fear Jehovah brought their cattle into shelter, and it was as well they did so; for when, the next morning, Moses stretched out his rod to the sky, there came such fearful hail, accompanied by terrible thunder and lightning, that everyone who was caught in it was killed, all the trees were shattered, and the flax and barley crops were ruined. Only in the district of Goshen was there no storm.

Pharaoh sent hurriedly for Moses and Aaron. 'I have sinned,' he admitted. 'We can bear no more. Pray to God to relieve us and I will let Israel go. You need wait no longer.'

Bracelet of Queen Ahhotpe, early Eighteenth Dynasty. The front is decorated with the figure of the vulture goddess, Nekhbet; she holds in her claws two hieroglyphs symbolizing universal rule.

43

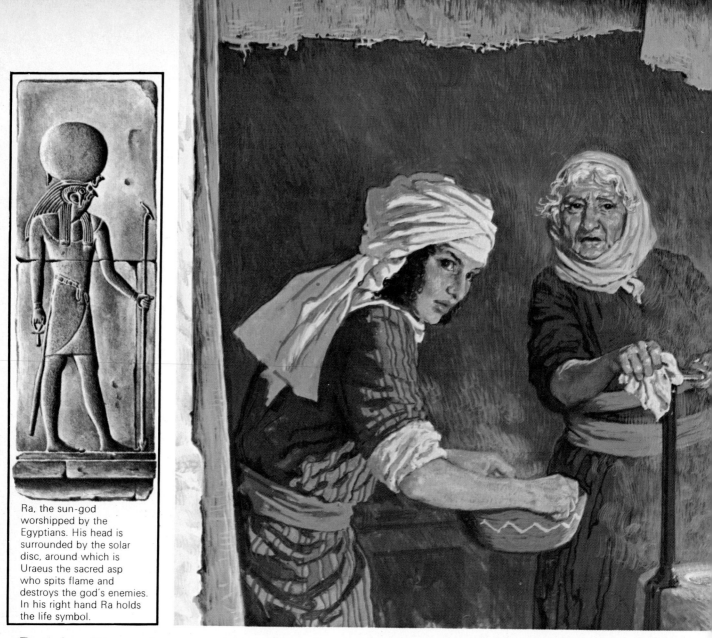

Ra, the sun-god worshipped by the Egyptians. His head is surrounded by the solar disc, around which is Uraeus the sacred asp who spits flame and destroys the god's enemies. In his right hand Ra holds the life symbol.

But when the sun shone once more, Pharaoh went back yet again on his word, and an eighth plague was sent upon Egypt.

This time it was locusts. The very threat of these was enough to make Pharaoh's ministers implore the King to let the Israelites go, and he called back Moses and Aaron. 'I will agree to let your menfolk go,' he said.

'No,' said Moses. 'Every man, woman and child is to go, together with everything we own.' But Pharaoh knew that if all of them went he would lose the nation of slaves that worked for him, and he refused, driving Moses and Aaron from his presence.

That night the Egyptians were awakened by the noise of a great wind blowing from the East, and in the wind could be heard a dry rustling of wings. When morning came, the whole land was black with locusts, a host of them such as had never before been seen. Everything the hail had not already destroyed, they ate. Not a blade of grass, not a leaf remained in all Egypt.

Yet again Pharaoh sent for Moses and Aaron. 'I have sinned against your God and against you,' he said. 'Pray to him and implore him to remove this deadly plague from me.' So Moses prayed. The wind blew again, this time from the West, sweeping the locusts out of Egypt into the Red Sea. But when Pharaoh again broke his promise, the wind grew more and more furious, whipping up the sand of the western desert, blasting out the sight of the sun and bringing so dense a darkness that men could not see one another and dared not move in the gloom. The darkness was particularly terrible to the Egyptians, for they worshipped Ra, the sun-god. Not only was the God of the Hebrews bringing plagues upon them, but it seemed that even their own god was hiding his face from them.

Pharaoh summoned Moses. 'Go,' he said. 'Take all your people, men, woman and children. Leave only your flocks and herds with us.'

'We shall take everything,' said Moses. 'Not a hoof must be left behind. What is more, you must yourself supply us with animals for sacrifice.'

Pharaoh's anger was terrible. 'I will never

44

let you go,' he shouted. 'Away with you from my presence! If ever you set eyes on me again, on that day you shall die.'

'You are right,' said Moses. 'I shall never see your face again.'

When he had left Pharaoh, Moses heard the voice of God once more. 'One last plague will I bring upon Pharaoh, so terrible that he will not only let you leave but will drive you out of Egypt. To make sure that they are safe from this final plague, this is what my people must do. Every household must kill a male lamb between sunset and dark, dip a bunch of hyssop in its blood and sprinkle it on the two doorposts and the lintel of the house in which they live. That evening the lamb is to be roasted, and eaten with unleavened bread and bitter herbs. None of it must be left until morning; anything which cannot be eaten must be burned. They must eat in haste. Not an Israelite is to leave his house until morning. For at midnight my destroying angel will pass through the land of Egypt, and the firstborn of every family shall die: from Pharaoh on his throne to the humblest slave, together with

the firstborn of all cattle. But when my angel sees the blood on the doorposts and lintel, he will pass over that house and spare the people within.'

So it happened. At midnight God struck down all the eldest sons in Egypt and all the firstborn of the cattle, and there was scarcely a home in the land where someone did not die. On every side agonizing wails of anguish were heard and the air was filled with lamentation.

While it was still night Pharaoh sent for Moses and said, 'Away with you out of my country and from among my people! Take everything you have and go. Sacrifice to your God and ask a blessing on me, too.' The Egyptians urged the Hebrews away, pressing upon them gifts of gold, silver, clothing and anything they asked.

So the Israelites left Egypt on a night they have never forgotten; for, to this day, the Passover is one of the most important festivals of the Jews, when they teach their children to remember that on that first Passover night, thousands of years ago, the Lord God brought them out of Egypt.

The Crossing of the Red Sea

Exodus 13, 17–22; 14; 15, 19–21

Although Canaan did not lie far from Egypt along the Mediterranean coast, the way was barred by Egyptian fortresses. Even if the Israelites, slaves for many years and therefore untrained for war, had overcome these, they would still have had to face warlike tribes in the south of Canaan. So God guided them towards the Sea of Reeds, an arm of the Red Sea stretching much farther north than it does today.

In ancient times guides sometimes carried a brazier full of burning wood before an army to show it the way. But the Israelites had no need of this, for Jehovah himself guided them in a pillar of cloud which moved before them by day and glowed with fire by night, so that they could travel without stopping. He led them to a place by the sea, hemmed in by wilderness. Here they could have been trapped, but they were confident that they had completely escaped the Egyptians.

Meanwhile Pharaoh and his courtiers were beginning to realize how much they had lost by allowing the Israelites to leave. 'What have we done?' they cried. 'We have let our slaves go! After them, quickly!' The king immediately ordered six hundred of the best chariots to be made ready, each carrying a commander, followed by all the other war-chariots in Egypt and, with his whole army, set out after the Israelites.

They moved fast. For a long time the Israelites failed to realize that the Egyptians were close behind them. Then suddenly they saw the long chariot-line sweeping towards them. Panic-stricken, they clamoured round Moses. 'Could you not have left us to die

Without hesitating, the Egyptians pursued the Israelites. When they reached the middle of the seabed, the wheels of the heavy chariots, each drawn by two horses and carrying two or three fully-armed warriors, began to clog in the ooze. The foremost chariots stuck fast, in spite of the efforts of the floundering horses to free them. Their riders, leaping down, tried to shoulder the wheels loose, sinking to their thighs in the mire. Those behind, unable to move because their path was blocked, sank into the mud or tried to turn, increasing the confusion. A storm of panic swept through the Egyptian ranks. 'Fly!' they screamed. 'God fights for Israel!'

It was too late. Moses stretched out his rod. The wind dropped and the tide had already turned. From both sides the waters roared back over the struggling horses, anchored to their chariots, and despairing men, weighted by their equipment. Every warrior in Pharaoh's host was drowned.

The Israelites celebrated Jehovah's triumph in a fervour of exultation. The men shouted praises and the women replied in chorus, dancing with tambourines—

'O praise the Lord, for he hath triumphed gloriously.

The horse and his rider hath he thrown into the sea.'

It was a deliverance they never forgot.

peacefully in slavery? See what you have done by bringing us out of Egypt!'

'Have no fear,' said Moses. 'Trust God. Watch how he will deliver you. You will never see the Egyptians again after today.'

He stretched his staff over the Sea of Reeds. A strong east wind blew all night driving the waters back on one side, while on the other, according to an Egyptian account, the ebb tide sucked back the sea. Simultaneously, the pillar of cloud moved behind the Israelites, bringing darkness and early nightfall, preventing the Egyptians from seeing them.

Soon a strip of land appeared across the sea, dry enough to take the weight of men and cattle. Before dawn, the Israelites were all marching safely across the sea. The pillar of cloud returned to its usual place at their head, for daylight showed the Egyptians that their intended victims were safely approaching the other side.

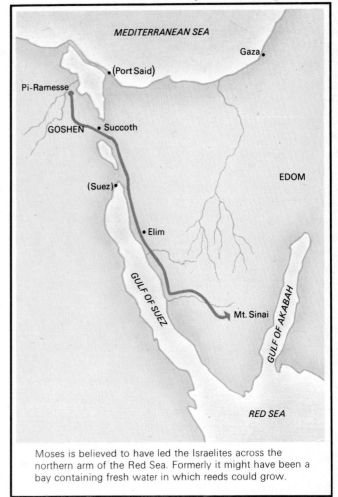

Moses is believed to have led the Israelites across the northern arm of the Red Sea. Formerly it might have been a bay containing fresh water in which reeds could grow.

The Law and the Covenant

Exodus 15, 22–25; 31, 12–35

The Israelites wandered through the desert, often rebellious and complaining, especially when water or food was scarce. They forgot how much they had suffered in Egypt and remembered only that there they had always eaten well. But God guided Moses to water, and food was provided sometimes by flights of quails and every day by manna, a white substance like frost, which was left on the ground when the dew had gone, and which tasted like a wafer made with honey.

They fought and won their first battle as a people against the Amalekites. Shortly after, Moses divided the people into smaller groups and appointed men to lead each one, since the task of governing Israel was now too heavy for one man on his own. When, after three months' wandering they reached Mount Sinai, they were starting to become an organized nation.

The mountain was at that time sacred to Jehovah. God summoned Moses up its slopes and said to him, 'Israel shall be my kingdom of priests, my holy nation. Tell the people to make ready and purify themselves, for three days from now I shall descend on the mountain in a cloud in the sight of all the people. You must put barriers round the mountain, and anyone who touches it shall be put to death.'

On the third morning, dense cloud covered the mountain's peak. From it thunder pealed, lightning flashed and trumpet-blasts were heard. The mountain smoked like a furnace and the blaring of the trumpet grew louder, terrifying the people assembled on the plain. They implored Moses to tell them what God said, for if they themselves heard the voice of Jehovah, they would die of terror.

'Do not be afraid,' said Moses. 'God has chosen to appear like this so that the awe of him may remain with you and keep you from sin.'

He approached the dark cloud where God was and disappeared into it. Long after he had gone, the thunder continued to echo round the mountain slopes, and the Israelites believed that it was the voice of Jehovah talking to Moses. From where they watched they could see the glory of the Lord shining out of the cloud like a devouring fire.

Many commandments were given to Moses. In keeping these, the nation of Israel would become God's chosen people. Chief among them were the Ten Commandments, some of which are the foundations of many of the laws of nearly all civilized nations today. God said –

'You shall not have any gods but Me.

'You shall not make and worship carved images of anything in heaven or earth or the sea.

'You shall not make wrong use of the name of God.

'Remember to keep the Sabbath day holy.

'Respect your father and mother.

'You shall not commit murder.

'You shall not commit adultery (which means, you shall love your own husband or wife and not someone else's).

'You shall not steal.

'You shall not tell lies, or stories which you do not know to be true about your fellow-men.

'You shall not long to take for your own

48

anything that belongs to someone else.'
Moses returned to the people and wrote
down all the laws he had been given by God.
The next day he built an altar at the foot of
Mount Sinai with twelve stones standing
round it, representing each of the tribes of
Israel. Bulls were sacrificed to Jehovah, and
Moses took half their blood and dashed it
over the altar. Then, in a loud voice, he read
out the laws he had written down and asked
the people if they would obey them. They
shouted in reply, 'We will do all that the Lord
has said.' Moses then sprinkled the other half
of the blood from the sacrificed bulls over the
people, saying, 'This is the blood of the covenant which the Lord has made with you,
based on the laws in this book.' From that

moment, Israel became the People of the
Covenant, a nation holy to God.

But God still had much to teach them.
Once more he summoned Moses to the moun-
taintop, first with the other Israelite leaders,
who were granted a vision of God, and then
by himself. Again he entered the cloud and
this time remained there for many days and
nights. He was given further laws and told to
make a holy chest, the Ark of the Covenant,
in which a copy of all the laws of God was to
be kept, and a holy tent, the Tabernacle,
where Jehovah was to be worshipped until a
permanent temple for him could be built.

Meanwhile, on the plain below, the people
waited impatiently for Moses to return. At
last, certain now that they would not see

him again, they went to Aaron.

'Make us a god to lead us,' they said. 'We don't know what has become of Moses.'

Aaron told them to give him their golden earrings and, after melting them down, he made them into a golden calf. He built an altar before the idol and proclaimed the next day a festival in honour of the god.

But in the mountain Jehovah's anger blazed out against the people who had so soon broken his covenant with them. 'I will destroy them,' he told Moses, 'and make a great nation of you.'

Moses pleaded with him. 'Why should the Egyptians sneer, "Their god took them into the desert to destroy them"? Remember your promise to Abraham, Isaac and Jacob to make a great nation of them.' So God relented, and Moses returned down the mountainside to his people, carrying two tablets of stone, on which the law of God was written.

Long before he reached the camp he heard the noise of merriment, and when he drew nearer, he saw the people dancing round the golden calf. Enraged, he flung down the tablets, breaking them into fragments. Halting at the edge of the camp he shouted 'Who is on Jehovah's side? Let him join me!' At once the tribe of Levi rallied to him.

'Gird on your swords,' he told them, 'and sweep through the camp from end to end, killing your kinsfolk, friends and countrymen.' The Levites obeyed him, killing about three thousand men.

Moses then burned the calf, ground it into powder, threw it into water and made the people drink it. Bitterly he reproached Aaron. 'What did the people do to you,' he asked, 'that you brought this great sin upon them?'

'Do not be angry with me!' cried Aaron. 'You know how determined this people is to do wrong. All I did was to collect their golden earring and throw them into the fire, and out came this calf!'

Moses, feeling that the people had been sufficiently punished, again went up into the mountain, carrying two blank stone tablets with him. Once more God renewed his covenant with the people. Once more his laws were engraved on the tablets of stone. And once more Moses carried them back to the Israelites.

This time the people did not dare to look at Moses, for his face glowed with light from having talked with God. From that time he wore a veil except when he went apart to speak with the Lord.

As for the people, they began to carry out God's command to build the Tabernacle, giving gold and silver, precious woods and fine materials, with willing hearts and minds now loyal to Jehovah.

The Tabernacle and the Ark

Exodus 25–27; 35–40

The Israelites gave materials so generously for the building of the Tabernacle that soon no more were needed, and their craftsmen set to work.

They built an enclosure one hundred cubits long and fifty wide. Sixty bronze columns on pedestals, fitted with silver hooks and connected by silver rods, formed the boundary; from them hung a continuous wall of curtains round the enclosure except at the eastern end. There a separate curtain, richly embroidered in violet, purple and scarlet, hung from the four centre pillars to form an entrance.

The Tabernacle, erected at the enclosure's western end, was thirty cubits long and ten wide. Its north, west and south sides were formed of forty-eight wooden boards covered with gold. These were ten cubits high and one and a half wide, and the base of each fitted with pegs into two silver pedestals. The framework was strengthened by five lines of wooden rods overlaid with gold, which ran through

golden rings fastened to the boards. Though they are not mentioned in the Bible, there must also have been rafters connecting the tops of the boards to support the covering of the Tabernacle.

The covering was made in four layers. The innermost consisted of linen curtains of violet, purple and scarlet, skilfully embroidered with cherubim. When linked together and suspended from the framework, these were large enough to cover the whole interior, except where a strip of the gilded boards gleamed beneath them. The embroidered cherubim stood along the walls and gazed down from the ceiling.

The second layer was made of woven goats' hair and was large enough to cover the whole of the outside of the Tabernacle to the ground. The third was of ram-skin leather, dyed red, and the fourth of a stronger leather to protect the tent against wind and storm. None of the layers covered the east end, which was closed

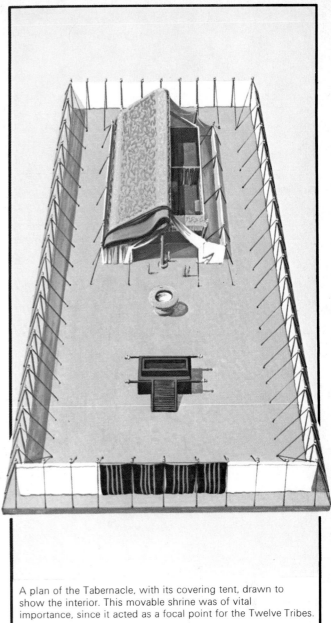

by a curtain hanging down from five pillars.

Every Israelite man (but no woman) was allowed to pray in the enclosure. In it was placed the Altar of Burnt Offering, where sacrifice was made every morning and evening to purify the people from their sins. Behind this was the Laver or basin containing water, for the priests to wash in before they entered the Tabernacle, which only they were allowed to do. The tent itself was divided into two rooms, the Holy Place and, separated from it by the Veil, a magnificent curtain hanging from four golden pillars, the Holy of Holies, exactly ten cubits square. The High Priest alone was allowed to enter here, and he only on the Day of Atonement, the holiest day of the Jewish year.

In the Holy Place there stood on the right a table bearing twelve sacred loaves of 'shew-bread' representing the tribes of Israel; on the left a lampstand with seven branches, each ending in a lamp. Before the Veil stood the Altar of Incense, on which incense was burned to God day and night.

Within the Holy of Holies stood the Ark of the Covenant. This was a wooden chest overlaid with gold. Into its sides were fastened four rings through which rods were passed by which to carry it, for to touch the Ark meant death. Inside it were the tablets of the Law. Two golden cherubim faced each other across the lid of the Ark, screening it with their wings, which were outspread and pointing upwards. When Jehovah came down to his people he descended between the wings of the cherubim.

Once the Tabernacle was completed, a cloud covered the tent, which was filled with the glory of the Lord. From then on the Israelites broke camp only when Jehovah gave the sign by lifting the cloud; and always at their head as they journeyed went the Ark of the Covenant containing God's laws, itself the symbol of his presence.

Wanderings in the Desert

Numbers 11–14; 20–25; 31; Deuteronomy 34

For many more years the Israelites wandered in the wilderness. They grew in strength and numbers, beginning to feel more united as a nation. But life was hard. There was often little food and less water, and many times they complained to Moses, and murmured against God. As the years passed, they remembered only the good things of their past lives in Egypt, the food, drink and houses they had enjoyed, forgetting the never-ending labour and the whips of the slave-drivers. Even Aaron and Miriam, his brother and sister, joined in the opposition to Moses, and several times God had to punish his people with pestilence and fire.

At last the time came when God saw that Israel was strong enough to invade the land of Canaan. Moses sent out twelve leaders, one from each tribe, including Joshua, the commander of the army, to spy out Canaan and bring back information about the land and the people. They travelled through it from south to north, and returned with enthusiastic accounts of the land, and showed their people wonderful fruit grown in Canaan. It was a beautiful, fertile country, they said; but the cities were walled and strong, the many tribes were too warlike for them to conquer, and some of the inhabitants were huge giant-like men. Only Joshua and a man called Caleb had faith enough to believe that Jehovah would lead his people to victory.

Once more God wanted to destroy Israel for their lack of faith and once more Moses pleaded with him successfully to spare his people. But the Israelites were condemned to wander many more years in the wilderness until all those over twenty years of age, except Joshua and Caleb, should have died. On hearing this, some of the people changed their minds and recklessly attacked the Canaanites. But, as Moses warned them, God was not with them and they were routed. Sadly the rest turned back into the desert.

Now that all hope of entering the Promised Land had gone for most of them, the Israelites became increasingly rebellious. Two hundred and fifty of their leading men, led by three arch-rebels, demanded a share in the priesthood which God had reserved for Aaron, his sons and the Levites. The earth opened beneath the three leaders and swallowed them up alive, while the others were consumed by fire sent from God.

Some time later, all the people complained against Jehovah and many of them were killed by a plague of poisonous snakes, until they implored Moses to help them. Com-

manded by God, he made a snake of brass and hung it on a pole. Anyone bitten by a snake, who looked with faith at the brazen serpent, lived. On a third occasion, the Israelites, camping near the country of Moab, were enticed by Moabite women to worship the idols of Moab. Moses publicly hanged the leaders, while a great plague carried off twenty-four thousand of the people.

But, as the years went by, the harsh life of the desert toughened the Israelites into ferocious fighters. They defeated the Midianites in spite of the efforts of Balak, a Midianite king, to bribe a great prophet named Balaam

to curse them. Whenever Balaam tried to utter the curse, Jehovah caused a blessing to come from his mouth instead. They defeated the Amorite kings, Sihon of Heshbon and Og of Bashan. They learned how to take walled cities as well as fight pitched battles.

Time passed. Miriam died. Aaron died. At the end of his life, God led Moses up to a mountain top from which God showed him the Promised Land. Moses knew that he would never enter it himself. But he had turned a mob of slaves into a great nation, and had brought them to the threshold of the land that was to be theirs.

Manna is understood to have been the sweet, edible drops of fluid secreted by two kinds of tiny insects living on tamarisk trees. The drops are secreted in the spring, then dry and fall to the ground, where they are still collected as food by the Bedouin Arabs.

In early autumn thousands of quails arrive on the shores of Egypt and the Sinai during migration from their breeding grounds in central Europe.

The Spies and the Crossing of the Jordan

Joshua 1–5

Moses was succeeded as the leader of the nation of Israel by Joshua, commander of the army. He at once prepared to lead his countrymen to the conquest of Canaan. God had spoken to Joshua himself. 'Be strong and very courageous,' he said. 'Do not be fearful or dismayed, for the Lord your God is with you wherever you go.'

Confident and resolute, Joshua addressed the people. 'In three days,' he told them, 'you will be crossing the River Jordan. Prepare food and be ready to march.' This time the Israelites had neither doubts nor fears, for they knew they would conquer Canaan.

Joshua sent two men to spy in Jericho and discover what they could about the people and the city's defences. They became acquainted with a woman called Rahab, who had a house built on an angle of the city wall. The King of Jericho heard that they were there and sent

soldiers to order Rahab to hand them over. But when she saw the soldiers coming, she hid the Israelites under the flax drying on the roof and said to the king's men, 'Yes, some men did come to me, but they left by the town gate when evening fell. You will overtake them if you ride fast.'

The soldiers galloped away, and the town gate slammed behind them. They rode as far as the Jordan before they gave up the search. Meanwhile, Rahab said to the two Israelites, 'We are all terrified here because everybody knows that God has given you the country. Now, since I have dealt kindly with you, deal kindly also with me. Promise that you will

spare the lives of my family and me when you take the city.'

'Tie this scarlet cord outside your window when we attack,' said the Israelites. 'Collect all your family inside the house during the battle for the town, and they will be safe – provided you do not say a word about our mission.'

The woman then lowered them down the city wall by a rope. It was too dangerous for them to take the road, so they fled across country to the hills, where they hid for three days till the hunt for them had died down. Then they returned to Joshua and said, 'God has indeed given you the country. The inhabitants are panic-stricken because of us.'

In the morning, Joshua led the Israelites to the west bank of the River Jordan. There he camped and the officers gave the army its

orders. 'Purify yourselves, for tomorrow the Lord will do wonders among you; and when you see the Levites carrying out the Ark of the Covenant, follow them, leaving an interval of two hundred cubits between them and you.'

The Levites bearing the Ark were told to advance to the brink of the Jordan and to stand still in the water as soon as their feet touched it. The moment they did so, the water that flowed from upstream was dammed at a place far up the valley; and downstream the river drained away. The entire Israelite army was therefore able to cross dryfoot.

One man, chosen from each tribe, carried a large stone taken from the place where the priests had stood, and piled them near the river as a memorial of the miraculous event.

When the whole nation had crossed the Jordan, Joshua ordered the bearers of the Ark to move on. Immediately the water flowed once more. The Israelites prepared for the siege of Jericho more certain than ever that Jehovah was fighting for them, while the men of the city felt their courage draining away, knowing that they were doomed.

The Fall of Jericho
Joshua 6

After the Israelites had crossed the Jordan, Joshua led them to Jericho. He began by besieging the city so that no one could go in or out. One day, he saw a man before him holding a drawn sword. He asked him, 'Are you for us or against us?' The man replied, 'I am here as captain of the host of God.' Joshua, realizing that he was in the presence of a messenger from God, worshipped him, asking, 'What commands have you for me?'

The man said, 'For six days you and your warriors must march round the city once every day, with seven priests carrying seven rams' horns as trumpets in front of the Ark of the Covenant. On the seventh day you shall march round the city seven times, and the priests shall then blow one long trumpet-blast. When they hear this, all the people must give a great shout. The walls will fall down flat, and every man of you can march in.'

Joshua returned to the camp and gave the soldiers their orders. 'The army will march round the city, with seven priests in front of the Ark in the centre of the column. Everyone must remain completely silent until the signal is given to shout. Then shout all together as loudly as you can.'

Examples of Hyksos pottery from the Middle Bronze Age *c.*1700 BC found in the ruins of the third city to have been built on the site of Jericho. At the top is shown a cross-section of a Hyksos tomb.

Cities in those days were much smaller than they are today. There were probably enough Israelite soldiers to go completely round Jericho, and their silence made them all the more frightening. The men of Jericho watched for an attack, but none came. The Israelites marched round the city and back to their camp.

Tramp, tramp, tramp, on the second day. Tramp, tramp, tramp, on the third. Still silence. Still no attack. The men of Jericho grew more and more nervous.

On the seventh day, when the army had marched round the city seven times, it halted. Following the long blast of the rams' horns, all Joshua's men shouted at the tops of their voices. The noise echoing back from the hills was too much for the weakened walls. They fell outwards and slid down the slope towards the Israelites. Joshua's soldiers scrambled over the rubble and attacked Jericho from all sides at once. In a short time the city was theirs.

Only where Rahab's house stood did the wall not collapse. She and her family were led to safety. The spies had kept their promise. Nobody else was spared, for the Israelites believed that God wanted them to destroy everyone in the city. They were then too savage to understand that God is love, and wants his worshippers to love even their enemies.

Bronze weapons and scarab-seals found in a tomb of the Hyksos period of the 17th century BC. The Hyksos came to Canaan c.1750 BC and remained there for about 100 years. Joshua lived c.1400 BC

59

A Plan and a Trick

Joshua 6, 18–19; 7–9

Not all the Canaanite cities were taken as easily as Jericho, and many years of warfare lay ahead of the Israelites before they conquered the whole country. Sometimes they brought defeat upon themselves by disobeying God.

Before Jericho fell, Joshua had ordered that all gold and silver and everything made of copper and iron in the city was to be given to Jehovah. No Israelite was to keep anything for himself. So all the precious things were carried out of the city before it was burned and piled up in a great heap to be kept only for the service of God. Then, when Jericho had been destroyed, Joshua sent men to spy out the next city, which was called Ai.

They came back with a contemptuous report of the town. 'It is only a small place,' they said. 'There is no need to send the whole army against it. Three thousand men are enough to take it.' But the men of Ai chased the three thousand Israelites far from their city, killing thirty-six of them in the rout. Joshua realized how seriously even a small defeat at the beginning of his compaign to take all Canaan could discourage the people and, in his disappointment, he turned to God for guidance. God told him that someone among the Israelites had sinned.

The next day, Joshua discovered by drawing lots who the guilty man was. He was called Achan, and he confessed that he had stolen some silver and gold and a beautiful Babylonian mantle for himself, hiding them in his tent. For his crime he was stoned to death.

Shortly afterwards Joshua captured Ai by a clever plan. He hid thirty thousand men in the hills behind the city by night. The next day, he attacked the city, approaching from the front, but pretended to run away when the men of Ai charged out against the attackers. Away fled the Israelites with the Canaanites after them in full cry, leaving their city undefended; and, at a signal from Joshua, the men in ambush entered the city and set fire to it. When the Israelites saw the smoke rising from the city, they turned on their pursuers. The men of Ai panicked, not knowing where to flee, and every one of them was killed.

But once, the Israelites themselves were tricked. A Canaanite tribe called the Gibeonites were terrified by what had happened to Jericho and Ai, where every man, woman and child had been killed by the ferocious invaders from the desert. They decided to save themselves from the same fate by a cunning plan. Several of them dressed up in old clothes and worn-out shoes. They loaded some donkeys with patched wineskins and torn sacks containing mouldy bread, and limped wearily into Joshua's camp.

'We have come from a country far, far away,' they said. 'Look at our old clothes and shoes, our torn wineskins and mouldy bread. They were new when we set out, and the bread was hot from the oven. You can see how long we have been travelling. We have heard all that God has done for you, and our rulers have sent us as ambassadors to make a treaty with you.'

So Joshua and the Israelite leaders made a treaty with them, to discover three days later that the Gibeonites lived only a short distance away. The army grumbled, furious with their leaders for allowing themselves to be tricked. They wanted to slaughter the Gibeonites. But the leaders refused to allow the oath to be broken. The Israelites therefore let the Gibeonites live, but made them their slaves, to draw water and cut wood for them and for the services of the Tabernacle.

A reconstruction of an ivory, showing Canaanite troops.

The People Choose Jehovah

Joshua 10–24

The rest of Joshua's life was spent in fighting. City after city fell into his hands until most of the south and centre of Canaan and part of the north were conquered. Here and there strong cities held out against the Israelites, and many Canaanite tribes were only half-subdued. Forced for a time to serve the Israelites as slaves, they became strong again after Joshua's death, and often recaptured the land and cities they had lost.

But seven years after they entered Canaan, the Israelites had conquered enough of it for every one of their tribes, except one, to be given districts in which to settle. The one tribe not allotted a district of its own was the Levites. They were given forty-eight cities throughout Canaan so that they could act as priests to the other eleven tribes, and show them how Jehovah should be worshipped. The city of Shiloh in central Canaan was selected as a permanent home for the Tabernacle, and there it remained for nearly three hundred years.

Six other cities were chosen to be Cities of Refuge. In those days, if a man accidentally killed another, the dead man's relatives had the right to kill the man who had slain their kinsman. But if the killer fled to a City of Refuge, he was safe from the Avengers of Blood, as the relatives were called, until he could be tried before a court. If the court decided that the killing had indeed been accidental, the man was allowed to live freely in the city; and when whoever was then High Priest died, he could return without penalty to his own city and home.

So, by the time Joshua was a very old man, the Israelites were firmly settled in Canaan, secure against the enemies around them. Knowing that his death was near, the old warrior called the people together and addressed them for the last time.

He reminded them of all that God had done for them from Abraham's time onwards, promising them that the Canaanites who still remained in the country would be driven out. The Israelites were not to mix with nor marry these heathen, for, if they did, the Canaanites would entice them to worship false gods and Jehovah would destroy them. They were to remain faithful to him, worshipping neither the gods their ancestors before Abraham had revered nor those their fathers had served in Egypt before Moses had told them of the Lord.

'If you do not want to worship Jehovah,' he ended, 'choose now the gods whom you will revere. But as for me and my family, we will serve the Lord.'

'God forbid that we should forsake the Lord for other gods,' the people answered, 'for it was he who brought us out of Egypt, who worked great wonders on our journey to this land and who drove out the Canaanites before us. We, like you, will worship the Lord.

Joshua warned them, 'The Lord will not forgive you if, having chosen him, you forsake him for other gods. If you do this, he will certainly destroy you.'

Again the people shouted, 'We will serve the Lord!'

'Then put away all foreign gods,' said Joshua, 'and worship the Lord God of Israel from your hearts.'

The people promised to obey Joshua, and he made a covenant with them, setting up a great stone in the sanctuary of the Lord. 'If you reject Jehovah,' he said, 'this stone shall be a witness against you.'

Shortly afterwards, Joshua died. But although the Israelites served the Lord during Joshua's life and for some years after, the time came when they turned away from Jehovah. So the Lord delivered them into the hands of their enemies.

The Defeat of Sisera

Judges 4–5

After Joshua's death, the Israelites continued to wage war successfully against the Canaanites, but did not drive them out; and when the generation that had invaded Canaan had passed away and another took its place, the memory of the wonderful things God had done for his people began to fade. The Israelites forsook Jehovah. They married Canaanite men and women and began to worship Canaanite gods, so the Lord gave them into the power of their enemies. Now and again, when they repented, God raised up heroic leaders who rescued them from their oppressors. The Israelites would then return to worshipping Jehovah, but when their rescuers died, once more they would abandon God, whereupon some other nation would conquer them.

After being subject in turn to the Kings of Mesopotamia, Moab and the Philistines, the Israelites fell under the rule of Jabin, King of Canaan. He had nine hundred iron chariots and was served by a great general named Sisera. Jehovah's people were cruelly treated for twenty years, until Deborah, a prophetess and judge of Israel, inspired a man called Barak to lead ten thousand men to Mount Tabor. 'The God of Israel,' she said, 'will bring Sisera out to fight you and will deliver him into your hands.'

'I will go if you will be my ally,' said Barak. Deborah agreed, but warned him that a woman would win the greatest glory.

When Sisera heard that the Israelites were rebelling, he marched with all his troops and chariots to attack them. Barak hid his men in the woods on Mount Tabor overlooking a plain through which ran the River Kishon. Deborah's tribe, the Ephraimites, advanced on the south of the plain; and when Sisera moved across the river, which was then in flood, Barak's army charged down from the mountain and cut him off from his city on the other side of the river. The river was swollen even more by a storm, and the valley was so marshy that the chariots were useless. The two Israelite armies drove Sisera and his men up the valley, forced him into a narrow gorge and cut his army to pieces. Sisera himself managed to escape.

Exhausted, and knowing that he would soon be hunted down if he did not find a hiding-place, he fled to the tent of Jael, the wife of a man named Heber who was a friend of Sisera's master, Jabin. She came out to meet him.

'Have no fear, my lord,' she said. 'Hide in my tent.' She gave him milk to quench his thirst, hid him under a rug and made him feel secure. But for some reason that we do not know, Jael betrayed Sisera. Perhaps she was afraid that she and her husband, as friends of Jabin, would be killed by the victorious Israelites. When Sisera was asleep, she took a tent-peg and mallet and hammered the peg right through his skull.

Soon after, Jael went to meet Barak who was in hot pursuit of Sisera. 'I will show you the man you want,' she said. She took Barak into her tent. There he saw Sisera dead, with the tent-peg through his forehead.

With his general dead and his army slaughtered, Jabin stood no chance against the Israelites. Again and again they attacked, pressing harder and harder upon him, until at last he was destroyed. After his death, the Israelites remained free for forty years.

The Story of Gideon

Judges 6–8

Again the Israelites forsook Jehovah. Again he gave them into the hands of their enemies. For seven years the Midianites, tribes from the desert, ravaged their crops, stole their cattle and drove them to hide in strongholds in the mountains.

A young man named Gideon, all of whose brothers had been killed by the Midianites, was one day threshing wheat, when suddenly he saw a man standing by him.

'You are a brave man,' said the stranger. 'God is with you.'

'If God is with us,' asked Gideon, 'why has he delivered us to the Midianites?'

'You shall destroy the Midianites,' he said.

'If you think so highly of me,' said Gideon, 'will you accept a gift of food from me?'

He prepared meat, bread and broth and brought it to the stranger. 'Put them on that rock,' the man said. When Gideon did so, he touched them with the tip of his staff. Instantly fire spurted out of the rock and burned up the food, and the stranger vanished. Gideon knew that he had met with a messenger from God, and was afraid; and on the spot where he had seen him, he built an altar to Jehovah.

That night, God told Gideon to replace the altar to the false god Baal which belonged to his father, Joash, with one to Jehovah, and to offer up a sacrifice on it. Next morning, when people discovered what Gideon had done, they were indignant and wanted to kill him. But Joash said, 'If Baal is truly a god, let him avenge himself,' and Gideon was spared.

Once again the Midianites and their allies prepared to attack Israel. Encouraged by signs from God and inspired by him, Gideon sent messengers to four tribes and assembled

an army of thirty-two thousand men.

'They are too many,' said God. 'They will say that their own strength, not I, gave them the victory. Tell all who are afraid to return home.' Gideon did so, and only ten thousand men remained with him.

'They are still too many,' said God. 'Take them down to the water and let them drink. Put on one side every man who laps the water with his tongue like a dog, and, on the other, all who go down on their knees to drink.'

Only three hundred lapped with their tongues. 'With them will I save Israel,' God said. 'Send the rest home.'

That night, Gideon divided his men into three companies. He handed every soldier a trumpet and a pitcher with a torch inside it, and gave them their orders. In the middle of the night, the three companies crept up to the Midianite camp from different directions, and when they were all in position, Gideon acted.

He and his hundred men gave a great blast on their trumpets. They smashed the pitchers. Their torches blazed high. They shouted together, 'A sword for the Lord and for Gideon!'

Instantly the other two companies did the same. The sudden trumpeting, the lights appearing all round them, and the shouts echoing from the hills, panicked the Midianites. They thought a great army was attacking them, and in the darkness and confusion began fighting among themselves. The panic and the fighting spread, and soon Israel's enemies were destroying each other.

They began to run. The Israelites poured from the mountains to join Gideon in the pursuit; and so great was their final victory that the Midianites were utterly subdued. Gideon slaughtered two chieftains who had killed his brothers with his own hand; and for the rest of his lifetime, Israel lived at peace, free from its enemies.

Baal, the Canaanite god personifying fertility, for whom the Israelites forsook Jehovah. In his hands he holds a club and a thunderbolt. The Israelites abandoned the worship of Baal when they went to war against the Canaanites to win land. The tribes united in the name of Jehovah, and so he was credited with the prestige of their victories, having proved in their eyes that he was the God of Palestine.

The Story of Samson

Judges 13–16

Of all the nations that oppressed the Israelites, the Philistines were the most warlike. They had invaded Canaan from the sea as Israel had from the land, and for centuries the two nations fought for the possession of the country.

At a time when the Philistines ruled the Israelites, a messenger of God appeared to the wife of a man called Manoah, and said, 'Although you have no children, you will give birth soon, to a son. No razor must touch his head for he will be consecrated to God, and he shall begin to deliver Israel from the power of the Philistines.'

In due course a son was born to them, and they called him Samson.

Samson grew up to be tall and enormously strong, and when he was fully grown he fell in love with and planned to marry a Philistine woman. Once, on his way to visit her, he met a young lion which he killed with his bare hands. Returning some weeks later, he saw a swarm of bees had made its home inside the lion's carcass. Samson broke off a piece of the honeycomb and ate it.

Later on, the marriage was arranged and he invited thirty Philistines to his wedding-feast. During the merrymaking Samson said, 'I will ask you a riddle. If you answer it during the seven days the feast lasts, I will give you each a fine linen shawl and a handsome robe. But if you cannot answer it, you must each give me a shawl and a robe.' They agreed, and Samson asked his riddle.

'What eater itself gave out something to eat?
'And out of the strong, what came forth sweet?'

Rack their brains as they might, the Philistines could not answer the riddle. So they threatened Samson's wife, saying, 'Find out the answer, or we shall burn down your house and you in it!' The girl asked Samson, and when he refused to tell her, she wept, complaining, 'You do not love me!' With tears and reproaches she nagged at him every day of the feast, until at last he told her, and she told her countrymen. Just before the wedding on the seventh day, they gave him the answer.

'What sweet thing than honey is sweeter?
'What stronger beast than the lion, the eater?'

Samson replied grimly,

'You used my heifer to pull your plough,
Or you would not have answered my riddle now.'

Enraged, he went to Ashkelon, a Philistine city. He killed thirty citizens, using their

money to buy the promised shawls and robes. These he gave to his thirty guests and returned to his father's house, forsaking the girl who had betrayed him.

But he still loved her, and some months later, during the wheat-harvest, he returned to her, only to find that she had married one of his thirty companions. He resolved to be avenged on the whole Philistine nation. He caught three hundred foxes, tied them together in couples by their tails and bound a lighted torch to each pair of tails. The animals, maddened by terror, ran crazily all over the countryside, setting fire to the crops, olive

trees and vineyards.

Finding out who had fired their harvest and why, the Philistines burned down the house of Samson's former bride. In revenge he attacked them and single-handed routed them, killing a large number. Then he withdrew to his own country.

The Philistines pursued him there. His countrymen resolved to give Samson up to them rather than be punished for sheltering him, and Samson agreed. 'But you must swear not to kill me yourselves,' he pleaded. They handed him over bound with two new ropes, and when the Philistines saw him apparently helpless, they shouted with triumph. But the Spirit of God came upon Samson. He snapped the ropes as if they had been thread, and, snatching up the jawbone of an ass which lay nearby, he killed a thousand Philistines.

After this, he became a judge, and for the next twenty years, governed Israel. During that time Samson visited the Philistine city of Gaza. His enemies thought their chance had at last come to kill him. They lay low during the night, planning to kill him in the morning.

But at midnight Samson arose, uprooted the city gate-posts and carried them away, posts, gate and all, and so escaped.

Samson's downfall was brought about by a woman. He fell in love with a girl called Delilah. The Philistine chieftains promised that, if she could discover the secret of his strength and how he could be mastered, they would give her a great quantity of silver. She asked Samson and he replied, 'If I am bound with seven new bowstrings, I shall become as weak as other men.' So while he was asleep, she hid Philistines in an inner room ready to seize Samson, bound him with the bowstrings and cried out, 'The Philistines are upon you, Samson!' He sprang up, snapping the bowstrings as a strand of hemp is destoyed by fire.

'You have lied to me,' cried Delilah. 'Now tell me truthfully how you may be bound and become like other men.'

'If I am tied with new ropes, my strength will fail.' Again she bound him while he was asleep. Again she cried, 'The Philistines are upon you, Sampson!' Again he broke the ropes like thread.

'You always cheat me,' Delilah shouted angrily. 'You always tell me lies,' and she nagged at him unceasingly to tell her his secret. 'If you weave my hair into the cloth on your loom and fasten it there,' he said at last, 'I shall become weak like other men.' But when Delilah did this and once more called, 'Samson, the Philistines are upon you!' he woke, dragging away the loom with his hair.

'How can you say, "I love you",' wailed Delilah, 'when you go on lying and lying to me.' And she gave him no peace – pressing and urging him every day, until at last he told her his secret. 'If my hair and beard are cut off, I shall be like any other man.'

This time Delilah knew that he was telling her the truth. She told the Philistine lords to be ready: and while they hid in the inner room, she lulled Samson to sleep. A Philistine cut away Samson's hair and beard, carefully with shears and razor. When he had finished, Delilah cried once more, 'The Philistines are upon you, Samson!' Thinking it was her customary joke, he got up to stretch and shake himself. But his strength was gone from him and the Philistines leaped upon him and bound him. They stabbed out his eyes and dragged him to their city of Gaza. There he was loaded with chains and made to grind corn in the prison.

But his hair grew quickly again, and, as it grew longer, his strength returned.

There came a day when the Philistines held a great festival in honour of their god, Dagon. The temple was crowded. All the rulers and great men of Philistia were there, and there were even three thousand people on the roof. They shouted for Samson to be brought to the temple so that they could mock him. When he was led in, they laughed and jeered at him. But now his beard and hair were fully grown again, and all his strength had returned. He told the boy who led him to guide him to the pillars that supported the roof.

When he felt his arms round the pillars, he prayed. 'O God, just once, just this once, give me back my old strength.'

Samson braced himself against the pillars. He shouted aloud, 'We shall die together, all you Philistines and I.' Then he bowed himself and strained with all his strength. The jeers and laughter of the Philistines turned to silence, then to moans and cries of fear. The pillars trembled. They bent and broke. The roof crashed on those below, killing all within the temple by its weight and hurling those upon it to their deaths.

Samson did not escape. But he killed more people at his death than he had in the whole of his life, and he was revenged for the loss of his two eyes.

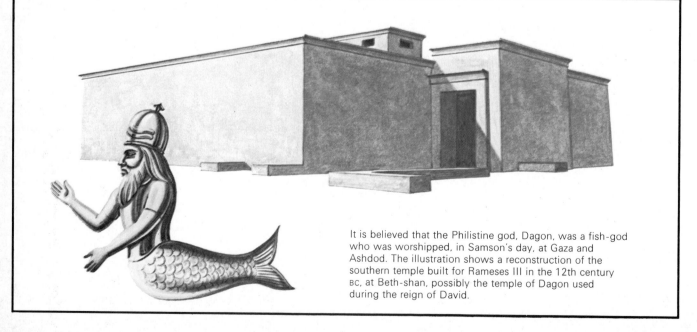

It is believed that the Philistine god, Dagon, was a fish-god who was worshipped, in Samson's day, at Gaza and Ashdod. The illustration shows a reconstruction of the southern temple built for Rameses III in the 12th century BC, at Beth-shan, possibly the temple of Dagon used during the reign of David.

Ruth

The Book of Ruth

Once, when the judges were ruling Israel, a famine drove Elimelech, a man of Judah, with his wife Naomi and their two sons, into the land of Moab. The sons married Moabite girls, one called Orpah, the other Ruth. But the men all died, leaving three lonely widows.

Naomi decided to return to her own people. She pleaded with her daughters-in-law to remain in Moab, for they were young enough to marry again. Orpah stayed, but Ruth would not forsake Naomi.

'Do not ask me to leave you,' she said. 'Wherever you go, I shall go. Your people shall be my people. Your God shall be my God. Death alone will separate us.'

So the two women journeyed back to Bethlehem where Naomi, sad and lonely, though comforted by Ruth's affection, was welcomed by her kinsfolk.

There was living at Bethlehem, a landowner, called Boaz, a relation of Elimelech's. Ruth, as was the custom among women, went out at barley-harvest time to glean – that is, to gather for her own use any stalks of barley which the binders of the sheaves might overlook. By chance she was gleaning in one of Boaz's fields when he saw her and asked who she was. He was told that she was the Moabitess who had returned with Naomi.

He spoke to her kindly. 'Glean with my girls in my fields and go nowhere else. My men will not interfere with you. If you are thirsty, help yourself to the water they have drawn for my workers.'

Ruth bowed before him. 'Why are you being so kind to me, a foreigner?' she asked.

'I have heard,' said Boaz, 'of all you did for

Naomi, and how, rather than desert her, you left your own people. May the God of Israel reward you richly for your kindness.'

'I am already rewarded,' Ruth replied, 'in the kindness you are showing me.'

When the time came for the harvesters to eat, Boaz called Ruth to join them, and gave her enough food to provide a meal for herself and for Naomi that evening. When she went back to her gleaning, he told his sheaf-binders privately, 'Pull out some handfuls of barley from your sheaves and leave them for her to glean.' That evening Ruth beat out about a bushel of barley from the stalks she had collected.

When Naomi heard that Ruth had been gleaning in Boaz's fields, she told her he was Elimelech's kinsman. 'Glean there throughout the barley-harvest and the coming wheat-harvest,' she said, 'and when the harvests are over, I will tell you what you must do.'

In those days, when a woman's husband died, she could claim protection from his nearest male relative. Naomi told Ruth that she was to go to Boaz when he was in good humour after the harvest festivities. She was to lie down by him on the threshing-floor where he would be sleeping, and was to cover herself with the skirt of his robe. This would be a sign to him that she claimed his protection.

When he awoke, Boaz was deeply moved by Ruth's coming to him. The next day he went to the city-gate, where all public business was done, and made certain that no one who had a better claim than himself to protect Ruth, wished to do so. Then he married her and cared for her all her life.

In due time Ruth had a son called Obed. He in his turn had a son called Jesse; and Jesse became the father of David, the greatest king that Israel ever had.

The corn was arranged in sheaves or bundles with the ears pointing in the same direction. The ears were then repeatedly struck with a stick, knocking off the grain and the chaff. The straw stems left in the hand were used for roofing or for all kinds of plaited work. Ruth would have taken home only the grains of the barley for herself and Naomi to eat.

73

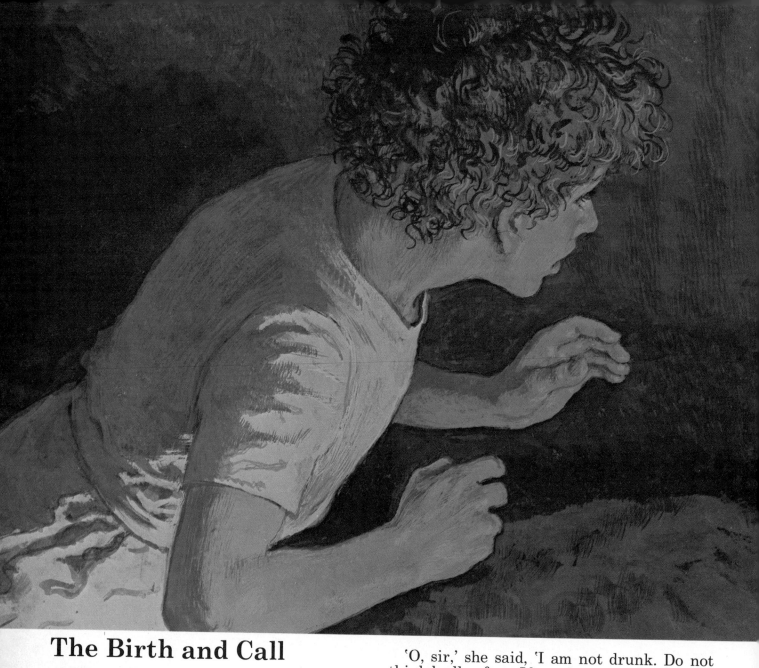

The Birth and Call of Samuel

1 Samuel 1–3

There was once an Israelite called Elkanah, who had two wives. One, named Peninnah, had several children, and she taunted Hannah, the other wife, who had none. Elkanah's entire family went yearly to the tabernacle at Shiloh to sacrifice to God. One year, after Peninnah had tormented her more cruelly than usual, Hannah, weeping bitterly, prayed to God outside the Tabernacle enclosure.

'Lord,' she prayed, 'if you will send me a son, I will give him back to you to serve you throughout his whole life.'

Eli, the High Priest, was sitting by the entrance to the enclosure. He saw Hannah swaying and her lips moving in silent prayer but could not hear her voice, and he thought she must be drunk. 'Be off with you,' he said harshly, 'and do not come back until you are sober.'

'O, sir,' she said, 'I am not drunk. Do not think badly of me. I have been pouring out my heart to God in grief and misery.'

'Go in peace,' said Eli, 'and may God answer your prayer.'

His kindness made Hannah happy. But her happiness then was nothing to the joy she felt when very soon after she knew that her prayer had been answered and that she was going to have a child. When the baby, a boy, was born, she called him Samuel, which means 'Asked of God', and as soon as he was old enough, she took him to Eli.

'I am the woman, sir,' she said, 'whom you thought was drunk. I was praying for a son, and God answered my prayer. Now I have come to lend him to the Lord, to serve God all his life.'

Hannah saw Samuel every year. She had five more children, and Peninnah could no longer mock her.

Hannah's children gave her joy, but Eli had two sons who made him unhappy. Although they were priests, they were greedy and wicked men. They robbed the pilgrims to the

Tabernacle of the best part of the offerings they intended to give to God, and brought evil customs into the religion of Jehovah from the worship of heathen gods.

Eli, now a very old man and nearly blind, could not control his sons, although he knew of their wicked ways. Because of this, the Israelites grew to despise the Tabernacle sacrifices, and this was perhaps why God did not appear openly in those days. Men neither heard the voice of God as Moses had done, nor saw his messengers as Joshua and Gideon had seen them. It seemed that God was far away.

But Samuel served the Lord faithfully in the Tabernacle. He used to sleep in the Holy Place, and very early one morning, before the seven-branched lampstand which shone all night had burned itself out, he heard a voice calling his name. He ran to Eli. 'Here I am,' he said.

'I did not call you,' Eli replied. 'Go back to sleep.'

Again Samuel heard his name called and again he ran to Eli. 'I heard you call,' he said, 'I am here.'

'Not I,' said Eli. 'Lie down again.'

'Samuel! Samuel!' called the voice a third time. Once more Samuel went to Eli who realized this time that it must be God who was calling Samuel. He said to him, 'Lie down, and when you hear the call, answer, "Speak, Lord; your servant is listening."'

Samuel obeyed him and the voice answered, 'Because Eli knew of his sons' evil ways and did not check them, my judgments against his family shall stand for ever. They shall never be forgiven for making my sacrifices despised and my worship unclean.'

The voice was silent. Samuel was afraid to tell Eli what he had heard until the old man called him. 'Hide nothing from me of what God told you,' he said.

Samuel told him everything. Eli said only, 'Let God do what he thinks good.'

This was the first of many occasions that God spoke through Samuel. He grew up to be known throughout Israel as a prophet who always spoke the truth. Once more the Lord had raised up a leader like the heroes of old through whom he could address his people.

The Philistines and the Ark

1 Samuel 4–6

Samuel grew up at a time when the Israelites and Philistines were fighting for the mastery of Canaan. After a defeat by the Philistines, the Israelite leaders said, 'Why did God allow us to be beaten today? Let us fetch the Ark of the Covenant and carry it into battle against our enemies. It will bring us certain victory.'

So the Ark was brought to the camp from Shiloh, attended by Eli's two wicked sons, Hophni and Phineas. The Israelite army welcomed it with a cheer so loud that it was heard by the Philistines.

When they discovered the reason for the shout, they were terrified. 'Their god has come into their camp,' they said, 'the mighty god who crushed the Egyptians. We are lost – who can save us from the power of such a god? Courage, Philistines! Fight like heroes. Do not become slaves of the Hebrews as they have been to you.'

They hurled themselves into the attack. To their astonishment, they carried all before them. Thirty thousand Israelites were killed, among them Hophni and Phineas. The rest fled, and worst of all, the Ark was captured.

A survivor reached Shiloh on the same day. When he told the news, a great groan of horror went up from the people, which Eli heard, sitting by the road outside the town. He was now ninety-eight years old, completely blind, and full of anxiety about the Ark of God.

He asked what the uproar meant and was told, 'The Philistines have routed the army. Our men have fled in panic. Your two sons are dead and the Ark of God is taken.' When he heard of the capture of the Ark, Eli fell to the ground, broke his neck and died.

Meanwhile, the Philistines had carried the Ark to the city of Ashdod and placed it in the temple of their god, Dagon. The next morning, when the priests entered the temple, they found Dagon's image lying on its face before the Ark as if worshipping it. With difficulty they raised the giant idol and restored it to its place. But the next day the image had not only fallen again; its head and two hands were broken off.

The city of Ashdod also suffered. A plague of rats destroyed the citizens' goods and the people were afflicted with agonizing tumours from which many of them died. The Philistines moved the Ark from city to city, hoping to find some place acceptable to the God of Israel. But everywhere the same dreadful plagues accompanied the Ark until at last the Philistines

urged their princes, 'Send the Ark of Israel's God away, back to its own place before it kills us all.'

The princes asked their priests what should be done, and they said, 'Make a new wagon. Harness to it two cows which have never before drawn a cart. Take their calves from them and shut them in their stalls. On the wagon place the Ark of Israel's God together with five golden images of the tumours and five golden images of the rats, one for each of the five

princes of the Philistines.

'Let the cart go where it will. If it goes to Israelite country, we shall know that the God of Israel has brought us these disasters. If not, we have been the victims only of chance.'

The Philistines did all their priests suggested. When they released the wagon, the two cows pulled it straight along the road to Israel's land, turning neither right nor left. The Israelites were havesting their wheat when the cart came into view. They were overjoyed at the sight. For seven long months they had been without the Ark, which for them represented the throne upon which God sat when he visited his people.

They made a fire of the wood of the cart and sacrificed the two cows upon it as a thank-offering to God. The Ark was housed in a nearby city where it remained for many years until King David brought it to Jerusalem. Meanwhile, after Eli's death, Samuel ruled and judged Israel.

Saul Anointed King

1 Samuel 7–10

Under Samuel's leadership, the Israelites forsook the idols many of them still worshipped and returned to their own true God. As a result, they were granted victories against the Philistines, and began to recover the cities and lands which the Philistines had captured from them.

But Samuel grew old, and his two sons who shared his work turned out to be almost as wicked as Eli's sons had been. So the Israelite leaders went to Samuel and said, 'We want a king to govern us.'

Samuel was displeased with their request and turned to God for guidance. 'It is not you they have rejected,' God said, 'it is I. Tell them that a king will take their men for his army, their women for his servants. The people will plough his fields and reap his crops. He will seize the best of their lands and give them to his favourites. He will tax them, taking a tenth of their grain, wine, slaves, flocks and herds for his own use and for his courtiers. He will end by making them all his slaves.'

But the people insisted, 'We want a king to rule us and lead us into battle.' God said to Samuel, 'Let them have their way.'

Soon after, a man of the tribe of Benjamin, called Kish, lost some donkeys, and sent Saul his son to look for them. After searching for several days, Saul was about to give up the task when his servant told him that Samuel would be coming to the nearby city for a festival to be held that very day. Perhaps the prophet would help them.

The moment Samuel saw Saul, God revealed to him that this was the man he had chosen to rule Israel. Samuel told Saul that the asses had been found, but that all Israel awaited him. The words puzzled Saul, for his tribe was small and his family unimportant. But the prophet honoured him at the feast that day, made him stay the night, and the next day accompanied him out of the city.

'Send your servant on ahead,' said Samuel, 'and I will give you a message from God.' When the boy had gone, Samuel poured a flask of oil over Saul's head. 'The Lord anoints you king over his people, Israel. You shall rule them and deliver them from their enemies. God will be with you. Now go. I shall join you in seven days and tell you what to do.'

As Saul turned to go, he knew that Samuel's words were true. He felt that he was a changed man. God was indeed with him, and he, an unimportant farmer's son, would be able to be a worthy king of Israel.

Once again Samuel summoned the nation to hear what he had to say. 'The God of Israel has spoken,' he said. 'I delivered you from Egypt and from the nations that oppressed you. But you reject me and demand a king. Take up your positions by tribes and families, and your king will be selected by drawing lots.'

Of all the tribes, Benjamin was chosen. Of all the families of Benjamin, the family of Matri, to which Kish belonged, was chosen. Of all the men of Matri's family, Saul was chosen. But when they came to look for him he was nowhere to be found.

Suddenly frightened by the greatness of the task that God was calling him to do, Saul had hidden himself. Eventually he was found and presented to the people. When they saw how majestic he looked – for he was head and shoulders taller than any other man in Israel – there was a tremendous shout of 'God save the King!'

Samuel told the Israelites what were the duties of a king and wrote them on a scroll. All but a few of the people, who despised the farmer's son, went home content. It would be easier to be loyal to a king whom they could see, they felt, than to a god whom they could not see.

The Rejection of King Saul

1 Samuel 11; 13–15

A month after Saul had been elected King, the Ammonites, ancient enemies of Israel, besieged a city called Jabesh-Gilead. The city was small and the Ammonite army so large and strong that the men of the city thought they had no choice but to surrender. But the Ammonite general said, 'We will allow you to surrender peacefully only on condition that we put out the right eye of every man in the city. In this way we shall disgrace Israel, the nation which could not save you.'

'Give us seven days to send messages throughout Israel,' pleaded the Gileadites. 'Then, if no one comes to our aid, we will surrender, and you can do what you like to us.' So certain were the Ammonites that no Israelite would risk his life to save Jabesh-Gilead that they allowed the messengers to be sent.

Saul heard the news when he was bringing back his oxen from ploughing – for, in spite of being king, he had returned to his ordinary life as a farmer. At once the Spirit of God seized him. Furious, he took two oxen, cut them in pieces, and sent them to every tribe in Israel with the message, 'The same shall be done to the oxen of any man who does not follow me into battle.'

A larger army than the Israelites had ever mustered before gathered within days. Saul sent messengers to tell the Gileadites that they would be rescued the next day. In their turn, the Gileadites tricked the Ammonites into a false feeling of safety by telling them that they would surrender on the morrow. But hours before the time the men of Gilead had promised to surrender, Saul attacked. He divided his huge army into three columns which assaulted the unsuspecting Ammonites from three different directions at once. They were taken by surprise and completely defeated.

After this first great victory of Saul's, his followers wanted to kill the men who had despised the farmer's son when he was elected King. But Saul forgave them. Such a victory, he said, should not be spoiled by putting to death any Israelite.

Saul had a valiant son named Jonathan under whose command he placed a thousand men while commanding two thousand himself. Jonathan killed the governor of a district where the Philistines still ruled; and the whole Philistine army gathered to crush the Israelite revolt. All Israel rallied to Saul.

But they were outnumbered by their enemies and were soon hard-pressed; and, to make matters worse, Samuel did not come on the day he had appointed to sacrifice on their behalf to God and pray to him for aid.

Saul's army began to melt away as the frightened people slunk back home. The king waited for seven days, and still Samuel did not come. Afraid that soon he would have no army left, Saul lost patience and offered the sacrifice himself, although only a priest was allowed to do this. Samuel arrived just as Saul had finished and said, 'You have acted foolishly. For what you have done, God will take the kingdoms from your family and give it to another whom he has already chosen.' Without a word more, Samuel left Saul and went angrily on his way.

Not more than six hundred men remained

80

with the king, and none of them had weapons other than axes and sickles; for the Philistines were determined to prevent the Israelites from making swords and spears and had allowed them to have no blacksmiths in the areas they governed. Only Saul and Jonathan carried arms.

The Israelites were camped on top of a cliff bordering a deep ravine, and their enemies were on the other side of the valley. Catching sight of Jonathan and his armour-bearer who were on their own, the Philistines called to them mockingly, 'Come up here – we have something to show you.' Jonathan had made up his mind that, if the Philistines told them to come up, this would be a sign that God had delivered them into his hands. So he and his companion clambered down the cliff, across the ravine and up the other side on their hands and knees. Once on top of the cliff, the two attacked the Philistines with the utmost fury, mowing down about twenty of them at the first assault. Some Hebrews, whom the Philistines had enrolled in their army, now changed sides and attacked their former masters from inside the camp. This added to the panic and confusion which Jonathan's whirlwind attack had already caused.

Saul and his army, seeing the tumult on the other side of the valley ran shouting to help Jonathan and his Hebrew allies. Other Israelites who had been hiding in caves nearby poured out of them and spread more alarm among the Philistines, who were now attacking each other, unable to distinguish friend from foe. Soon they were running for their lives. Saul's men pursued them, slaughtering

A sarcophagus coffin-cover representing a Philistine warrior. The headpieces of horizontal bands decorating these man-shaped clay coffins represented the typical feathered head-dress of the Philistines.

81

as many as they could before evening fell.

In his zeal to destroy his enemies, Saul proclaimed, 'A curse on anyone who stops to eat before nightfall, until I have taken vengeance on my foes.' Not knowing of his father's order, Jonathan ate part of a honeycomb he found and was refreshed. In the evening, when this was discovered, Saul decreed that he must die. Jonathan was ready to submit. But the people were horrified that the hero who almost single-handed had inspired that day's victory should die. They ransomed him, either with money or a sacrifice, and so Jonathan was saved.

Saul became a great warrior king, and fought against Israel's enemies on every side. He defeated the armies of Moab, Ammon, Edom, and Zobah, as well as the Philistines, brave and fierce warriors. Although he defeated another people, the Amalekites, his victory over them made God finally abandon him.

For Samuel had brought Saul a message from Jehovah, 'Because the Amalekites attacked Israel on their way to Canaan from Egypt, you must destroy them completely and everything they possess.' So Saul mustered all the fighting men of the country and attacked the Amalekites. He killed every man, woman and child, but he allowed their king, Agag, to live, and the best of the sheep and the cattle.

When Samuel found out what had happened, he reproached Saul bitterly for having disobeyed God's command. Saul tried to excuse himself by saying that the sheep and oxen had been kept to be sacrificed to the Lord. But Samuel replied, 'To obey God is better than sacrifice. To disobey him is worse than witchcraft. Because you have rejected the word of the Lord, he has rejected you as king.'

Saul was struck to the heart by Samuel's words and begged him to ask God for his forgiveness. But Samuel refused and turned to go. As he did so, Saul caught hold of his robe and it tore in his hand. 'As you have torn my cloak,' said Samuel, 'so God has torn the kingdom from you and given it to another who is a better man than you. You cannot turn God by force.'

'Honour me just this once before my people,' pleaded Saul, 'and I will repent and submit to God.' So Samuel returned with Saul as if nothing had happened between them. Saul killed Agag, the last Amalekite left alive. Then Samuel went back to his home and Saul to his; and never did the two of them see each other again. But Samuel mourned for Saul, pitying from his heart the fine man whom the Lord had rejected from being king over Israel.

David is Chosen

1 Samuel 16

There came a time when Samuel realized that he must stop grieving for Saul whom God had rejected from being king over Israel. He knew that a better man had been selected to take his place; and in the course of time, God guided him to the man he had chosen.

'Fill your horn with oil,' God said to him, 'and go to Bethlehem to a man called Jesse. I have chosen a king from among his sons.'

'How can I go?' said Samuel. 'If Saul hears that I have gone to anoint a king in his place, he will kill me.'

'Take a calf with you,' God said, 'and go to Bethlehem to sacrifice to me. Invite Jesse to the sacrifice. I will tell you what you must do, and show you the man whom I have chosen to be king.'

So Samuel went to Bethlehem, leading a calf for sacrifice. The chief men of the city were alarmed when they saw him coming for, although a king now ruled the land, Samuel still had power to judge a city and punish it for offences against God.

'Why have you come?' they asked him anxiously. 'Is anything wrong?'

'Do not be alarmed,' Samuel replied. 'All is well. I have come to sacrifice to God on your behalf. Purify yourselves for a festival and rejoice with me today.'

Samuel himself went to Jesse and invited him to the feast. 'Call your sons,' he said. 'I shall purify you and each of them in turn for the sacrifice.'

The eldest was a fine, handsome man, and as he knelt before Samuel, the prophet thought, 'This must be the one whom the Lord has chosen.' But at once God brought another thought into his mind. He remembered Saul. 'God does not judge a man by his handsome face or by his height,' he reflected. 'God does not see as men see, but he sees what a man is really like within.' Samuel knew that Jesse's eldest son was not the man he was looking for.

Six more sons came before Samuel to be purified and he knew that none of them was the one chosen by God. But as no more came forward Samuel asked Jesse, 'Are all your sons here?'

'There is still David, the youngest,' answered Jesse. 'He is looking after the sheep.'

'Fetch him,' replied Samuel. 'We must not sit down to the sacrificial feast until he comes.'

When the young man arrived, Samuel knew at once that this was the king whom God had chosen to succeed Saul. David was good-looking, with ruddy cheeks and bright, alert eyes. Samuel took the horn of oil and anointed David in the presence of his brothers. But they did not know what the anointing meant. It may have seemed to them that Samuel had anointed their brother as his follower, to become a prophet like himself. But David felt the Spirit of God rushing over him like a great wave, and from that day on, it never left him.

From Saul the Spirit of God had finally departed. Its place was taken from time to time by an evil spirit which terrified him and brought madness upon him. The madness went as suddenly as it came. But while it possessed Saul, he either sat in gloomy silence or raved within his house, his actions a danger to everyone around him.

When his courtiers came to him and said, 'Let us find for you a man who can play skilfully upon the harp. Let him play for you when the evil spirit comes upon you so that the music may make you better,' Saul agreed to their suggestion. One of them said, 'I know the very man. His name is David. He is the son of Jesse of Bethlehem, and not only does he play the harp skilfully, but he has the makings of a brave fighter. He is handsome and intelligent, and God is with him.'

So Saul sent for David, little knowing that this was the man who would be king of Israel after him. The moment he saw him he loved him and made him welcome at his court. And whenever the evil spirit overpowered Saul, David played the harp until the king's madness left him and he had recovered.

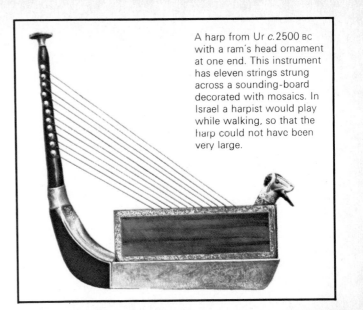

A harp from Ur c.2500 BC with a ram's head ornament at one end. This instrument has eleven strings strung across a sounding-board decorated with mosaics. In Israel a harpist would play while walking, so that the harp could not have been very large.

The Giant from Gath

1 Samuel 17

But David was still young and did not spend all his time at Saul's court. When the Philistines started invading Israelite territory once again, he was at home, shepherding his father's flocks. One day his father, Jesse, sent David to take food to his three eldest brothers who were in Saul's army.

He reached the Israelite camp just as the army was going out in battle array. David left the food in the camp and ran to find his brothers. While he was greeting them the whole army started to rush back to their camp.

'Why are you running?' asked David, bewildered by the sudden flight.

'Look,' said a soldier, pointing behind him as he ran. David turned and saw a huge man striding ahead of the Philistines. He was almost twice as tall as an ordinary man, clad in bronze armour, and carrying the largest spear David had ever seen.

'What need is there of a battle, you Israelite slaves?' he roared after the fleeing Israelites. 'Choose a champion from your ranks to fight me, Goliath of Gath. Let us settle our business by single combat. If he kills me, we Philistines will be your subjects. But if I kill him, you shall serve us. I defy you, dogs of Israelites. Send a man to fight it out with me.'

David was enraged when he heard Goliath's challenge. 'Who is this heathen that he dare insult the armies of the living God?' he cried. When the soldiers saw his anger and fearlessness, some of them told Saul, who sent for him.

'I will fight this Philistine for you,' said David.

'You cannot fight him,' said Saul. 'You are only a youth and he is an experienced warrior as well as a giant.'

'If a wild beast seizes one of my father's sheep,' replied David, 'I rescue the sheep and kill the beast if it attacks me. I have killed both lions and bears, and this Goliath shall meet the same fate as they for insulting the armies of Jehovah. God who preserved me from lions and bears will save me also from this Philistine.'

'Go then, and God be with you,' answered Saul. He gave David armour, but the boy found it too clumsy and took it off. Trusting to the weapons he knew, he chose five smooth stones from the nearby brook, and armed with only a sling and club he went out to fight Goliath.

'Do you think I am a dog,' roared the giant when he saw him, 'that you come with a stick to beat me? Come here, and I will give your flesh to feed to the vultures and jackals.'

'You threaten me with sword and spear,' David retorted, 'but I come against you in the name of Israel's God. He will deliver you into my hands, and it is Philistine flesh that will feed the birds and beasts today. The world shall learn that battles are not won by sword and spear but that victory belongs to God.'

As the Philistine started to move towards him, David ran to meet him. He took a stone from his pouch and slung it with all his strength and skill. It pierced Goliath's forehead. The giant wavered, his arms flung wide, then toppled forward on his face. David ran to him, struck off Goliath's head with his own sword, and held it high.

Aghast, the Philistines turned and fled. The Israelites chased them to the very gates of their cities, slaughtering them by the hundred. Victory, as David had said, belonged to God alone, and he granted it with a pebble from a stream.

David's sling would have been of twined wool with a 2-inch wide middle piece, reinforced to hold smooth, riverbed stones. Goliath's bronze coat of mail was made with great technical skill: it had to be lightweight, and provide protection as well as freedom of movement.

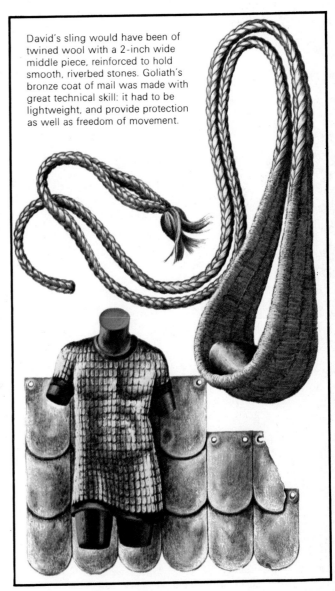

David and Saul

1 Samuel 18; 19, 1–18

The Israelite army marched home flushed with victory. From every city along the way women came out to greet Saul, singing and dancing with cymbals and tambourines.

'Saul of thousands has been the bane,
But tens of thousands has David slain.'

The song filled Saul with jealousy. He thought to himself, 'They give David tens of thousands but only thousands to me. They will be giving him the kingdom next!' From that day on he watched the young warrior with hatred and suspicion.

The very day after their return from pursuing the Philistines, Saul was attacked by a fit of madness. Hastily David was summoned to play the music which usually soothed the king. But Saul had a spear in his hand, and, without warning, he hurled it at the young man, trying to pin him to the wall. David twisted out of the way and courageously continued to play. But soon after, Saul leaped for the spear, snatched it out of the wall and again hurled it at David, once more missing the boy.

The madness passed, but Saul, knowing that the Spirit of God had left him and was now with David, was afraid. Jealous though he was of David, and glad though he would have been if he had died, he did not want to commit the sin of murdering him himself. The king put the young warrior in command of a regiment of his troops, hoping that in a skirmish with the Philistines he might be killed while leading his men. But David was so skilled and successful that his soldiers idolized him, and the ordinary people, too, admired him as he went about the king's business.

Michal, Saul's daughter, fell in love with David. She told her father and he was delighted, for he saw a way in which he could bring David to his death. He told his attendants to say to him, 'The king loves you. Why do you not ask him if you can marry Michal?' But the young soldier replied, 'I am a poor man and belong to a family of no importance. I have neither the wealth nor the rank to become the king's son-in-law.'

'Ah,' they replied, 'but the king wants no dowry for the bride except one hundred dead Philistines. Bring proof that you have killed them and you can marry Michal.' Saul hoped that David would be killed in the attempt. But David and his men slew two hundred Philistines and the king was forced to allow him to marry Michal.

In the continuous border-fighting between Israel and Philistia, David played a significant part. He was so successful that Saul gave up all hope of his being killed in battle, and at last gave direct orders to Jonathan and his officers to kill David.

But Jonathan, a hero and warrior himself, loved David with all his heart and spoke vigorously against his father's commands. He pointed out all that David had done for Israel and shamed Saul into repenting for his evil thoughts against his son-in-law. The

king gave his promise that David should be safe at court, and Jonathan brought his friend back to serve his father.

But this happy period did not last. Another great victory of David's renewed Saul's jealousy, and again, in a fit of madness, he tried to spear him. David fled home. Resolved now to finish him once and for all, Saul sent men to watch the house all night and kill David in the morning. But Michal saw them, and, when it became dark she lowered her husband from a window. In his bed she placed an image, covering it with bedclothes.

When Saul discovered that David had escaped he was furious with his daughter. 'Why did you let my enemy go?' he shouted. 'He threatened to kill me,' Michal sobbed. 'What else could I do?'

Saul sent his men in pursuit, but by that time David was far away. He went to Samuel, where, for the time being, he was safe, and told him all that the king had done.

Psalm 23 (Authorized Version)

A Psalm of David

*The Lord is my shepherd; I shall not
   want.*
*He maketh me to lie down in green
   pastures:*
He leadeth me beside the still waters.
He restoreth my soul:
*He leadeth me in the paths of
   righteousness for his name's sake.*
*Yea, though I walk through the valley
   of the shadow of death,*
I will fear no evil: for thou art with me;
Thy rod and thy staff they comfort me.
*Thou preparest a table before me in the
   presence of mine enemies:*
*Thou anointest my head with oil; my
   cup runneth over.*

*Surely goodness and mercy shall
follow me all the days of my life:*
*And I will dwell in the house of the
   Lord for ever.*

The Twenty-Third Psalm

The best-known of psalms the Twenty-third, was inspired by David's work as a boy, for it describes a day in his life as a shepherd.

In the morning the shepherd takes his crook and cudgel (rod and staff), his sling and stones. He does not drive his sheep but calls them to follow him. He knows each of them individually and every one of their names. They trust him completely because they know that, even though he may ˙lead them through difficult or dangerous places, he will look after them. He guides them to rich grass, where they can lie down peacefully when they have fed, and to quietly-flowing water, avoiding noisy mountain-streams which frighten them.

The best pastures sometimes lie through ravines in the mountains, so dark and narrow that sunshine never reaches to their depths. Their gloom and cold terrify the sheep. But the shepherd cheerfully rattles his crook and cudgel against the rocks on either side, encouraging his sheep by calling out their names.

There are two dangers from which the shepherd must particularly protect his sheep. One is poisonous herbs, which they cannot distinguish from good grass. But the shepherd can, and he watches his sheep continually. If he sees one of them about to eat a poisonous plant, he calls it by name. Sometimes the plant looks so good that the sheep takes no notice of his warning. Then the shepherd quickly puts a stone in his sling and sends it hissing under the sheep's nose to save it from its own stupidity. Eastern shepherds have to be very skilful with their slings and spend a great deal of time practising with them.

Snakes are the other chief danger. They lie almost completely covered in sandy hollows, such as those made by the hooves of animals in desert places through which the sheep sometimes have to pass. The shepherd, walking in front of his sheep, stirs the sand round with the end of his crook in places where a snake may be hiding. If he finds one, he kills it with his cudgel, and the sheep follow in safety.

When, in the evening, the sheep return to the fold, the shepherd calls each of them to him in turn and, holding his crook level with the ground, makes every one jump over it. This shows him if any sheep is either lame or exhausted. He refreshes tired sheep by pouring oil on their heads and soothes their hurts by rubbing oil into scratches and cuts. Next, the shepherd fills a large, two-handled bowl to the brim with cool water from a cistern which he always keeps full. Beginning with the tired or hurt sheep, he gives a drink to each in turn. He refills the bowl after every sheep has drunk so that none of them needs strain to reach the water. All of them have a cup which 'runneth over'.

At last the working day is over. Sitting at the opening of his tent, the shepherd sees running towards him a man hunted by two others. They nearly catch him; but in desperation the fugitive hurls himself into the shepherd's tent. The shepherd knows that his unexpected guest has killed someone, accidentally or intentionally. He knows, too, that his two pursuers are Avengers of Blood, probably relatives of the dead man, who have the right to kill the killer in turn. But the Eastern law of hospitality forbids the killing of a man when he has taken refuge in another man's home. The Avengers must wait outside until the killer leaves the tent.

The shepherd sees even in this a picture of God's loving-kindness. The Lord's goodness and mercy are like two Avengers of Blood. We may fly from them because we do not understand God's love. But they will drive us into the tent of the Good Shepherd himself, and, by waiting for us outside, will see that we never leave it.

David and Jonathan

1 Samuel 20

From his hiding-place David sent a message to Jonathan, arranging to meet him secretly. 'Why does your father want to kill me?' he asked. 'What have I done wrong?'

'He cannot want to kill you,' said Jonathan. 'He tells me everything he intends to do, and he has not told me this.'

'The king knows that we are friends,' replied David. 'He would not grieve you by telling you that he plans to kill me. I know I am only one step away from death.'

'What do you want me to do?' asked Jonathan.

'Tomorrow at the festival of the new moon,' said David, 'I am expected to eat at the king's table with the rest of the court. But I will hide in the country. If your father asks where I am, say, "David asked my permission to go to Bethlehem where a yearly sacrifice is being held for his family." If he answers, "Good," I shall know I am in no danger. But if he is angry, I shall take it as a warning that he is plotting some mischief against me. Can we plan some way in which you can tell me what the king does without anyone knowing?'

'Yes,' said Jonathan. 'My father will not be surprised if you miss the first day of the feast. But he will begin to wonder on the second day, and on the third he is bound to ask where you are.

'You know the heap of stones where I practise my archery. Hide near it on the third day close enough for you to hear me calling. I will shoot my arrows as if I were aiming at a mark and send my boy to collect them. If I call, "The arrows are here, on this side of you," you will know that you have nothing to fear. But if I shout, "The arrows are beyond you," you will know there is danger, and you must hasten away with all speed.'

The two friends bade each other goodbye. 'God be with you,' said Jonathan. 'If I die, promise me that you will always show kindness to my family. May God save you from all your enemies.'

When the new-moon festival began, the only empty seat at the king's table was

Drawings made from Assyrian reliefs of the 9th and 8th centuries BC of a bow and a quiver of arrows.

David's. Saul said nothing on the first day, but on the second he asked Jonathan where David was. Jonathan gave his father David's message about his going to his family festival and watched to see how Saul would take the news.

He did not have to wait long. Saul's anger blazed out against Jonathan as ferociously as if he had been David himself. 'You son of a rebellious mother!' he cried. 'I know you are David's friend. Don't you see that as long as he is alive, your crown and kingdom are in danger? Bring him to me. He shall die.'

'Why, what has he done?' asked Jonathan. Saul brandished his spear as if to strike his own son. Hot with anger at the insults Saul had hurled at him, Jonathan left the table and

refused to eat. He knew that David was right. Saul was determined to kill him.

The next day, accompanied by his boy, he took his bow and arrows to the place where he had arranged to signal to David. He gave the agreed sign, and when the boy had collected the arrows and had been sent away, David left his hiding-place and bowed to Jonathan in friendship and gratitude. They embraced each other and wept. At last Jonathan said, 'Go in safety. God keep our friendship firm, and let it continue between your children and my children for ever. Farewell.'

So David went away to hide from Saul. Jonathan watched him till he was out of sight. Then he returned sadly to the town.

David the Refugee

1 Samuel 21–22

David fled to a city of priests where he was met by Ahimelech, their chief. He pretended to be on a secret mission from Saul, and as he had neither food nor weapons, Ahimelech gave him the shewbread, which only priests were allowed to eat, and Goliath's sword, kept there in the shrine. But as Doeg, one of Saul's bodyguard, saw him, David thought it wise to go.

Thinking he would be safe among Saul's enemies, he went to the city of Gath. He was recognized, and to save his life he pretended to be mad; for madmen were regarded as holy and no one living then would have dared harm one. When his chance came, he escaped into the wilderness. There he was joined by his family and by men in distress or debt or other kinds of trouble, until he had a band of four hundred men.

Meanwhile Doeg told Saul that Ahimelech had helped David, and, at Saul's command, he attacked and killed Ahimelech's whole clan. Only one son escaped to tell David of the massacre.

Then the Lord guided David to attack the Philistines who were besieging the Israelite city of Keilah. Defeating them, he gained much plunder and relieved the city, which he and his men entered.

But he did not stay long. God warned David that the men of Keilah would hand him over to Saul, and he left the city at once with his band, which now numbered six hundred, and lived in the wilderness.

There Saul hunted him like an animal. Once he so nearly caught him that he happened to be on one side of a hill when David and his men were on the other. Had not a messenger arrived summoning Saul to attack at once the Philistines who were ravaging Israel, David would have died that day.

When Saul had defeated the Philistine raiders, he set out once more in pursuit of David. While David was hiding in the depths of a long dark cave on one occasion, Saul entered it, not knowing he was there. David's companions whispered that he should kill Saul, but he refused. Instead he crept silently up to Saul and cut off a piece of his robe without his knowing. When the king left the cave, David followed him.

'My lord!' he called. Saul spun round, startled. David bowed, held up the cloth and said, 'Why do you believe those who say I wish you harm? See, you were in my power. I could have killed you.'

Saul's conscience was troubled and he wept at David's words. 'You have returned

A water flask, found at Gezer, and a spearhead, dating from the Early Iron Age c.11th–12th centuries BC. A flask was an essential piece of equipment for anyone marching through desert country, and like this one, usually had two small handles through which a cord could be passed. The spear was the standard weapon of the hunter or warrior, its bronze head fastened to a wooden shaft by a spiral of metal.

good for evil,' he said. 'One day, I know, you will be king of Israel. Swear that you will not destroy my family.'

David gave Saul his word, and the king returned home.

But Saul's madness returned and again he hunted David in the wilderness. One night when Saul was asleep with three thousand men around him, David and a friend stole through the lines of sleeping men to where Saul lay, took his spear and water-jug, and silently crept out of the camp.

Next morning David shouted down to Saul's camp from the top of a neighbouring hill, 'Where are the king's spear and water-jug?' Saul recognized his voice and once more acknowledged that he had done wrong. 'Come back,' he cried. 'I will never harm you again.'

But David knew that Saul could not control himself when the madness came upon him, and that his promises were worthless. So he returned to Gath where he pretended to side with the Philistines in raiding Israelite territory. Instead, he attacked the countries of the Amalekites and other enemies of Israel, leaving no one alive to tell the truth, and remained in favour with Achish, King of Gath.

The End of King Saul

1 Samuel 28; 31

While Saul was hunting David in the deserts and the mountains, Samuel died and was mourned by all Israel. Shortly afterwards the Philistines mustered a huge army and prepared once more to attack. Saul summoned the Israelites to meet them and camped at Mount Gilboa. But when he saw the size of the enemy army, brave as he was, his courage failed him. He prayed to God for guidance, but no answer came, either by dreams, signs or prophecy.

Desperate, Saul said to his courtiers, 'Find me a wise woman that I may consult her.' He was told that such a woman lived at Endor; so he disguised himself and went to her that night.

Now Saul had expelled from Israel all who practised witchcraft and wizardry and all wise women who claimed to be able to talk to the spirits of the dead, for he believed that worshippers of Jehovah should have nothing to do with such people. When, therefore, he said to the woman, 'Bring forth the spirit of the man I shall name to you,' she replied, 'You know that King Saul has driven out all wise women and wizards from the country. Why are you laying a trap for me, then, to have me put to death?'

Saul swore by almighty God that she should be safe. But when she asked, 'Whom shall I bring forth for you?' and he answered, 'Samuel,' the woman screamed with fear. 'Why have you deceived me?' she cried. 'You are Saul!' 'Have no fear,' he said, 'I have promised you your safety. What do you see?'

'I see an old man covered with a mantle,' she said. Saul knew that it was the spirit of Samuel and bowed low.

'Why have you disturbed me and called me forth?' asked the spirit.

'The Philistines are attacking Israel,' said Saul, 'and God is silent and will give me no sign. What shall I do?'

'Why do you ask me?' the spirit replied, 'God has abandoned you as I prophesied he would. Tomorrow you and your sons will fall in battle, and your army will be defeated.'

Aghast, Saul fell fainting to the ground. Not only was he overcome with the horror of what he had been told, but he had eaten nothing all that day and night and was weak with hunger. When he had recovered a little, the woman persuaded him and his attendants to eat, and after the meal they rode off to rejoin the army.

The next day, the Philistines attacked. All that Samuel's spirit had told Saul came true. The Israelites fled and were cut down in hundreds upon Mount Gilboa. Jonathan and two other sons of Saul were slain, and the king himself was gravely wounded by the Philistine archers. To avoid being captured by the enemy, Saul fell upon his own sword and died.

The defeat was crushing. The Israelites fled from the border towns without striking a blow, surrendering them to the victorious Philistines. The next day the Philistines found the bodies of Saul and his sons and rejoiced greatly, sending messengers through-out their country carrying the good news. They strung up the bodies to the walls of their town of Beth-shan. But brave warriors from the town of Jabesh-Gilead, where Saul had won his first victory as king years before, remembered that he had saved them from having their right eyes put out by the Am-monites. They marched all night, took down the bodies from the walls of Beth-shan, carried them back and buried them honour-ably, fasting and mourning over them for seven days.

David Becomes King

2 Samuel 1–4; 5, 1–5

Three days after the battle of Mount Gilboa, an Amalekite brought David news of the disaster that had befallen Israel. He carried with him Saul's crown and armlet; and, thinking that David would reward him, claimed that he had himself killed the king. Saul, he said, had asked him to kill him when he saw the Philistine chariots and horsemen closing in upon him and realized there was no escape. But David cried, 'How dared you slay God's anointed king!' and ordered the Amalekite to be executed for his crime. He then tore his clothes and mourned over Jonathan and Saul, for whom, in spite of all the king's hostility to him, he still felt loyal affection.

Judah, David's own tribe, immediately anointed him king over them, but Abner, Saul's commander-in-chief, remained faithful to his old master's family and made Ishbosheth, Saul's son, king of the other eleven tribes. There was a struggle for the throne which began with a battle between Abner and Joab, who commanded David's forces. Joab won the battle, in which, however, his brother Azahel was killed by Abner. The victory was the first of many which Joab won, and as the war continued, David's men gradually gained the upper hand.

The end came for Ishbosheth when Abner married a woman who had been one of Saul's wives. To marry a wife of a former king was in those days almost like claiming the throne, and Ishbosheth rebuked Abner for the marriage.

'Am I a dog,' exclaimed Abner, 'that after all my service to you, you find fault with me over a mere girl? From now on I will transfer my loyalty to David.' Ishbosheth was too weak and frightened of Abner to stop him, and his former general at once sent messengers to all

the Israelite princes urging them to join David. When they replied favourably to him, he met David in peace and arranged to travel round Israel on his behalf, to rally the whole nation to his support.

Shortly after Abner's departure, Joab returned bringing plunder from a raid. When he heard that Abner had only just left the king, he went at once to David. 'Do you not realize,' he said, 'that Abner came only to deceive you and spy on you?' Then, unknown to David, he sent a messenger after Abner to recall him. Taking him aside as if to speak to him privately, he suddenly stabbed him, crying out, 'Azahel, my brother, is revenged!'

When he heard of the murder, David was appalled. 'I am innocent of this crime,' he proclaimed. 'It was committed without my knowledge. A curse on Joab and his family for this deed.' He gave Abner an honourable burial and fasted for him all that day. His army and subjects approved what he did, realizing that he was indeed innocent of Abner's death.

With Abner's desertion and death, Ishbosheth and his followers lost heart. Two of his captains decided that they would now join David; and, in order to win his favour, they stole into Ishbosheth's palace one drowsy afternoon, stabbed him, cut off his head, and took it to David.

The king was furious. 'When the Amalekite told me that he had killed Saul, I executed him on the spot. How much more is it my duty to wipe villains like you off the earth, who have murdered an innocent man in bed in his own house?' So David executed the traitors, cut off their hands and feet, and hung them up as a dreadful warning to all would-be murderers.

With Ishbosheth dead, David had no rival for the throne of Israel. Every tribe rallied to him, and he reigned gloriously over a united nation for many years, waging successful war against all his enemies.

David and Bathsheba

2 Samuel 5–12

David's reign was a glorious one of continuous victories against the Philistines and other enemies of Israel. He brought the Ark to Jerusalem and planned to build a temple to Jehovah which his son, Solomon, erected. He showed kindness to those who were left of Saul's family. David was a great and good king.

But like all men, however good, he sinned. One day, from the roof of his palace in Jerusalem, he saw in the courtyard of a nearby house a woman so beautiful that he instantly fell in love with her. He learned that she was called Bathsheba, and that her husband, Uriah, was in his army besieging the town of Rabbah.

Although she was married, David could not forget her and summoned her to his palace. Her beauty inflamed him more than ever, and she, on meeting him, loved him, too. Soon David was so much in love that he was capable of any wickedness, no matter how horrible, in order to win her for his wife. So he wrote to Joab commanding him to place Uriah where the fighting was fiercest, then suddenly to retreat, leaving him alone so that he should be killed. Joab placed Uriah at a spot where he knew the men of Rabbah would resist most strongly. As he expected, they attacked. The Israelites drove them back, but came under a hail of arrows from the city walls. Uriah was killed.

Bathsheba mourned for her husband for the customary time. Then David married her, and she bore him a son.

But David's sin was not hidden from God. One day there came to him Nathan, a prophet, who told him this story.

'Living in a certain town were two men, one rich, the other poor. The rich man possessed large flocks and herds, but the poor man had only one lamb, which grew up as a pet with his children, almost like another child itself. A traveller came to visit the rich man who, instead of serving one of his own sheep to feed his guest, took the poor man's lamb and roasted that.'

David was furious. 'The man deserves to die,' he cried. 'He must at least give back four lambs for the one he stole.'

'You are the man!' thundered Nathan. 'Hear what God has to say to you. I saved you from Saul; I made you king; you had the pick of Israel's women for your wives. Why have you done this dreadful thing, murdering Uriah and stealing his wife?

'This shall be your punishment. Never shall your household have rest from the sword.

Your own family will rebel against you. You have sinned in secret, but all Israel shall see trouble come upon you openly.'

David was overwhelmed with remorse. 'I have sinned against God,' he said.

'Your immediate punishment,' said Nathan, 'is that your son will die.'

Nathan had scarcely gone when Bathsheba's baby became very ill. David prayed and fasted for a week in such despair that his servants dared not approach him. On the seventh day, when the child died, they were terrified of telling him. But he guessed the truth from their behaviour.

'Is the boy dead?' he asked. 'He is,' they acknowledged. David rose, washed, put on clean clothes, worshipped God and ordered food to be served. His servants were astonished. But he explained, 'While the boy lived there was hope that God might answer my prayers. But now fasting and mourning will not bring my son back to me.'

David comforted Bathsheba, and in due course she bore him another son, Solomon, who was to succeed him as king and build the Temple at Jerusalem.

David and Absalom

2 Samuel 13–18

Nathan's prophecy that David would be troubled by quarrels within his family soon came true. When a man had as many wives and children as David did, there was often much jealousy and rivalry among them. One of David's sons, Amnon, grievously wronged his half-sister, Tamar, and her full brother, Absalom, murdered him in revenge two years later and then fled abroad. But David yearned for Absalom, whom he loved in spite of his crime, and after five years father and son were reconciled.

But Absalom was ambitious and tried to attract David's subjects to support him by promising them favours. When he thought himself popular enough, he proclaimed himself king of Israel at Hebron, and was joined by an ever-increasing number of Israelites, including even Ahithophel, one of David's most trusted counsellors. So threatening did the revolt become, that David and his supporters left Jerusalem to avoid being trapped there. David left behind a trusted friend called Hushai who was to pretend to join Absalom, so that he could discover his plans and perhaps persuade him by giving him wrong advice to do foolish things which would result in his defeat.

Absalom marched triumphantly into Jerusalem with his followers. Ahithophel advised him to attack David at once while he was on the run. Only David need be killed, he said; once he was dead, the whole country would rally to Absalom. But Hushai said, 'No. Your father is an old soldier, experienced in open warfare. Wait until you have gathered all your supporters throughout Israel, and are strong enough to make your victory certain.' Absalom preferred Hushai's advice, and Hushai sent messengers secretly to David to tell him of Absalom's plans. They were nearly caught, but reached David safely and gave him their message. Meanwhile, when Ahithophel saw that his advice had been rejected, he realized that Absalom's rebellion would certainly fail, and he killed himself.

David had the breathing-space he needed to organize his forces, and by the time Absalom and his army were ready to attack, the royalist troops were prepared. But his men would not allow David to risk his life in the fighting. If they lost the battle, he could still recover his throne by winning another; but if he were killed, all would be lost.

In spite of Absalom's treachery, the king still loved him, and before the battle David told his commanders that, whatever happened that day, they were to deal kindly with his son. The struggle took place in a wild forest and resulted in overwhelming victory for David's men. Absalom himself, riding fast from David's bodyguard with whom he clashed in the confusion of the battle, was caught by his long hair in the branches of an oak. He remained helplessly suspended while his horse galloped away from beneath him. One of his pursuers hurried to Joab and told him of the young man's plight, whereupon Joab snatched up three spears and, riding to where Absalom was hanging, struck them into his body. His act was a signal for ten men who were with him to hack at the prince until all sign of life had gone.

Two messengers ran to David, waiting in a nearby city. The first told him the joyful news that the battle had been won, but pretended to know nothing of Absalom's fate. The second told David that Absalom was dead. On hearing this, all David's joy in the victory left him. He went to a room where he could be alone and lamented as if his heart would break. 'Oh, my son, Absalom! my son, my son, Absalom! Would to God I had died in your place, Oh, Absalom, my son, my son!'

Uriah the husband of Bathsheba was a Hittite— he was probably a migrant as the Hittite Empire did not extend as far south as Israel. A Hittite war chariot of the first millenium carrying an archer. Right, a Hittite warrior holding his long spear and shield.

The Wisdom of Solomon

1 Kings 1–4

When David was a very old man, he let it be known that he wished Solomon, Bathsheba's son, to be king after him. But Solomon did not become king without a struggle. His half-brother, Adonijah, tried to seize the throne even before David died, so David forestalled Adonijah by having Solomon proclaimed and anointed king immediately. Once a man had been consecrated king, he was regarded as sacred. Only a very bold rival dared raise his hand against the Lord's Anointed.

After giving Solomon his last wishes, David died. Without losing time, the young king set about making his throne secure by revenging himself on David's old enemies whom his father had spared during his life time. Although he was faithful to the worship of Jehovah, Solomon sacrificed at shrines in different parts of the country, since as yet there was no central Temple built to be the only place to worship the God of Israel. One of the greatest of these places was Gibeon, where the king used to offer a thousand victims at a time.

After one such sacrifice, God appeared to Solomon in a dream and asked, 'What would you like me to give you?' Solomon asked for wisdom and a thoughtful mind with which to govern the people over whom God had made him king; for he felt he could not bear such a responsibility without strength and wisdom given him by God.

Jehovah was pleased with the request and answered, 'You shall have your wish. Never again shall there be your equal for wisdom on the throne of Israel. And I will give you, too, what you might have asked for but did not, wealth, honour and, if you remain faithful to me, long life.' When Solomon awoke he realized Jehovah had talked to him in a dream; but the dream did, in fact, come true.

Soon after, his wisdom had its first test. Two women came to him for judgment. The first said, 'We two women live alone in the same house. We both had babies within three days of each other. During the night, her child died, and she got up and exchanged her dead child for my living baby. When I woke in the morning and looked at the baby, I saw at once that it was not mine.'

'No,' insisted the other woman, 'the living child is mine.'

'It's not. It's mine,' retorted the first woman, and the two wrangled in front of the king.

'Fetch me a sword,' ordered Solomon. When it was brought in, he said, 'Cut the living child in two and give half to each of the women.'

At this, the real mother gave a shriek of horror. She pleaded tearfully with the king. 'No, no, my Lord. Do not kill the child. Rather let her have it. Anything would be better than killing the baby!' But the other woman said, 'Divide the child, oh King. Neither of us shall have it.'

Solomon replied, 'Give the weeping woman the child. She is its mother.'

All Israel heard of the judgment and was filled with wonder at the king's wisdom.

Solomon was not only wise in judgment. He wrote three thousand proverbs, some of which can be read in the book of Proverbs. Like his father David, who wrote many of the psalms, he was a poet and a composer of over a thousand songs. He was learned in the ways of nature and knew much about plants, animals, birds, fishes and reptiles. People came from all over the world to consult Solomon and listen to his wisdom. Above all he was wise in making and keeping peace, and he was able to fulfil David's great dream of building a superb Temple in Jerusalem to the honour of the God of Israel.

Building the Temple

1 Kings 5—9

One of Solomon's closest allies was Hiram, King of Tyre, who had been a friend of David's. The district of Lebanon, famous for its cedar trees, was part of his kingdom; and when Solomon began to build the Temple, he arranged with Hiram to float cedar logs down the coast to him by sea. Begun four hundred and eighty years after the Israelites had left Egypt, the Temple was completed in seven years.

The building was planned like the Tabernacle, and was twice the size. It was sixty cubits long, twenty cubits broad and thirty high, and there may have been another storey on top of its main hall which doubled the height. At one end of the building was a porch ten cubits long, running along its whole width. This was one hundred and twenty cubits high, according to one description, and soared above the main building like a steeple.

The walls of the Temple were made of stone, prepared in the quarries so that they could be fitted into each other on the site of the building; not a single iron tool was heard in the Temple while it was being built. Inside, the walls and ceiling were lined with boards and beams of cedar wood and the floor was made of planks of fir. The Holy Place was forty cubits long, the Holy of Holies twenty cubits, and in the latter were two cherubim ten cubits high carved out of olive wood and overlaid with gold, their inner wings touching each other and their outer wings touching the walls. A veil hung from golden chains across the shrine of the Holy of Holies which was also separated from the Holy Place by beautifully carved olive wood doors, and there were similar doors to the Holy Place overlaid with gold. The whole of the interior of the Temple was also overlaid with gold.

Inside the Holy Place was a golden altar, a golden table for the shewbread and five golden lampstands on each side. The Ark of the Covenant was placed in the Holy of Holies beneath the wings of the cherubim.

The Temple walls were built in steps outside, and three storeys of rooms constructed on beams rested on the steps. On each side of the entrance to the porch was a bronze pillar eighteen cubits high, and in front of it were the Altar of Burnt-Offering, a huge basin filled with water ten cubits across resting on the backs of twelve bronze oxen, and ten trolleys carrying water-pots, also of bronze. The Temple courtyard was enclosed by a wall of three layers of stone topped with one of cedar wood.

When the Temple was finished and the day came for it to be dedicated to God, Solomon called all the Israelite chiefs together. After sacrificing many thousands of animals, he prayed to the God of Israel. He knew, he said, that Jehovah was too great to live in a house made with human hands. But if, as a result of sin, Israel was defeated and carried into captivity, or suffered drought, famine, pestilence or plagues of mildew, locusts or caterpillars, let them repent sincerely of their sin and look and pray in the direction where the Temple lay. Then let God in his heaven listen to their prayers and rescue them and the foreigner living among them from their distress.

After his prayer of consecration Solomon turned and blessed the assembled Israelites. The cloud of the glory of the Lord filled the new Temple as it had the old Tabernacle, and for seven days the nation held high festival, rejoicing in the prosperity the Lord their God had granted them.

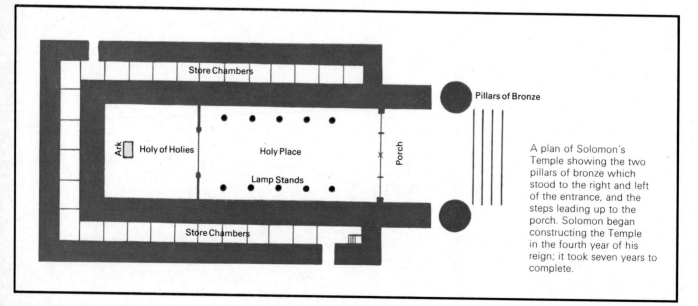

Store Chambers

Pillars of Bronze

Ark | Holy of Holies | Holy Place | Porch

Lamp Stands

Store Chambers

A plan of Solomon's Temple showing the two pillars of bronze which stood to the right and left of the entrance, and the steps leading up to the porch. Solomon began constructing the Temple in the fourth year of his reign; it took seven years to complete.

The Dividing of the Kingdom

1 Kings 9–12

Solomon built not only the Temple but also palaces and public buildings in Jerusalem. All over Canaan he constructed store-cities and other towns. He used the survivors of the nations which the Israelites had conquered when they captured their country to work in his forced labour gangs, and employed the Israelites themselves as his army and in positions of authority. He built a navy, using it to trade, and grew so rich in gold, silver, spices and other precious things that he outdid all the kings of the world in splendour.

Eastern kings in those days showed their greatness by the number of wives they married, and Solomon had a thousand. Many of these were foreign women who brought with them the worship of their own gods, and they persuaded Solomon to worship them, too, as well as Jehovah. Because he did this, God was angry with him.

'Since you have been disloyal to me,' God said, 'I will tear the kingdom from you and give it to another. I will not do it during your lifetime for David's sake, but in the lifetime of your son.'

And so it happened. One of Solomon's courtiers, an energetic young man called Jereboam, made so great an impression upon the king that Solomon put him in charge of all the labour gangs in a certain district. Shortly after, Ahijah, a prophet, met Jereboam alone in the open country. Ahijah was wearing a new robe, and he dramatically took it off, tore it into twelve pieces and gave ten to Jereboam.

'Hear the word of God,' said the prophet. 'I shall tear the whole kingdom except for the tribe of Benjamin-Judah from Solomon because he has forsaken me. This tribe will remain his for the sake of David and my holy city of Jerusalem. But ten tribes shall be yours; and if you are as loyal to me as David was, I shall establish your family on the throne of Israel for ever.'

Although Ahijah and Jereboam were alone when this happened, it soon became generally known that Jereboam would inherit the kingdom. Solomon tried to kill him, and the young man fled to Egypt where he remained until the king died after an apparently glorious reign of forty years.

Splendid though the reign had been, Solomon's buildings, and his wives and his chariots and horses and navy had cost more than the people of Israel could afford. The burden of taxation and forced labour was enormous, and when Solomon died the Israelites sent for Jereboam and asked him to be their leader. They went together to Solomon's son, Rehoboam, who now sat on the throne, and said, 'Your father taxed and worked us unmercifully. But lighten the load, and we will serve you loyally.'

'Come back in three days,' said Rehoboam, and he consulted his advisers, the wise older men first, and then those of his own age. The

108

older men advised him to answer the people kindly and agree to lighten their burden; but the younger men counselled him to 'put the rebellious dogs in their place' and show them who was master by replying to them harshly. Rehoboam foolishly took the advice of the younger men. 'Tell the people,' he said, 'that I will make your load heavier than ever my father did. He used whips on you; I will flay you with scorpions.'

Hearing this harsh reply the people shouted, 'Back to your homes, Israelites! We will no longer serve the family of David!' Only the tribe of Benjamin-Judah remained faithful to Rehoboam. He raised an army to recover the kingdom by force; but God forbade him through Shemaiah, a prophet, to make war upon his kinsmen, and the unhappy division became permanent. From that day on there were two kingdoms, Israel and Judah, each pursuing its own destiny, and sometimes even fighting against each other.

Jehovah or Baal?

1 Kings 16, 29–34; 17–19

Over sixty years passed. Four kings ruled over Judah and six over Israel, and the seventh, Ahab, was possibly the greatest king Israel ever had; yet the Bible condemns him, for he did evil in the sight of Jehovah. He married Jezebel, daughter of the King of Sidon, who worshipped Baal and persuaded Ahab to worship him also. Almost the whole country deserted God and followed the example of their king.

During Ahab's reign there lived a great and brave prophet of Jehovah called Elijah. Sent by God to the king, he said, 'This is a message to you from God – there shall be no rain nor dew in Israel for three years.' When Elijah left Ahab's presence, he was guided by God to hide in a cave by the brook Kerith. There he was fed morning and evening by ravens, and drank from the stream until it dried up in the drought. Then God guided him to the home of a widow who had nothing but a handful of flour and a little oil to keep her from starving. But as long as Elijah stayed with her, the flour and oil were never used up, and the woman, her son and the prophet were fed by them for as long as was necessary.

All this time Ahab searched unsuccessfully for Elijah. In the third year God told the prophet to show himself to the king for he would bring rain to the land. When the two met, Elijah challenged Ahab.

'Call all Israel to meet me on Mount Carmel,' he said. 'Summon also the four hundred and fifty prophets of Baal and the four hundred prophets of the goddess Asherah whom Jezebel pays. Let us see who is the true god: Baal and Asherah or Jehovah.'

Ahab did as Elijah requested. When all the people and prophets were assembled, Elijah said to them, 'How long will you hesitate between gods? If Jehovah is God, follow him; if Baal, worship him.' None of the people answered. Then Elijah issued his challenge.

'Let the prophets of Baal prepare a bull for sacrifice,' he said, 'without lighting a fire. I, the only prophet of Jehovah left against their four hundred and fifty, will prepare another. Let them call upon their god to send fire to burn their sacrifice. I will pray to Jehovah to do the same. The god who sends fire in answer to the prayer is the true God.'

'Yes, yes!' shouted the Israelites. 'There are many of you,' said Elijah to his rivals. 'Call upon your god first.' The prophets prepared their bull, and from morning to midday called upon Baal to answer them. There was no reply. Elijah mocked them, saying, 'Call louder. Remember, he is a god with other concerns than you. He may be thinking, or occupied in some business of his own, or travelling somewhere. Perhaps he's asleep and needs waking.' Baal's prophets danced madly round their altar, working themselves up into a frenzy, gashing themselves with knives till they were covered in blood. All the afternoon they continued, but nothing happened.

Just before the time of the evening sacrifice, Elijah took his turn. He built Jehovah's altar with twelve stones representing the tribes of Israel and dug a trench round it. He prepared his sacrifice and ordered a large quantity of water to be poured over it. This was repeated twice more until not only was the sacrifice soaked but the ditch round the altar was filled.

The hour of sacrifice came. Elijah stood before the altar and prayed. Scarcely had he finished speaking when the fire of God hissed from heaven and burned up the bull, the wood, the stones and the earth round it. The water in the trench vanished in a cloud of steam. The Israelites fell on their faces in terror, crying, 'Jehovah is God, Jehovah is God.'

When they had recovered a little from their fear, Elijah told them to take the prophets of the false gods and slaughter them to the last man. Then he said to Ahab, 'Prepare to go home quickly, for rain is on the way.' He himself went to the top of Mount Carmel with his servant, whom he told to watch the western sky. 'There is nothing there,' said the man. Seven times Elijah told him to look, and the seventh time he said, 'There is a little cloud, small as a man's hand, coming from the west.' 'It is the rain,' said Elijah. 'Tell Ahab to mount his chariot and drive home before the rains prevent him.'

Soon the sky was black with clouds. Ahab drove fast, but his horses could not match Elijah's speed. For the Spirit of the Lord, which gives men great strength, endurance and swiftness, came upon the prophet, and he ran before Ahab's chariot all the way to the king's royal city of Jezreel.

Ahab was afraid to do anything to a prophet of God, but when he told Jezebel how Elijah had had all the false prophets killed, her fury overcame any fear she might have felt. She sent a message to Elijah. 'The curse of Baal and Asherah upon me,' she said, 'if I do not slay you before this time tomorrow.'

Elijah fled for his life. In despair he went into the desert, for it seemed to him that, in spite of the victory Jehovah had won at Carmel, he was the only Israelite still faithful to the God of Israel, and that there was no hope that the nation would ever turn to the one true God again. He prayed for death. But God miraculously fed him, and he travelled

many days through the desert until he came to Sinai, where Moses had received the Law. There he entered a cave and slept.

Suddenly God spoke to him, 'What are you doing here, Elijah?' 'I am here,' he answered, 'because I alone am faithful to you, and they want to kill me.' Outside the cave the wind was rising and it seemed to call to Elijah, 'Come out and stand on the mountain before the Lord.' So Elijah stood while the wind rose to a shrieking storm, but God was not in the wind. Then came an earthquake, but God was not in that, nor was he in the volcanic fire which flamed out of the mountain after its shaking by wind and earthquake. But after the fire Elijah heard a low quiet voice which was somehow more frightening than every-thing that had gone before. He covered his face and stood in the entrance to the cave.

The voice of God came to him. 'Go to Damascus and anoint Hazael king of Syria, and anoint Jehu king of Israel. Anoint Elisha prophet in your place. They are to be my avengers. He who escapes Hazael's sword will be killed by Jehu, and he who escapes Jehu will fall by Elisha. And you are not alone. I have seven thousand men true to me in Israel who have not worshipped Baal.'

So Elijah recovered his courage and returned to play his part in the struggle to win Israel back to God. He was alone no more; for he anointed Elisha to be prophet after him, and Elisha was his friend and companion for the rest of his life.

Naboth's Vineyard

1 Kings 21

There lived in the town of Jezreel an elder and city councillor called Naboth, who owned a vineyard very close to Ahab's palace. Ahab wanted Naboth's land for the palace garden; so he said to the elder, 'Let me have your vineyard. I will either give you a better one in exchange or will pay you for it.'

But Naboth refused. 'I cannot sell the vineyard. It has belonged to my family for many years,' he said.

Ahab returned home sullen and angry. He behaved like a sulky child, throwing himself on the bed, covering his face and refusing to eat. After a time his wife Jezebel came to see what was the matter. He told her how he had asked Naboth to exchange or sell his vineyard and how the man had refused.

'Do you call yourself a king?' said Jezebel. 'Come, cheer up and eat. I will give you a present of Naboth's land.' She wrote a letter in Ahab's name, sealed it with the royal seal and sent it to the city council of Jezreel.

'Proclaim a fast day,' she wrote, 'and give Naboth the place of honour. Then, when he is prominent among the people, produce two men to witness falsely against him. Let them accuse him of cursing God and speaking against the king. Make sure their witness agrees exactly, as the law requires. Then take Naboth out of the city and stone him.'

The city council was too afraid of Ahab and Jezebel to disobey. They did all that was ordered in the letter and then sent word to Jezebel that Naboth was dead.

The moment the queen heard the news, she said to Ahab, 'Naboth has died a criminal's

Small shelters resembling summer-houses were often built in fruit gardens and vineyards, consisting of a roof made of branches supported on rough posts. These were watchmen's booths built on top of watch-towers, which were used during the ripening of the fruit and harvest.

death. His goods, therefore, belong to you. Up, then; take possession of his vineyard and make it a garden for you palace.'

But too many people knew of the crime for it to remain hidden. The news soon reached Elijah. He knew at once that it was God's will that he should go to Ahab and reproach him bitterly for the great evil he had done.

He found Ahab in the very vineyard itself. The king was already planning his garden when Elijah stormed through the gate.

'Have you murdered Naboth and are you now helping yourself to his land? Listen to God's word to you. The dogs will lick up your blood in the very spot where they licked up Naboth's blood.'

Ahab said wearily, 'Are you here again, you who are always my enemy?'

'Yes, I am here again,' replied Elijah, 'and because you have given up yourself to do nothing but evil in God's eyes, he will utterly destroy your family, as he destroyed the families of those kings of Israel before you who did not do his will. Jezebel shall be eaten by dogs at the city-wall of Jezreel. Those of your family who die in the city will likewise be eaten by dogs, and those who die in the country will be food for vultures.'

Evil as he was – and to the worshippers of Jehovah he was the most evil king who ever sat on the throne of Israel – Ahab was shocked into repentance by Elijah's words. He tore his clothes in sorrow, put on sack-cloth and wandered muttering to himself in anguish of spirit. When Elijah saw that his repentance was sincere, God spoke through him again to Ahab. 'Because Ahab has humbled himself before me, tell him this. I will not bring disaster upon him, but upon his son.'

Yet even so, Elijah's prophecies came true.

The Death of Ahab
1 Kings 22

Israel was often at war with Syria, the kingdom to the north. But for three years there had been peace between the two nations, as there was between Judah and Israel. Jehoshaphat, King of Judah, was in fact so friendly with Ahab that he agreed to join him in an attack on Syria to recover the Israel border-city of Ramoth-Gilead, which Ben-hadad, the King of Syria, had taken. 'Treat my army as if it were yours,' said Jehoshaphat, 'only let us first ask guidance from God.'

Ahab called together four hundred prophets, all but one of the prophets of Israel. 'Shall I attack Ramoth-Gilead or not?' he asked them. To a man they replied, 'Go. God will give you the city.' But something about them made Jehoshaphat distrustful. 'Is there any other prophet we can consult?' he asked.

'There is one called Micaiah,' replied Ahab, 'but he prophesies only evil for me.' Seeing, however, that his guest wanted to hear Micaiah, he sent a servant to fetch him quickly. When he arrived, Ahab asked him, 'Shall we attack Ramoth-Gilead?'

Micaiah, warned by Ahab's messenger that all the other prophets had given a favourable answer, replied, 'Attack. The city is yours.' But Ahab could see that he was not sincere. 'In the name of God, tell me the truth,' he said.

'I saw the armies of Israel scattered on the mountains like a shepherdless flock of sheep,' said Micaiah.

'You see,' said Ahab, 'he never says anything good of me.'

But Micaiah had not finished. 'I saw God on his throne,' he continued, 'asking his angels how Ahab could be persuaded to attack Ramoth-Gilead. A spirit answered him, "I shall persuade him by entering his prophets and giving false prophecies of success through them." "Go, and be successful," said God.'

When Micaiah had related his vision, one of the other prophets slapped him across the face. 'How can the Spirit of God say such things through you when he has said the opposite through us?' he demanded.

'When the news of Israel's defeat arrives,' retorted Micaiah, 'and you run terrified to hide yourself in an inner room, you will know through which of us God truly speaks.'

'Lock Micaiah up and feed him on bread and water till I come home victorious,' said Ahab. 'If you do return victorious,' replied Micaiah, 'I am not God's spokesman.'

So Ahab and Jehoshaphat marched against Ramoth-Gilead. In the battle for the city, Jehoshaphat wore his royal robes, but Ahab put on the armour of an ordinary soldier.

Ben-hadad had ordered all the captains of his chariots to attack no one but the king of Israel; and when they saw Jehoshaphat in his royal robes they mistook him for Ahab and attacked him. But he shouted, 'I am not Ahab,' and they withdrew and searched about them for the king of Israel.

They could see him nowhere. But it happened that a Syrian archer, shooting at random into a mass of Israelites, hit Ahab. His arrow found the very chink in the armour where the breastplate joined the shoulder-plates. The king, sorely wounded, ordered his driver to take him out of the battle-line; and in the evening, Ahab died in his chariot facing his Syrian foes. When his death was known, the Israelite army disbanded, and every man returned home. Ahab was brought to his capital city and buried there. The chariot full of his blood was washed out in a pool close to the spot where Naboth had been stoned to death, and the scavenger dogs licked up Ahab's blood as they had done the blood of Naboth. So Elijah's prophecy was fulfilled.

The Chariot of Fire

2 Kings 2

The time came for Elijah to end his earthly service and to go to God. As he and Elisha were travelling together, Elijah said to his friend, 'Stay here, for God is sending me to Bethel.' But Elisha, sensing that his master was about to depart from him, said, 'No, I will not leave you.'

They arrived at Bethel where they were met by the company of prophets who lived there. 'Do you realize' they said to Elisha, 'that God is going to take away your master today?' 'I know it,' he replied. 'Talk to me about it no more.'

'Stay here,' Elijah said again. 'God is sending me to Jericho.' But Elisha would not leave him, and the two continued their journey together. There they were met by another company of prophets. 'Do you know that God is about to take away your lord?' they asked Elisha. 'Only too well,' he said. 'Say no more.'

Elijah tried a third time to persuade Elisha to stay behind. 'Remain at Jericho,' he said. 'God is sending me to the Jordan.' But again Elisha refused, and they went to the river followed at a distance by fifty of the prophets from Jericho.

They saw Elijah take off his mantle, twist it into a roll and strike the water with it. Just as had happened centuries before when the Israelites first entered Canaan, the waters parted. A path of dry land stretched across the river. Elijah and Elisha walked across it, and when they reached the far bank, the waters flowed back and the pathway disappeared.

When the river was far behind them, Elijah said, 'I am about to leave you. Ask me for a last favour.' Elisha replied, 'Treat me as your

in ever-increasing strength, drawing up the chariot into the sky, so that the horses seemed to gallop round in circles as they ascended. While Elisha watched they grew smaller and smaller as the distance between them and earth increased, until at last they had gone.

As he saw his master ascending, Elisha cried out, 'My father, my father, worth an army of chariots and horsemen to Israel!' Then he tore his clothes in sorrow.

On the ground lay Elijah's mantle which had fallen from him. Picking it up, Elisha strode back to the Jordan. He struck the waters of the river with it, crying out, 'Where is God, the God of Elijah?' The river parted. The God of Elijah was with him.

When the prophets saw Elisha returning alone and the miracle of the parted waters, they said, 'Elijah's spirit is in Elisha!' They bowed in reverence before him and asked his permission to search for Elijah. 'Perhaps God has simply caught him up and taken him elsewhere,' they said. Elisha at first refused but when they urged him earnestly he at last consented. They searched for three days, but could not find Elijah; and when they returned Elisha said, 'I told you not to go.' But they had satisfied themselves that God had indeed taken Elijah, and that they would never see him more.

eldest son receiving a double portion of his father's goods. Give me a double portion of the Spirit of God within you.' 'That is hard to give,' Elijah answered, 'but if you see me when I am taken from you, the gift will be yours. If you do not see me, you will not receive it.'

Suddenly, as they were talking, there appeared a chariot of flame drawn by horses of fire. It drove between them, forcing them apart; then Elijah was caught up into the chariot as if by a whirlwind. The wind circled

119

The Leper General

2 Kings 5

Naaman, commander-in-chief of the Syrian army, was a great and victorious general. But he suffered from what was then an incurable disease. He was a leper.

His wife had as maid an Israelite girl, captured by the Syrians in a border raid. One day she said to her mistress, 'If only my lord Naaman would visit the prophet Elisha – he would heal him.'

As Syria and Israel were then at peace, Naaman travelled to the King of Israel armed with a letter from his own king demanding that his general be cured of his leprosy. When the King of Israel read what was written, he was appalled. 'Am I God,' he cried, 'to heal this man of his disease? Syria wants an excuse to attack us!' He tore his clothes in despair. But news of the visit reached Elisha, and he sent the king a message, 'Let Naaman come to me.'

So Naaman drove up with all his chariots and servants to Elisha's house. But the prophet, unimpressed by his display, did not even come to the door. He sent the general a curt order, 'Wash in the River Jordan seven times and you will be cured.'

Naaman was enraged. 'I expected him to come out, call upon God and wave his hands over the leprous places. There are bigger and better rivers in Syria. Why should I wash in this puddle of a Jordan?'

But his servants tried to reason with him. 'My lord, if the prophet had told you to do something difficult, would you not have done it? Why not, then, obey his easy command to wash?'

Naaman realized the sense of their argument. Six times he dipped himself in the Jordan and nothing happened; but when he came out the seventh time, his servants gasped with amazement. Every trace of leprosy had gone; and the skin of his whole body was as soft and clean as a child's.

Syrian tribute-bearer brings objects of precious metal—bowls and armlets—to the Persian king. The figure comes from a relief from the stairway of the Tripylon at Persepolis, 5th century.

The general returned to Elisha, this time with gratitude and humility, and implored him to accept a fortune of gold and silver. But the prophet had no need of such things.

'Then let me take enough of Israel's earth back with me,' said Naaman, 'to make a little platform where I may worship Israel's God on his own soil.' It was the belief then that gods, like kings, ruled over their own lands and could be worshipped only on the earth of the land they ruled. 'And may Israel's God forgive me,' continued Naaman, 'when my king orders me to accompany him to the temple of the Syrian God, Rimmon, and I have to pretend to worship him.'

When Naaman had gone, Gehazi, Elisha's servant, thinking it a shame that so much gold and silver should have been refused, galloped after the general. Naaman turned back to meet him.

'Just after you left,' Gehazi lied, 'two young prophets visited my master. He wanted nothing for himself; but he would be glad if you could spare something for them.' Naaman was delighted to show his gratitude and gave Gehazi a fortune, far more than he had asked.

When he returned, Gehazi went into Elisha's room. 'Where have you been?' asked the prophet.

'I? Nowhere,' Gehazi said.

'Was not I with you in spirit when a certain chariot turned back to meet you? You have money enough now to buy yourself great possessions. Yes, and you have bought Naaman's leprosy, too. It shall remain with you and your descendants for ever.'

Gehazi saw the skin of his hands turn to the dead white of leprosy before his eyes. He felt a crawling, itching sensation over his entire body. He knew, as he stumbled in horror from Elisha's presence, that he was a leper from head to toe.

Jehu the Avenger

2 Kings 8, 29; 9–10

Ahab's son, Jehoram, was ruler of Israel while his nephew, Ahaziah, reigned over Judah. Both kings worshipped Baal. Ahaziah went to visit Jehoram, wounded in a war against Syria; and Elisha saw his chance of carrying out the doom which God had pronounced on Ahab's whole family. Summoning a young prophet, he said, 'Hurry to Ramoth-Gilead where the Israelites are fighting the Syrians. Seek out a general called Jehu, take him aside privately, anoint him with oil and say, "God makes you king over Israel." Then fly for your life.'

At Ramoth-Gilead the young prophet found all the generals at a council of war. Taking Jehu into an inner room, he did as Elisha had said, and then ran back past the generals and away. When Jehu followed him slowly out of the inner room, his companions said, 'What did that madman say to you?' 'Oh, nothing important,' he said. 'You know what nonsense such fellows talk.' But they could see from his manner that there had been more to the interview than idle chatter. 'Tell us the truth,' they said, and he told them what had happened.

The other generals did not hesitate. They laid their cloaks under Jehu's feet, thus doing him royal honours; then they summoned the army with a trumpet-blast and proclaimed, 'Jehu is king!'

'See to it that no one leaves the city,' ordered Jehu, and sped away in his chariot to Jezreel with a squad of soldiers at his back. A sentinel on the city walls saw them coming and told Jehoram, who sent a mounted man to meet them.

'Is all well?' asked Jehoram's messenger. 'What has that to do with you?' snapped Jehu. 'Fall in behind me.' A second messenger was sent with the same result. The sentry told the king what had happened, and said that he thought the chariot was being driven by General Jehu, who always drove like a lunatic.

'Harness my chariot,' said Jehoram, and he and Ahaziah drove out in their chariots to meet Jehu. When they were within speaking distance, Jehoram called, 'Is all well?' 'How can all be well,' retorted Jehu, 'when your mother, Jezebel, survives to carry on her idol-worship and witchcraft?'

Jehoram wheeled his chariot round, and fled, crying, 'Treachery, Ahaziah!' But Jehu's bow was already raised. His arrow pierced Jehoram's heart, and the general ordered his body to be flung into what had been Naboth's vineyard. Then he furiously pursued Ahaziah before wounding him to the death. So the kings of Israel and Judah died on one day.

Jehu drove back to Jezreel. Jezebel, royal to the last in courage, dressed herself as beautifully as she could and cried scornfully from an upper window to Jehu as he entered the palace courtyard, 'Do you come in peace, murderer of your master?' Jehu looked up. 'Who is on my side?' he called. Two or three men signalled from the windows. 'Throw her down,' ordered Jehu. They seized Jezebel and hurled her from the window, and the horses

trampled her under foot. Jehu and his men left her there while he dined within the palace, and later, when he gave orders for her to be buried, nothing remained of her but a few fragments. The scavenger dogs had eaten her. So was fulfilled Elijah's prophecy that Jezebel should meet the same fate as her victim, Naboth – that dogs should devour her where Naboth himself had fallen.

Jehu continued his campaign of slaughter till he had wiped out Ahab's whole family, numbering over a hundred men. Then, by a trick, he murdered every worshipper of Baal. But although he was a follower of Jehovah, he was not perfect in his worship of God; and when, years later, the Israelites understood better what God was like, they realized how terrible Jehu's killings had been, and that murder is always wicked, even if committed in the name of the Lord.

The Prophets

1 Samuel 10, 10–14; 19, 18–24

After the Israelites had settled in Canaan and were fighting for their lives against the Philistines, strange bands of men could sometimes be seen wandering round the land. To the throb and clash of primitive musical instruments they leaped, danced, spun round in circles and chanted praises to God in ecstasy. This wild frenzy was partly patriotic, for their object was to make every Israelite feel he was a member of the nation which was God's Chosen People; partly religious, to inspire the Israelites to fight for God against the heathen who still lived in Canaan and to destroy the false gods that continued to be worshipped there. If a bystander had gone close to them, he would have seen that their eyes were glazed and unseeing, and if he had talked to them they would not have heard him, for they worked themselves up into trances which lasted for hours and sometimes even for days.

These men were the earliest prophets. They sometimes had a strange effect on people who came into contact with them, for their ecstasy could be infectious. After Saul had been anointed king by Samuel, for example, he met a band of these prophets. He was immediately caught up in their ecstasy and joined them, dancing and prophesying, so that his friends said to one another, 'What has happened to Saul? Has he also become a prophet?'

On another occasion, Saul sent messengers to arrest David. But they met a company of prophets prophesying with Samuel at their head, and the messengers became prophets, too, and joined in the dancing and chanting.

The same thing happened to two further sets of messengers sent by Saul; and when in anger Saul went himself, the spirit of prophecy fell upon him as well, and after shouting and ecstatically praising God, he lay in a trance for a whole day and night.

As times grew more settled, the prophets behaved more calmly. One or two of them became attached to the king's court and gave the monarch warnings and advice, telling him what was the will of God when he had to make important decisions. Because they were holy men, the king did not dare punish them for anything they said, and they could defend private men against royal oppression and injustice. So, as we have seen, Nathan was able to pronounce God's punishment on David when he stole Uriah's wife, Bathsheba, and Elijah condemned Ahab for having Naboth murdered.

By Elijah's time, prophets were found living in communities in all the big cities. They did not foretell the future, as is often thought, but they revealed the will of God so that the king or nation might be guided in times both of prosperity and difficulty. It is almost certain, too, that they collected and edited the history of their country. It is thought that among them was a great writer and editor called the Deuteronomist, who gathered together most of the books and writings which make up the Old Testament. To him we owe the stories which you have been reading in this book.

Then, in about 750 BC, came the first of the writing prophets, Amos, whose book is in the Bible. For nearly four hundred years after him, prophet after prophet wrote wonderful poetry and, much more important, taught people more of God and how to live better lives. They came from every kind of profession and background. Some were farmers, some statesmen, some came from prophetic or priestly families. Some were humble men, others aristocrats, related to the king.

Even when Israel and Judah disappeared as kingdoms and their inhabitants were exiled in far-off lands, the prophets trusted in God's purpose for his Chosen People. They kept his worship alive when it might have died as other religions have done. They looked forward to a time when the Messiah would come to restore the kingdom to the House of David and make Israel the ruling nation of the world. The Holy Spirit of God spoke through them with more meaning than they realized; and each in his own way prepared for the coming of Jesus Christ, a monarch of David's line, who would found the Kingdom of God which would never have an end.

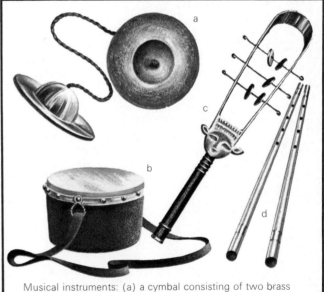

Musical instruments: (a) a cymbal consisting of two brass bowls which were struck against each other; (b) a portable drum which served to beat time for singing or dancing; (c) a bronze sistrum, a form of metal rattle, and (d) flutes made of reed.

Hezekiah the Good

2 Kings 18–19; Isaiah 36–39

Over a hundred and fifty years after Jehu's revolution, Hezekiah became King of Judah. He was more loyal to Jehovah than any king since David, and he destroyed every idol he could find. He rebelled successfully against Assyria, which had subjected Judah, and conquered the Philistine district of Gaza. He was supported in all he did by Isaiah, one of the greatest of the prophets.

After reigning for fourteen years Hezekiah became dangerously ill, and Isaiah told him he would die. When the prophet had gone, the king prayed earnestly that he might be allowed to live; and before Isaiah had left the palace grounds he knew that Hezekiah would be given a further fifteen years of life. As a sign that this would indeed happen, the shadow on the palace sundial moved back ten degrees, a truly remarkable miracle, for it meant that the earth had spun backwards for a time.

Shortly after Hezekiah's recovery, the King of Babylon's son visited him; and the Jewish king, flattered by the attention paid him by the representative of a nation far greater than his own, showed him all his treasures. Isaiah was not pleased with what Hezekiah did. 'God has told me,' he said, 'that the time will come when everything you have shown the Babylonians will be carried off to Babylon and your sons will be servants in the King of Babylon's palace.'

Soon after, Sennacherib, King of Assyria, determined to bring back the rebel kingdom of Judah under his sway. He marched into Judah taking city after city. As he drew nearer to Jerusalem, Hezekiah tried to save his capital by paying an enormous sum of gold and silver, even stripping the Temple doors of their gold; but in spite of the payment, the Assyrians continued to march on Jerusalem.

A strong army under Sennacherib's chief commanders camped outside the city. They were met by Hezekiah's ministers. The Assyrian spokesman shouted to the Jewish officials in Hebrew so that all the soldiers on the city-wall could hear. 'On whom is Hezekiah relying? Does he think Egypt will help him? Egypt is like a pointed stick which pierces a man's hand when he leans on it. Does he think his God will help him? Why, he has destroyed all his shrines and altars, telling everyone they can worship only at Jerusalem. Does he rely on his own strength? You are so weak that we will give you two thousand horses if you can put as many riders on them. And it is your God who has told us to march against Jerusalem and destroy it.'

Hezekiah's envoys were afraid that the Assyrian's words might discourage the listening soldiers. 'Speak to us in Aramaic,' they said, 'not in Hebrew.' But the officer shouted all the louder in Hebrew to the soldiers themselves. 'Do not let Hezekiah fool you. Surrender to us and live in peace until arrangements are made for you to live elsewhere. Hezekiah says your God will save you. But show me one god who has saved his country from the Assyrians.'

The people said nothing. Hezekiah's envoys returned carrying the Assyrians' insults in a letter. Taking it into the Temple, the king laid it before the altar and prayed to God to deliver the city. Hardly had he finished when a message came from Isaiah. 'Your prayers are heard. The King of Assyria will never reach Jerusalem. He will return to his own land where he will perish by the sword. Soon you will sow and reap in peace.'

Isaiah's prophecy came true. Sennacherib had to return home because the King of Ethiopia suddenly attacked Assyria. There he was murdered by two of his sons. And the very night after Hezekiah's prayer in the Temple, a terrible pestilence swept through the Assyrian army, killing 185,000 men. The few survivors crept away home and Jerusalem was saved.

Details from a relief showing the siege of Lachish from Sennacherib's palace at Nineveh, 7th century.

The End of Israel

2 Kings 17–18

While Hezekiah was ruling in Jerusalem, Hoshea was King of Israel. He ruled over a land which had utterly forsaken the true God. When, centuries before, Jereboam had rebelled against the house of David, he feared that the Israelites might desert him through going up to Jerusalem to worship; and he set up two golden calves, one in the north of Israel, the other in the south. These, he said, represented Jehovah who had delivered them from Egypt; but though the Israelites served their own God, they worshipped him through idols, which the second commandment forbade them to do. As a result, Jereboam became known as the king who caused Israel to sin.

Cut off from Jerusalem, the Temple and the Ark of the Covenant, which were the centre of their national life and religion, the Israelites turned more and more to the false gods of the nations whose remnants still lived in Canaan. They built shrines on every hilltop and set up sacred poles and pillars, emblems of male and female gods. Everywhere they worshipped idols in spite of the warnings of the prophets sent by God. Some bowed down to the sun, moon, and stars; others practised magic and consulted the spirits of the dead. Worst of all, some sacrificed their children by burning them alive, making them 'pass through the fire', as it was called, to the fierce and cruel god, Moloch.

So God destroyed Israel as a kingdom. Its downfall began with an attack by Shalman-ezer, King of Assyria, upon Hoshea. The Assyrians were among the most ferocious of peoples, and they tried to terrorize all who opposed them by savage cruelty. But they were so cruel that their methods had the opposite effect; the nations they conquered rebelled against them in despair, and their empire lasted a very short time. They were eventually overwhelmed by Babylon.

But this was yet to be. Hoshea, defeated by Shalmanezer, became his subject, paying tribute to him each year. Like other nations conquered by the Assyrians, he soon discovered how cruel his masters were, and began to plot with Egypt.

Egypt was at this time the other great empire, and small nations, like Israel, Judah, Moab and Syria, were often forced to ally themselves either with Egypt or Assyria in the struggles between the two great kingdoms. But the Egyptians were not nearly so energetic in helping their allies as the Assyrians were in attacking them; and the moment Shalmanezer knew that Hoshea was plotting with Egypt, he marched into Israel. After a three year siege, he captured the capital city of Samaria. Then he did what was often done by conquerors in those days. He took all the Israelites out of their own country, transported them hundreds of miles to the east and settled them in other parts of the Assyrian empire. In this way he tried to destroy their sense of belonging to a land or a nation. They became people without roots.

In their place he settled inhabitants from other districts in his dominions. These became the ancestors of the people known in Jesus' time as Samaritans, who were hated by the Jews. Many of them were killed by lions when they first settled in Israel and believed that this happened because they did not know how to worship the god in whose land they were living. So Shalmanezer sent back a priest of Jehovah to teach them how to worship him. But their worship was not pure, for they continued to worship their own gods as well.

Strangely enough it was in exile that Israel and, later, Judah came to understand better the teachings of the great prophets and develop the most spiritual religion known in the world until Jesus came.

Sargon (King of Assyria 722–705BC) completed the capture of Samaria, begun by his predecessor, Shalmanezer.

The Reforms of Josiah

2 Kings 21–22

Sixty years after Hezekiah died, his eight year old great-grandson, Josiah, began his reign. He worshipped Jehovah faithfully, and when he was eighteen ordered the Temple to be repaired. In it the workmen discovered an old book of the law hidden away, probably by a follower of Jehovah during the reign of Manasseh, Hezekiah's son; for he had been as evil as his father was good, and had persecuted worshippers of God. Shaphan, Josiah's secretary, took him the book and at his command read it to him.

The book was almost certainly Deuteronomy, which contains the laws given to Moses in the wilderness together with some later ones. Listening, Josiah realized that Judah had broken every law given them by God. He was appalled when Shaphan read, 'If you do not obey these commands, you will be afflicted with pestilence, drought, locusts and plagues of insects. Defeated and slaughtered by your enemies, your corpses will be food for jackals

and vultures. You will build houses and never dwell in them; breed cattle and grow crops which other men will eat. Your children will be made captive and never seen again. Such disasters will come upon you that they will drive you mad.'

Tearing his clothes in repentance, Josiah sent his court officials to consult Huldah, a prophetess of Jehovah, to see if there were any way in which God's anger might be averted. But she held out no hope. 'Tell Josiah,' she said, 'that God will bring upon the people of Judah the disasters mentioned in the book because they have forsaken him and worshipped other gods. But because the king repented when he heard the book, they will not happen until after his death.'

When he heard the message, Josiah summoned all the leaders and people of Judah and read them the whole book. He swore a solemn oath that he would obey God and all his laws honestly and sincerely, and his subjects did the same. He followed this with the most thorough reforms that Judah had ever seen.

First he purified the Temple, for even there the worship of false gods had crept in. He took every object out of it used in the worship of Baal and Asherah and burned them outside Jerusalem. He removed all the heathen priests who worshipped on the hilltops and destroyed their shrines. He even took action beyond the boundaries of his own kingdom, slaughtering the priests of the hill-shrines in Samaria upon their altars and making their holy places foul by burning human bones upon them. He abolished the worship of the sun, moon, planets, and stars and destroyed chariots holy to the sun (the sun was supposed to travel across heaven every day in a fiery chariot). He destroyed temples of Baal, Ashtoreth, Kemosh and Milcolm which went back to the time of King Solomon. He filled the valley of Hinnom where worshippers burned their children alive in sacrifice to Moloch with the bones of dead men. He abolished from his kingdom all who tried to call up spirits of the dead, and allowed none of his subjects to keep in his home household gods and idols. He destroyed the shrine of the golden calf which Jereboam had made at Bethel. For the first time since Judah became a kingdom, Jehovah was worshipped without rivals.

Then Josiah held the feast of Passover as the book of the law said it should be observed. Never since the Israelites had entered Canaan had such a Passover been kept. But the reformation did not last long. Thirteen years later Josiah was killed in battle, and his reforms died with him; for the kings that followed him did evil in the sight of God, and the kingdom of Judah soon vanished as Israel had already done.

Jeremiah and the End of Judah

2 Kings 23, 26–37; 24–25;
2 Chronicles 35–36; Jeremiah

Jeremiah, perhaps the loneliest and saddest of the prophets, though one of the greatest, was a descendant of Eli, the priest who looked after the boy Samuel. As a young man of about twenty-five, he felt the call to become a prophet of God. He did not want to be a prophet, because he was a shy and gentle man to whom a prophet's career would mean distress and sorrow; but the call burned like a fire within him and he had no choice but to obey. His life was lonely because God forbade him to marry; he had an affectionate nature that would have made him a loving husband and kindly father. As it was he experienced nothing but hostility and failure.

Jeremiah forced himself to speak out boldly against the wickedness of his countrymen and, although a patriot, he had to advise his country to surrender to a nation more powerful than itself. Some of his early prophecies, too, seemed to be false, and he could do no miracles.

When he was a young man, the Scythians, a fierce race of people, marched from the north towards Judah, and Jeremiah prophesied that God would use them to punish his country for deserting Jehovah. But after advancing down the coast to the west, they withdrew, and it seemed that Jeremiah had prophesied wrongly. But his prophecy of danger from the north applied equally well to the new power of Babylon which defeated both Assyria and Egypt; and it was obvious to Jeremiah that, unless it turned to God, Judah, too, would fall to Babylon.

At first his life was contented. He had been a prophet for about five years when the book of the Law was discovered in the Temple, and he approved of Josiah's reforms. He was glad, too, when Babylon destroyed Assyria nine years later, and that his king sided with Babylon against Egypt. But Josiah was killed fighting against Egypt, and the good time came to an end. Jehoahaz, the next king, reigned for only three months and was replaced by Jehoiakim, under whom Jeremiah was attacked by priests and people alike. In the first year of Jehoiakim's reign God told Jeremiah to prophesy in the Temple that if the people of Judah did not repent, the same destruction would fall upon them as had come upon Israel. There was a great outcry against him, and the Temple priests and prophets wanted to execute him. But he was saved by the people and the court officials, although

Jehoiakim killed one of his fellow-prophets for giving the same warning as Jeremiah.

In spite of his narrow escape, Jeremiah preached again in the Temple, proclaiming that since the people of Judah had not repented, destruction would now certainly come upon them. Pashur, the chief officer of the Temple, had Jeremiah flogged and imprisoned in the stocks one night. Jeremiah said to him, 'This is what God says: you will be called Terror-Let-Loose because you will be a terror to yourself and your friends. Since you are a false prophet, you will be carried captive to Babylon. There you will die.'

Jeremiah had one close friend, his secretary, Baruch, who wrote down all his prophecies on a parchment scroll. This was read by some of the nobles to the king. Jehoiakim was sitting in his palace with a lighted fire by his side, for it was cold; and as he listened to the prophecies of disaster, he cut off bits of the roll in fury as it was read and burned them in the fire, until there was nothing left. He wanted to arrest Jeremiah and Baruch, but they had been well hidden; and later Jeremiah dictated the whole book again to Baruch, who rewrote every word.

When Jehoiakim died, he was succeeded by Jehoiachin, who was carried off to Babylon after only three months. Zedekiah, Josiah's youngest son, reigned instead. He was a kind man who would have liked to rule well; but he was weak, and influenced by whoever was with him at the moment. Sometimes he consulted Jeremiah and agreed to submit to Babylon, which would have been the sensible thing to do. Sometimes he listened to the princes of Judah who trusted the treacherous friendship of Egypt.

The Babylonians became tired of Zedekiah's ever-changing mind, and, when he had reigned nine years, they beseiged Jerusalem. Jeremiah prophesied that the city would fall, and went about wearing a yoke as a sign of the coming slavery. Zedekiah imprisoned him for disheartening the people; but Jeremiah showed his ultimate faith in the restoration of Judah by buying a field belonging to his cousin for a considerable sum of money. When Egypt for once showed a little energy and advanced to help Judah, the Babylonians retreated; but

God warned Zedekiah through Jeremiah that the Egyptians would soon return to their own land, the siege be renewed and the city captured.

Jeremiah, trying to leave Jerusalem, was accused of deserting to the enemy and imprisoned for a long time. Zedekiah released him secretly and asked him if God had anything new to say to him. But Jeremiah had only the old message of disaster and captivity. The Jewish nobles, wanting to kill the prophet, threw him into a deep dungeon thick with

mud at the bottom, into which he sank. But he was rescued by a kind Ethiopian member of the king's household, who hauled him out with ropes. Once more Zedekiah asked Jeremiah's advice.

'If you surrender to Babylon,' said the prophet, 'you will live and the city will escape destruction; but if you do not, neither you nor the city will escape.' Zedekiah still hesitated – until, suddenly, it was too late. Jerusalem fell. All the nobles of Judah and Zedekiah's sons were killed before his eyes, and he himself blinded and made captive with all the best of the people. Only the very poor were left behind. Jerusalem was burned and its walls broken down. Everything that Jeremiah had prophesied came true.

The Babylonians treated Jeremiah kindly because he had supported them against Egypt. They sent him to help Gedaliah, whom they made governor of Judah. But soon Gedaliah was treacherously murdered and there was chaos once more in the land. The few remaining Jews wanted to fly into Egypt where they thought they would be sure of peace. But Jeremiah told them, 'If you stay in Judah, God will look after you and build you up again. Even if you are taken to Babylon, you will one day return. But if you go into Egypt, you will meet destruction and death.'

The men of Judah did not believe him. Against his will they dragged him into Egypt, and with their going the kingdom of Judah disappeared. We do not know what happened to Jeremiah, but there is a tradition that he was stoned to death.

Before Jeremiah, the Israelites believed that they were safe because they belonged to the Chosen People, and that Jerusalem would never be taken because the Temple was a kind of magic charm. Jeremiah's true greatness as a prophet was that he was the first to realize that a man was not saved just because he belonged to the Chosen People. Every individual was responsible for his own goodness and wickedness and had to learn to love God and resist evil for himself. He had to ask God to be his personal friend and guide, and show him by his thoughts and conscience what was right and wrong. God's law, said Jeremiah, must be written in every man's heart. It was not till Jesus came that men learned more of God than this.

Babylon was famous throughout the ancient world for its splendid buildings and massive fortifications. This is a reconstruction of the ornamental Gate of Ishtar, and the 'Street of Processions' which led to Nebuchadnezzar's palace. The Gate was faced with coloured, glazed bricks representing wild oxen and legendary serpents with legs. The animals were modelled on a panel of clay. While still soft, the panel was cut up into small bricks which were glazed, fired and reassembled on the facade.

The Vision of Dry Bones

Ezekiel 37, 1–14

Among the inhabitants of Judah carried captive into Babylonia in 597 BC was a priest named Ezekiel, aged about twenty-five. When he reached thirty, regarded by the Jews as the age of complete manhood, he became a prophet. He lived in a small Jewish community in Babylon called Tel-abib. His countrymen wanted cheerful prophecies of speedy restoration to Judah, but Ezekiel knew that Jerusalem would have to fall before God's people realized they must repent.

For six years he prophesied, detested and disbelieved by his countrymen. But when he was proved right by the Babylonians' capture of Jerusalem in 586 BC, his message changed to one of hope. His fellow Jews were lost and bewildered when their Holy City was taken, their Temple destroyed and almost all their people exiled. 'We are cut off from all that gave us life and meaning,' they cried. 'We no longer belong to a land or a nation.'

But like Jeremiah, whom he had probably known, Ezekiel told his confused countrymen that they could save themselves – not by belonging to the Chosen People but by each of them living a good life. God would help those really willing to do this by taking away their hearts of stone and giving them hearts of flesh. And even though their position then seemed hopeless, one day the Chosen People would be restored. Ezekiel told them of a vision he had seen.

'The Spirit of God carried me away to a plain covered with bones as far as the eye could see. I walked among them all and found them bleached by the sun and very dry. "Do you

think these bones could ever live again?" God asked me, and I replied, "Only you, Lord, can tell that." "Speak to the bones," God told me. "Say to them, 'Dry bones, hear the word of the Lord. Be joined together by sinews. Let flesh appear upon you. Be covered with skin. Then God will breathe life into you.'" I did as God commanded; and as I spoke, I heard a rustling sound, as the bones came together and fitted into one another. I saw appearing sinews and flesh and skin until all around me there lay an enormous army of lifeless bodies. Then God said to me, "Tell the wind to come from every quarter and breathe life into these dead bodies." I did so. All the bodies began to breathe and stir and clamber to their feet. God told me, "These bones are the nation of Israel. They say, 'We are nothing but dead bones, cut off from our nation and land and everything that gave meaning to our life.' But

tell them this, Ezekiel. 'Hear God's word. He will one day restore you to your own country, the land of Israel. You shall know then that your God is truly the Lord of the world. He will put his Spirit into you and you shall live, settled once again upon your own soil. This is God's promise to you.'"

Many years later, Ezekiel's prophecy came true, though not until after he had died. But his achievement and that of prophets like him was to keep faith in Jehovah alive during all the weary years of exile. The religions of other nations who were taken into captivity and were cut off from all they held dear disappeared for ever and are now no more than names. But the religion of the Jews was purified by exile and suffering and not only became itself one of the great religions of the world but prepared the way for the coming of Jesus Christ.

The Mission of Jonah

2 Kings 14, 25; The Book of Jonah

Some Israelites who knew they were God's Chosen People believed that the only way they could keep their religion pure was by having nothing to do with foreigners. Others realized that the God of Israel was the God of the whole world and hoped that one day all men would worship him. They believed that they should tell foreigners about the Jewish faith and try to persuade them to worship Jehovah.

It was probably one of these who wrote the story of Jonah, some three hundred years after the prophet died. God ordered him to go to Nineveh, capital of Assyria, a very wicked city, to tell its inhabitants about Jehovah and to persuade them to repent. Jonah did not pity the thousands who might never learn of God if he did not go. What did he care for foreigners, especially Assyrians? So he boarded a ship bound for Spain, deliberately travelling as far as possible away from Nineveh.

Barely was the ship out of sight of land when a tremendous storm arose. All on board called upon their gods to save them except Jonah, who was asleep. The ship's captain woke him up so that he, too, might pray, but still the storm continued. The sailors therefore cast lots to discover whose fault it was the tempest had come, and it was found to be Jonah's. He confessed he was running away from doing something his God had ordered him to do, and advised the sailors to throw him overboard. Before they did so, they made every effort to row to land, but all their attempts were in vain. Praying to God to forgive them, they threw Jonah overboard. Soon the storm ceased, and the sailors were saved.

Jonah, too, was saved; for God had prepared a huge fish which gulped him down as he sank into the sea. In the fish's stomach he prayed to God for deliverance, and after a time the fish vomited him on to dry land. When he had recovered from his terrible experiences, God sent him once more to preach to Nineveh. He travelled a day's journey into the city, so immense that it took three days to cross it, preaching as he went. 'If Nineveh does not repent,' he said, 'it will be destroyed in forty days.' To his surprise and anger – for the Assyrians were the cruellest of all the nations that conquered the Israelites – the people listened to his warning. The King of Nineveh ordered his subjects to forsake their evil ways and to repent, praying God that he would turn away his anger from them.

Jonah behaved like a sulky child. Leaving the city, he made himself a shelter of branches and waited to see what would happen next. 'I knew you were a merciful God who would make these cruel and wicked Ninevites repent, and save them. Now take away my life. I would be better off dead.'

'So you are angry, are you?' God said to him, deciding to teach the resentful prophet a lesson. He caused a swift-growing plant to spring up by Jonah's shelter. In a very short time it covered the whole hut, so that he was shielded from the sun's heat. Jonah was grateful for its shade. But the following day God caused insects to destroy the plant so that it withered, exposing Jonah to the blazing sunlight. He also sent a burning wind from the desert which so distressed Jonah that again he prayed for death.

'Are you angry because your plant has died?' asked God.

'Yes,' Jonah moaned, 'bitterly furious.'

'If you pity a mere plant,' said God, 'ought not I to pity the thousands of ignorant people in Nineveh and all their poor animals?'

So, by this story, the Israelites were taught that God cared for all men as he did for them, that he was the God of all nations as well as of Israel, and that animals as well as men were his concern.

Nebuchadnezzar's Dream

Daniel 2

The Book of Daniel, from which this and the next three stories are taken, was probably written about a hundred and sixty years before Jesus was born. At that time the Jews were being savagely persecuted on account of their faith. The book was written to encourage them and to teach them that one day God's kingdom would replace the empires of the world and that all men everywhere would worship the one true God.

Daniel, a young Jew carried captive into Babylonia, entered the service of its king, Nebuchadnezzar. One night the king had a dream which so terrified him that he could not sleep again. In the morning he summoned all his magicians, astrologers and wise men to tell him the meaning of the dream.

'Tell us your dream, O King,' they said, 'and we shall tell you its meaning.'

'No,' said Nebuchadnezzar, 'prove that you are really magicians by telling me both the dream and its meaning. If you cannot do this, I shall know that you are tricksters who will conspire together to tell me a pack of lies. You will all be executed, and everything you possess shall become mine. But if you can tell me both the dream and its meaning, you will be richly rewarded.'

'What you ask,' said the dismayed magicians, 'is impossible. Only the gods could do what you demand of us.' Nebuchadnezzar, enraged, ordered all his wise men to be killed.

Among them was Daniel. When he discovered why the king had ordered his execution, he went to Nebuchadnezzar and begged for time in which to pray to God and ask him to reveal the secret. The king granted him his request; and that night Daniel saw in a vision what Nebuchadnezzar had dreamed.

The next day he came into the king's presence and said, 'God has revealed your dream to me, O King. You saw a huge image, its head of fine gold, its breast and arms of silver, its belly and thighs of bronze, its legs of iron and its feet half of iron and half of clay. You then saw a stone hewn out of a mountain but not by human hands. It flew against the feet of the image, shattering them into pieces. The great image crashed to the ground and was smashed into tiny fragments which were blown away like chaff until not a trace of it remained. But the stone which had destroyed the image grew and grew into a huge mountain, filling all the world.

'This is the meaning of your dream, O King. You and your empire are the head of gold.

140

After you shall arise another empire, worse than yours as silver is inferior to gold. This will be succeeded by a third kingdom of bronze which shall rule the whole earth, and this by a fourth as strong and forceful as iron. The fifth kingdom, of iron and clay, shall be partly strong, partly weak. Finally, God's kingdom will replace all those that have gone before and will last for ever. This is the stone, cut not by human hands, which became the mountain that filled the earth.'

Nebuchadnezzar, astonished that Daniel could tell him both the dream and the meaning, acknowledged that his God must indeed be Lord of all gods; and he promoted Daniel to be governor of the province of Babylon and chief of all his wise men.

The first four empires were those of Babylon, the Medes, the Persians, and Alexander the Great. Alexander's empire was divided into two and ruled by rival lines of kings, the Ptolemies and the Seleucids. All human empires were eventually to be replaced by the kingdom of God's Messiah.

Ordeal by Fire

Daniel 3

Daniel had three friends called Shadrach Meshach and Abed-nego who were also faithful servants of Jehovah. When he was made governor of the province of Babylon, he asked Nebuchadnezzar to put them in charge of the province under him. Their promotion naturally caused jealousy among officials over whose heads they were placed; and in due time an opportunity came to their enemies to try to bring the three young Jews to their deaths.

Nebuchadnezzar made a gigantic golden idol sixty cubits high and six broad which he set up on a plain near Babylon. He ordered all his high officials to come to the dedication of his image, and a herald made a royal proclamation: 'All nations in the empire of Babylonia are commanded, whenever a certain signal is given on any musical instrument or by singing, to fall down and worship the golden image set up by the king. Anyone refusing to do so will be thrown into a fiercely burning furnace.'

So it happened that whenever the notes were sounded, all those within hearing turned towards the golden image and worshipped it. But certain of Nebuchadnezzar's wise men came to him and said, 'Shadrach, Meshach and Abed-nego, whom you chose to rule the province of Babylon, have disobeyed your command. They refuse to serve your god and worship the golden image.'

In a fury the king sent for the three Jews and asked them if it was true that they would not worship his idol. If it was, they would be thrown into the furnace; and where was the god who could deliver them from that?

Shadrach, Meshach and Abed-nego replied, 'If there is a god who can save us from the fire, it is the God whom we serve. But even if he chooses not to save us, you must know, O King, that we will not serve your god nor worship your golden image.'

The defiant reply enraged Nebuchadnezzar still more. His face twisted with anger, he ordered the furnace to be heated seven times hotter than it had ever been fired before. All the clothes the three Jews possessed were tied round them so that not even an article of clothing should be left by which they might be remembered; and Nebuchadnezzar ordered his strongest warriors to throw Shadrach, Meshach and Abed-nego into the fire. The flames licked out so fiercely from the furnace that they killed Nebuchadnezzar's men with their heat, and the Jews fell bound into the searing heart of the inferno.

But Nebuchadnezzar, watching, leaped to his feet in terror. 'Did we not throw three bound men into the fire?' he cried. 'How is it that I see four men walking free and unharmed in the very middle of the flames, and the fourth looks like a god?' Then the king went as close as he could to the furnace-door and called out, 'Shadrach, Meshach and Abed-nego, servants of God most High, come out!'

The three men walked out of the fire. Their bodies were untouched by the flames. Not even their hair was singed nor did they smell scorched.

'Blessed is your God,' said Nebuchadnezzar, 'who has sent his angel to save you. You were willing to disobey my royal command and die in the furnace rather than be unfaithful to him. Therefore, from now on, if any man of any nation says anything against the God of Shadrach, Meshach and Abed-nego, he shall be torn in pieces and his property forfeit; for no other god can save his followers like this.' And the king gave the three faithful Jews even higher authority than before in the province of Babylon.

Under Nebuchadnezzar II (who reigned from 605 to 562 BC) Babylon reached the height of its glory as the centre of a vast empire. In this reconstruction from available material, the drawing shows the area of the King's palace constructed on both sides of the Euphrates River. A section of the Hanging Gardens is partially shown, and across the river, the temple of Marduk, and tower of the E-temananki can be seen.

Belshazzar's Feast
Daniel 5

Belshazzar, called in the story Nebuchadnezzar's son, though he was in fact the son of King Nabonidus who seized the Babylonian throne, gave a feast for a thousand of his nobles and his many wives. He used the gold and silver goblets which had been taken from the Temple at Jerusalem years before by the Babylonians. These were sacred to the service of Jehovah but Belshazzar and his guests drank from them at the feast.

While they did this, they praised their own idols which were not gods but only images of metal or stone. Suddenly there appeared a hand by itself, the fingers of which wrote on the wall opposite the king's seat *Mene mene tekel u-pharsin*. Terrified, Belshazzar shrieked for his magicians and wise men to be called, for, though he understood the words, there seemed to be no sense to them. When the sages came, he promised that whoever could tell him the meaning would be clothed in royal purple and be third in the kingdom, after his father who was king, and himself who actually ruled; for Nabonidus was a scholar who left the government to his son.

But the wise men were as puzzled as Belshazzar, and the mystery might never have been solved if the queen (probably Belshazzar's mother rather than his wife) had not entered the hall. 'Why are you so puzzled and alarmed?' she asked. 'There is a man whom King Nebuchadnezzar made chief of all the magicians and wise men of Babylon, so gifted was he in understanding dreams and riddles such as this. Summon Daniel. He will tell you the meaning.'

Belshazzar at once sent for Daniel, by now an old man. 'I hear that the spirit of the holy gods is in you,' said the prince, 'and that you can read riddles such as the words written there on the wall by a mysterious and terrifying hand which appeared by itself. If you can tell me the meaning, you shall be the third man in Babylon after my father and myself.'

'Keep your honours,' said Daniel, 'or give them to someone else. I will tell you the meaning of the writing without reward. God gave King Nebuchadnezzar a great empire and such power that all the peoples of the world feared him. But he grew so proud that God brought madness upon him. For a time he became like a wild animal, without understanding, eating grass, his body drenched

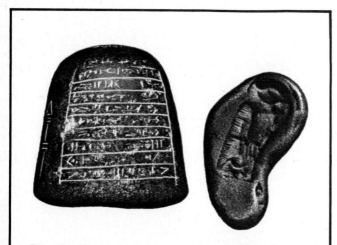

Taken literally the words *mene*, *tekel* and *pharsin* denote weights which were used as units of exchange before coins were introduced. Shown here are a Babylonian *mina* made up of sixty *shekels* from the reign of Nebuchadnezzar II, and right, a Persian *shekel*.

144

with rain and dew, until he realized that God controls the power and glory and kingdoms of men.

'But you, O Belshazzar, remained proud although you knew of Nebuchadnezzar's fate. You have exalted yourself against God himself. You, your nobles and your wives have drunk out of vessels holy to God. You have praised your idols and not given glory to the true God who holds your life and deeds in his hands. It was he who sent the hand you saw and this is the meaning of the words it wrote. *Mene* meaning "numbered", shows that God has numbered the days of your kingdom which are now ended, *tekel* – a shekel or weight – means that you have been weighed in the scales of God's judgment and have been found too light; *u* means "and"; *pharsin* has three meanings, "halves", "divisions" and "Persians" and the word here means that your kingdom has been divided and will be given to the Medes and Persians.'

In spite of the gloomy nature of the prophecy, Belshazzar honoured Daniel, decreeing that he should be the third most important person in the kingdom. But that very night, the Medes broke into the city of Babylon, killed Belshazzar, and brought the empire of Babylonia to an end. Daniel, however, survived, honoured by the new rulers.

Daniel and the Lions
Daniel 6

Although Daniel had faithfully served the kings of Babylon, he was also favoured by the emperors of the Medes and Persians who replaced them. Darius appointed over his dominions three chief ministers, inferior only to the emperor himself, of whom Daniel was one; and he was so much better than the other two that Darius planned to give him the government of the whole empire. The other Persian officials, jealous of Daniel, tried to catch him out in every possible way. But they could find nothing wrong with the way he governed. He was an efficient and just ruler who took no bribes and favoured no man. In the end, the Persian officials said, 'We shall never catch this man out unless we can accuse him in some way because of his religion.'

So they went to Darius. 'We, the officials of the kingdom, have talked this over together and have come to ask you to make a law that for the next thirty days no man shall ask for anything from any god or man except you, O King,' they said. 'If any man does so, then he shall be thrown to the lions.'

King Darius did not know the reason for this strange request, but, since nearly all his officials had agreed upon it, he ordered his scribes to write out the law and proclaim it to his people.

Daniel lived in a house with a room built on his roof. In the wall facing towards Jerusalem he had had windows made; and three times every day he knelt facing Jerusalem and praised and prayed to God. His enemies knew this and watched until they caught Daniel in the very act of praying. At once they went to Darius and reminded him of the decree he had made. The king replied, 'Yes, the decree was made. And once a law is made by a king of the Medes and Persians, it cannot be altered.'

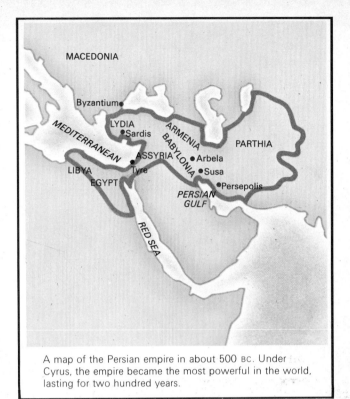

A map of the Persian empire in about 500 BC. Under Cyrus, the empire became the most powerful in the world, lasting for two hundred years.

'In that case,' said the officials, 'you must throw Daniel to the lions; for, in spite of the law you have made, he still prays to his god three times a day.'

The king realized, too late, that he had been tricked. Greatly distressed, he tried in every way he could to save Daniel; but whatever he said, he was met always by the reply, 'O King, a law of the Medes and Persians, once made, cannot be changed.' In the end Darius was forced to have Daniel thrown into the lions' pit. 'God, whose faithful servant you are, will save you,' said Darius; then Daniel was lowered into the pit, and over it a stone was placed, sealed with the seals of the king and his nobles so that no one might rescue him.

That whole night Darius remained sleepless and without food; and as soon as the day dawned, he hurried to the pit, terrified of what he would find. 'Daniel,' he called, 'has your God saved you?' To his great joy, Daniel called back, 'Long life to you, King Darius! God sent his angels to keep the lions from hurting me because I have done no wrong either to him or to you.'

Darius at once ordered Daniel, completely unharmed, to be raised from the pit. Instead of him, his accusers and their families were thrown to the lions, and before they so much as reached the bottom of the pit, the ravenous animals tore them to pieces.

Darius then made another proclamation that throughout his dominions all men should worship the God of Daniel who had saved him from the lions. Daniel lived an honoured life throughout his reign and that of Cyrus, his successor, and died peacefully, a very old man.

Return and Restoration
The Books of Haggai, Nehemiah and Ezra

In the years after the fall of Jerusalem and the end of the kingdom of Judah, the Jews lived in exile in Babylonia. There, like other nations taken from their native lands, they might have worshipped the Babylonian gods who seemed to have conquered their own. Their Temple, the only place on earth where they believed sacrifices could rightly be offered to Jehovah, had disappeared. They were living in an 'unclean' land where complete worship could not be offered to their God. But instead of giving up, they continued to obey such parts of the Law as could still be kept, such as observing the Sabbath. Through the lack of outward worship they may have been driven to more intense private prayer. They met together in synagogues, which date from this time. These were partly churches, where they prayed and where the Law was studied, and partly councils, where Jewish affairs could be debated and local decisions taken.

Realizing that as a nation they had sinned, the Jews at last began to learn what the prophets had tried to teach them – that they should turn from all other gods and worship Jehovah alone. Because of the Exile, they became a better, purer and more holy people.

During the last years of the Babylonian empire, there arose in the east a new power, Cyrus, King of the Medes and Persians. It was he who captured Babylon and his victory was hailed with delight by the Jews. He was a brave and good man, regarded by the Jewish nation as a servant of God, even though he did not worship Jehovah, who would restore them to their native land.

No sooner had Cyrus conquered Babylon than he issued a proclamation that all those Jews who wished should return to Jerusalem and rebuild the Temple. Not all went back. During the years of exile many of those who had left Judah had died, and a new generation had grown up who knew no other way of life than the Babylonian. Probably only a few went back immediately, although, during the next hundred years or so, many thousands followed them.

Cyrus appointed a governor of Jerusalem called Sheshbazzar to take the exiles back to their homeland. He was entrusted with all the gold and silver vessels which Nebuchadnezzar had taken from the Temple, so that they could be used again in the worship of God. He probably returned to Cyrus after settling the exiles in Jerusalem; for his place as leader of the people was taken by Jeshua, a priest, and Zerubbabel, a descendant of King David.

These two first built the altar of burnt-offering in the open air among the ruins of the old Temple, in the presence of a great crowd of Israelites assembled from the towns in which they had settled. Then, although the foundations of the Temple had not yet been laid, they offered once more all the sacrifices which the Law of Moses required.

148

As it was the right season of the year, the setting up of the altar was followed by the Feast of Tabernacles; and a short time after, the foundation of the new Temple was laid. There was tremendous rejoicing, psalms of praise being sung to the accompaniment of trumpets and cymbals. But there was sadness, too. Many of those old enough to have known the original Temple in all its glory wept when they remembered it. The noise of rejoicing and weeping was so great that it was difficult to distinguish the one from the other.

The Jews were surrounded by the Samaritans who had been settled in Israel and Judah when they themselves had been taken into exile. These men worshipped Jehovah after a fashion as the god of the land in which they had settled; but their worship was mingled with the worship of other gods. The Jews were afraid of them because they were far more numerous. But when the Samaritans asked to share in the Temple rebuilding, the Jews had the courage to refuse. They had learned in exile that the worship of God had to be kept free from all idolatry, and if the foreigners had helped with the building of the Temple, they would have had the right to worship in it and bring into it the adoration of the false gods they revered besides Jehovah. The refusal angered the Samaritans. They made trouble for the builders so successfully that the Jews, discouraged, gave up their work almost at once. 'It is not God's will that we build the Temple now,' they deceived themselves. 'The time is not ripe.'

But life proved hard for the returned exiles. As Haggai, a prophet of the time said, they sowed much and reaped very little, they had not enough food, drink and clothing, and their money disappeared as if it had been put into a purse with a hole in it. The reason for this, said Haggai, was that they had not built God's Temple – and it was for this purpose that they had returned from exile. Because of the reproaches of Haggai and another prophet, Zechariah, Zerubbabel and Jeshua began once more to build the Temple. Again they were opposed by the hostile Samaritans. But in reply to a letter written by the governor of the province to Darius II, king of Persia, the news came that a decree had been found among the royal laws and proclamations, in which Cyrus had ordered that the Temple should be rebuilt. So, in spite of all the Samaritans could do, the rebuilding went on. Four years later the Temple was completed among tremendous rejoicing. Hundreds of sacrifices were made; and the priests and Levites were divided into groups to carry out the daily worship of God for all the years to come.

Soon after the completion of the Temple, the Feast of Passover was held. All the returned exiles purified themselves and celebrated the feast with great joy, because God had caused the king to show them favour.

But although the Temple had been rebuilt, the city and walls of Jerusalem remained for many years heaps of ruins. News of this came to Susa, the capital city of Persia, to a Jew called Nehemiah who had achieved high rank in the service of the king, Artaxerxes I. As the king's cupbearer who handed him his wine, he was in his presence at every meal. When Nehemiah heard of the terrible state of Jerusalem, he was so sad that he could not hide his sorrow from the king.

'Why are you looking so sorrowful?' asked Artaxerxes. 'I trust you are not ill.'

Nehemiah replied that he was sad because the city of his ancestors still lay waste. 'Do you want to ask me a favour?' said the king. Nehemiah hesitated a moment, sending up a swift and silent prayer to God; then he said, 'Send me to Jerusalem in order that I may rebuild it.'

To his great joy, the king granted him permission. He also gave him letters of authority to the governors of the province where Jerusalem lay and to the keeper of the royal forests so that he might obtain all the timber he needed to rebuild the city. Immediately he arrived in Jerusalem, Nehemiah made a survey of the ruined walls by night. Not until he had seen what needed to be done did he tell the leaders of the Jews of the favour he had received from Artaxerxes. The people were enthusiastic and vigorously set about the rebuilding of the walls.

But they soon met opposition. The foreigners living round about, led by a certain Sanballat, jeered at them. 'Are you preparing to
rebel against the king?' they sneered. 'What
do you feeble Jews hope to gain with that wall
of yours? Why, if a fox jumps up at it, it will
knock it over!' Worse than contemptuous
words were their actions; for they banded
together to attack the men working on the
walls. The builders, already discouraged by
the immense piles of rubble, were still more
alarmed by the threat of attack.

But Nehemiah was a match for his enemies.
He divided his workers into two groups, one
of which built while the other stood by them
fully armed, carrying the weapons of the
workers as well. The men who had to carry

loads balanced them with one hand and
carried a sword in the other. Rallying-points
were arranged so that, if an assault were made,
trumpet-blasts could summon the workers to
whatever section of the wall was being
attacked. When Sanballat and his allies saw
that the threat of force had failed, they tried
to trap Nehemiah by cunning; but the Jewish
leader was far too clever for them, and all
their plots failed. Nehemiah's counter-meas-
ures were so effective that the walls were
completed in fifty-two days.

The walls were finished before any of the
houses inside Jerusalem were rebuilt. There
were not enough people living inside it to
defend the city, and Nehemiah ordered the
gates to be closed each day until the sun was

high and all the citizens astir. The leaders of the people were settled in Jerusalem; and later the rest of the Jews selected by lot, one in every ten to live in the city, providing it with a large enough population. Like the Temple, the walls were dedicated with songs, dancing and general rejoicing. Two great choirs, each at the head of half the most important men of Judah, walked in procession round the city, one to the right, the other to the left, meeting afterwards in the Temple where a great sacrifice was held. There the Law was read. The Israelites, realizing that the Law ordered them to keep themselves from foreigners, separated from the nation all who had foreign fathers or mothers.

His work done, Nehemiah returned to his royal master in Susa, but later came back to Jerusalem to see what progress was being made. He found that the first enthusiasm was already dying. Even Eliashib, the High Priest in charge of the Temple store-rooms, had given one to a foreigner with whom he was connected by marriage. The Levites who looked after the Temple services had not been given their livings and had consequently deserted the House of God and returned to their farms. Men were working on the Sabbath, and Jews, including one of the high priest's grandsons, had married foreign girls again. Nehemiah put everything to rights, purifying the nation from all foreign influences and seeing to it that the Temple services were properly conducted.

Nehemiah's work was carried on by Ezra, a descendant of Aaron and a man deeply learned in the Law. He came to Jerusalem from Babylon in the reign of Artaxerxes II with a company of two or three thousand Israelites. With him he brought a letter from the king authorizing him to collect supplies and appoint officials and judges over the Jews. Before Ezra and his company started on their journey, they fasted and prayed to God that he would keep them from all dangers, as they were travelling without soldiers and horsemen to guard them. Their prayer was answered and they arrived safely in Jerusalem.

A short time after Ezra arrived, some leaders of the people came to him to report that many Israelites had failed to keep Nehemiah's commands and had married women from the surrounding nations. The chief offenders in this had been the leaders and magistrates. Ezra was appalled. He rent his clothes, tore his hair and beard and sat in front of the Temple in silence until the time of the evening sacrifice. All who felt as he did rallied to him and sat with him. At the time of sacrifice he knelt in prayer and in tears confessed to God all that the nation had done wrong.

The people were deeply moved by his sorrow. Shekaniah, one of their leaders, acknowledged the nation's guilt but added, 'There is still hope. Let us promise God to put away all foreign wives and their children. Let us do what the Law requires. Lead us and we shall follow.'

So all the Israelites were summoned to assemble at Jerusalem within three days. They met in heavy rain, shivering both with cold and fear of what was going to happen. It was agreed that in every city all who had married foreign wives should present themselves to the elders and judges, and that the foreign wives should be divorced and sent away. So the Jewish race was kept pure, though at a cost of tremendous sorrow and pain; for many of the Jewish husbands must have dearly loved their foreign wives and were wretched at having to send them away.

This was not the end of Ezra's reforms. Once again all the people were summoned to Jerusalem and he read them the whole Law of Moses, taking from early morning till noon. He stood on a wooden platform so that all could see and hear him, and the Law was explained to different sections of the crowd as he read it by Levites who thoroughly understood it.

The people wept when they heard the Law and realized how far short of it they had fallen. But Ezra said, 'Do not weep. This is a holy day. Let it be a day of feasting and gladness, not of mourning – for it is joy in God which makes you strong.'

The reading of the Law revealed to the people that the Feast of Tabernacles, the great harvest festival of the Jews, occurred at the very time that the Law was being read. So for seven days they joyfully held the feast, which had not been celebrated properly since the days of Joshua, the conqueror of Canaan; and every day they listened to the reading of the Law. On the eighth day the feast was closed with the ceremony which the Law demanded.

A solemn fast followed the feast. Now that all the people had heard the Law of Moses read to them several times and explained by learned men, they all knew what God required of them. After prayers in which they acknowledged all that he had done for them since leading them out of Egypt and their continual sinfulness towards him, they made a firm vow once more to separate themselves from all foreigners and never to intermarry with them again. They would keep the Sabbath day holy.

They would loyally maintain the Temple services. They would faithfully observe the whole Law.

So at last the remnants of Israel and Judah had become a nation holy to God. From the days of Nehemiah and Ezra onwards they became more and more concerned with keeping their religion pure. Although they became far too rigid and unloving as the centuries went by, they did in their own way prepare for the coming of Jesus.

From the Old Testament to the New

While Nehemiah and Ezra had been restoring the worship of Jehovah in Jerusalem, Persia had been fighting a series of wars against the Greeks. These continued until, just over three hundred years before Jesus was born, Alexander the Great invaded Asia. In turn his brilliant general conquered Syria, Egypt, Babylon and Persia itself. He advanced into India, and when he died at the early age of thirty-three, he had founded the greatest empire the world had seen until that time.

As part of Alexander's dominions, Judaea came under the influence of Greek civilization. Alexander showed respect for the gods of the people he conquered, and he allowed the Jews to observe their laws and religion. But a number of Jews, especially the younger ones, admired Greek philosophy and culture and were influenced by them away from their own religion.

Those who remained faithful to Jewish thought and customs opposed them with all the energy they could. From the hellenized Jews, as the supporters of Greek culture were called, descended the Sadducee party, who did not believe in a life after death and valued worldly power, position and learning. From the orthodox Jews, as the faithful were called, came the Hasidim, or 'Separated Ones', who were rigidly faithful to the Law and the ceremonies of Judaism. They developed later into the Pharisees, who played such a prominent part in opposing Jesus.

When Alexander died, his empire broke up. Egypt, to the south-west of Judaea, was seized by one of his generals called Ptolemy, and Syria, to the north, by another called Seleucus. For a hundred years the Ptolemies and Seleucids fought for Palestine. Eventually, two hundred years before Christ, the Seleucids gained the final victory and Judaea became part of their empire.

During the reign of a Seleucid king, Antiochus Epiphanes, the hellenized Jews, supported by the king, tried to stamp out orthodox Judaism. They were fiercely resisted. An old priest named Mattathias killed a Jew trying to offer sacrifice on a heathen altar, and he and his five sons fled to the mountains where they quickly gathered together a heroic band of faithful Jews. For a time they lived a kind of Robin Hood existence, raiding the forces of Epiphanes when and where they could. Under the leadership of Judas Maccabaeus, the son of Mattathias, the band grew strong enough to take and fortify several towns. These successes were followed by others in pitched battles in which Judas defeated armies many times larger than his own. He eventually fell in battle, but not until he had freed Jerusalem and purified the Temple.

Judas Maccabaeus' brothers, Jonathan and Simon, carried on the struggle, and Simon all but freed the country from Seleucid rule. He was appointed both High Priest and ruler of the Jews, and became the founder of a line of kings called the Hasmoneans who were also High Priests. They gained an independance for the Jewish state which lasted sixty-six years, conquering lands round Judaea, including Galilee, the inhabitants of which were forced to become Jews. (It was in this district that Jesus grew up and from which he drew his first followers.) But the Jewish people came to hate the way in which their rulers sought the worldly power of kings rather than the holiness of high priests: and the Hasmonean line came to an end in a struggle for the throne between two brothers called Hyrcanus and Aristobulus. Hyrcanus, supported by a certain Antipater, allied himself with the rising empire of Rome. The Romans made him High Priest and ruler, but not king: because under them Judaea ceased to be a kingdom and became part of the Roman province of Syria.

Some time later, the Parthians, bitter enemies of the Romans, attacked and overran their province of Syria, captured Hyrcanus and made his nephew king. The Romans, in opposition, proclaimed Antipater's son, Herod, King of the Jews. It took him some years to win this throne, but in 37 B.C. supported by a Roman army, he besieged and captured Jerusalem. His rival was beheaded, and Herod became the Herod the Great who was King of the Jews when Jesus was born.

Elizabeth and Mary

Luke 1

During the reign of King Herod the Great, about four hundred years after the end of Old Testament times, there lived a Jewish priest called Zechariah and his wife, Elizabeth. Both of them were good and virtuous people, following the commandments of the Lord. Their only sorrow was that they had no children, and were by now well on in years.

At last, an event which happened only once in a priest's lifetime occurred. Zechariah's turn had come to enter the Temple at Jerusalem on his own, to burn the incense on the golden altar in the Holy Place. All the other worshippers remained at prayer outside.

Suddenly, on the right of the altar of incense, an angel appeared. Zechariah was overcome with fear, but the angel reassured him. 'Your prayers have been heard,' he said. 'Elizabeth will bear you a son, whom you must call John. He shall be great in the sight of the Lord and shall be filled with the Holy Spirit and turn many Israelites to God; for he shall prepare the people for the coming of the Lord.'

But Zechariah, remembering that he and Elizabeth were too old to have children, asked, 'How can I be sure of this?' The angel answered, 'I am Gabriel, a messenger from God. I have been sent to tell you this good news. Because you have doubted me, you will be unable to speak until the day this happens.'

Outside, the people began to wonder why Zechariah was so long in the Temple, and they were even more surprised when he came out at last unable to speak. He could only make signs, and they realized that he must have seen a vision in the Temple.

Soon, to Elizabeth's great joy, she knew that she was going to have a baby.

Six months later Gabriel was sent by God to a town called Nazareth, where there lived a girl called Mary. Mary was betrothed to Joseph, a descendant of King David.

The angel greeted Mary, saying, 'All joy to you, favoured one! The Lord is with you!'

Mary was startled, for she could not understand what this greeting meant.

'Fear not, Mary,' the angel said, 'for you have found favour with God. You are to bear a son, whom you will call Jesus. He will be known as Son of the Most High. God will give him the throne of David, and there shall be no end to his reign.'

'But how will this happen?' asked Mary.

'The Holy Spirit will come upon you,' Gabriel answered. 'The power of the Most High will overshadow you. Your son will be holy and will be called the Son of God. And what is more, your cousin Elizabeth has conceived in her old age, which shows that nothing is impossible with God.'

'I am here to serve God,' said Mary quietly. 'Let it be as you have said.'

When the angel had left her, Mary set out to visit Elizabeth and found that what Gabriel had said was true. Her cousin was indeed expecting a baby. Mary stayed with Elizabeth for three months before returning home.

Soon afterwards Elizabeth gave birth to a boy who, she said, was to be called John. All her relations were surprised, for no one in the family had ever been called John before. They asked Zechariah what he wanted the baby called, and gave him a writing-tablet. Then on it he wrote, 'His name is John.' No sooner had he done this, than he found he was able to speak again, and he began to praise God.

Everyone present was filled with wonder, and the story of these happenings soon spread throughout the entire country. People asked each other, 'What will this child John become?'

As time went on, John grew and became strong in character, and he lived in the desert until the time came for him to appear publicly to Israel.

The Birth of Jesus

Matthew 2; Luke 2

At the time when Gabriel appeared to Zechariah and Mary, Judaea was part of the Roman Empire. The Empire had been much troubled with civil war but was now at peace under the Emperor, Augustus Caesar. As it was necessary to raise money, the Emperor ordered every man to go to the town to which his family belonged, to be registered, so that he could pay taxes. Everywhere there were travellers returning to their own cities from other places where they had gone to live or work. In several towns the inns were full, and it was impossible to find anywhere to sleep.

About six months had passed since John's birth. Mary and her husband, Joseph, had to travel from Nazareth, where they were living, to Bethlehem, which had been King David's city, because Joseph was a descendant of David. The city was so full of people who had come to register that there was no room at the inn. Joseph pleaded with the innkeeper.

'My wife is expecting a baby,' he said, for the time had come when Mary's baby was due to be born. 'Isn't there a corner where she could sleep?'

'There is only the stable,' said the innkeeper. 'It shouldn't be too bad, however. There is plenty of hay to keep her warm.'

So Joseph and Mary sheltered in the stable. There, in the bitter cold of the night, without blankets or hot water, or any comfort or help save that which Joseph could give, Mary gave birth to the son of whom Gabriel had told her. The child who was King of Kings and Lord of Lords, the Messiah who had been foretold by all the prophets, the Saviour who was to save the whole world from its sins, was born in a a manger because there was nowhere else for him to go.

Though weary, Mary was full of joy, for the birth of her son was a wonderful event and the fulfilment of God's promise to her. Joseph rejoiced with her, because he shared her secret; he, too, had been told by an angel in a vivid dream that the Holy Spirit would come

upon Mary, and that she was to be the mother of the Son of God.

'You are to call him Jesus,' the angel had said, a name which means "God is salvation". 'For this child will save his people from their sins.'

On the night that Jesus was born, there were shepherds watching over their flocks in the fields outside Bethlehem. Suddenly an angel of God stood before them, and all round them shone a great glory of light. They were terrified at first, but the angel said, 'Do not be afraid. I bring you good news of great joy which is coming to all people. This very day a Saviour, who is the Lord Messiah, has been born in the city of David. You will find him wrapped in swaddling clothes, lying in a manger.'

As if this were a signal for a great outburst of joy through the whole universe, there suddenly appeared a great company of angels singing the praises of God:

'Glory to God in the highest heaven,
And on earth peace among men who
 love God.'

Then, as suddenly as they had come, the angels vanished. Nothing but silence and the darkness of night remained. But to the shepherds it was as if the light outside had become a glory of joy within. Had not the people of God waited for centuries for the birth of the Messiah, the great Deliverer of Israel promised by prophet after prophet? And they, humble shepherds though they were, were among the very first to be allowed to see him. Leaving only one or two men to watch their sheep, they ran excitedly to where the lights of the town were shining on the hillside.

Sensibly they went at once to the inn, where they knew that they would be likely to hear gossip of anything happening in Bethlehem.

'Baby in a manger?' said the innkeeper. 'I don't know anything about that. But there's a couple in the stable in the yard. The wife's time was pretty close by all accounts, and that was the best I could do for her. Perhaps they're the ones you're looking for.'

The shepherds ran to the stable. There, by the light of a lantern, they gazed in awe at the Messiah who was to be the salvation of his people, Israel, and – although they did not know it – of the whole world. Their entry woke Mary from a light sleep, and they told her and Joseph of the vision they had seen and what the angels had said and sung. They told many others, too, before the night was out, and all who heard them rejoiced. And Mary considered these things and thought about them in the days to come.

The shepherds returned to their flocks praising God for all they had seen because it had happened exactly as the angel had told them.

Since ancient times gold has been one of the most valuable articles of currency, as well as a favoured material for ornaments. The gift of gold by the Magi symbolized Christ's kingliness.

Frankincense, a whitish-yellow resin obtained by incising the bark of certain trees related to the terebinth, which smells extremely fragrant. The presentation to Christ of frankincense has been interpreted as symbolizing his priestly office.

Myrrh is a resinous gum which drips from the stems and branches of a low, shrubby tree growing in the Arabian desert and parts of Africa. Traditionally used as an ingredient of the holy anointing oil, myrrh was presented to the infant Jesus as a symbol of the relief from the pain he would suffer at his crucifixion.

The Visit of the Magi
Matthew 2

The shepherds were not the only ones to visit Jesus. After his birth, wise men from the East who were astrologers, arrived in Jerusalem asking, 'Where is the child born to be King of the Jews? We have seen his star rising and have come to pay him homage.' On hearing this, King Herod was greatly alarmed, fearing that the child would be a threat to his throne. He discovered that it had been prophesied that the Messiah was to be born in Bethlehem and, summoning the astrologers privately, he told them where to find the baby. 'When you have found the child,' he said, 'tell me, that I, too, may pay him homage.'

The wise men set out that night for Bethlehem, and the star, as if leading the way, travelled comet-like across the sky ahead of them. When they were in sight of the town, it seemed to them to linger on the skyline above a certain house. In it they found Mary and her baby; for when the crowds registering for taxation had returned home, she and Joseph had moved out of the stable to a proper home. Overjoyed to find the star had led them straight to their goal, the three wise men bowed before Jesus as before a King. Then

they opened their treasures and offered him gifts of gold, frankincense and myrrh. That night, they were warned in a dream not to return to Herod but to go home by another way.

When the wise men had left, the Lord appeared to Joseph in a dream saying, 'Rise up and flee into Egypt with Mary and the baby, and stay there until I tell you it is safe to leave. Herod means to kill the child.' Joseph rose at once, and taking Mary and the baby travelled by night to Egypt.

Herod fell into a terrible rage when he realized that the astrologers had tricked him, and he ordered that every child in Bethlehem under the age of two years should be slaughtered. The killing of the young children in Bethlehem was all the more tragic since Jesus was far away by the time Herod's soldiers arrived to carry out their grisly task.

Until Herod's death, Joseph, Mary and Jesus remained in Egypt. Then Joseph was once again guided by a dream to return to their own country, Israel. But learning that Herod's son Archelaus, was now King of Judaea, he was afraid to live there, and withdrew to Nazareth, a town in the northern province of Galilee. There Jesus spent his childhood.

Jesus in the Temple

Luke 2, 41–52

Jesus grew up healthy and strong, and his knowledge and intelligence increased day by day. When he was twelve years old, he accompanied his parents to the Feast of the Passover at Jerusalem, probably for the first time. From then on it would be his duty as a devout Jew, bound by the Law of Moses, to attend Passover every year if he possibly could. For when a Jewish boy reached his thirteenth birthday, he became a 'Son of the Law' and subject to all its regulations.

Nazareth was several days' journey from Jerusalem. Every year Joseph went with a company of his friends and relations and others from the town to swell the great crowds of pilgrims which filled the roads leading to the Holy City. Women were not compelled to go, and it is a sign of Mary's special devotion that she appears always to have accompanied her husband.

The full Passover feast lasted a week. But the worshippers were not obliged to stay for more than the first two days, and many busy farmers and others whose work needed them, departed early. Joseph and Mary and a number of their friends from Nazareth may have been among those who left after two days.

Pilgrims to and from the city used to travel in groups, sometimes several hundreds strong for defence against bands of robbers; so, at the beginning of their journey, his parents thought that Jesus was somewhere in their party, perhaps with boys of his own age, and they travelled contentedly for a whole day without seeing him.

In the evening they began to enquire for him, at first casually and then, as they unsuccessfully asked family after family and

group after group, with anxiety which grew into fear. Jesus was nowhere to be found, and they realized that he must have remained in Jerusalem, probably with friends celebrating the whole week of the feast. But they could not be certain of this. Very early the next day, they set out on the journey back to Jerusalem.

Tired and worried, Mary and Joseph went from place to place where they knew Jesus could be staying, but found no sign of their son. Next day, after they had spent a sleepless night, their search continued. Perhaps it was chance that led them to the Temple; perhaps they thought that the majestic building would attract Jesus, as a great city cathedral today might attract a sightseer from the country. Whatever the reason, there they found their son at last, seated among the great teachers and doctors of the Law, the most learned men in the whole country. Jesus was listening carefully to their instruction and asking them

questions; and, as part of their teaching, they were asking him questions in their turn. Everyone who listened to his questions and replies was amazed at his understanding.

His parents shared their astonishment, but they were also angry and upset. 'My son,' said Mary, 'why have you behaved like this to us? Your father and I have been searching for you everywhere. We have been dreadfully worried.'

'Why did you look for me?' Jesus replied. 'Did you not know that I would be here, in my Father's house?'

His answer puzzled them and they did not know what to think of it. But Mary added his words to the other sayings and wonders which she remembered from the time Jesus had been a baby, and often thought about them. Jesus returned with his parents to Nazareth, and obeyed them as a good son should; and as he grew up to manhood, he increased in favour with both God and man.

John the Baptist

Matthew 3; Mark 1, 1–11; Luke 3, 1–18
John 1, 19–34

When Jesus was about thirty years old, his cousin John began to preach near the River Jordan. He was a wild figure, dressed like one of the ancient prophets in a rough coat of camel's hair belted with leather, who lived on locusts and wild honey. His fiery preaching caused a great stir, and thousands of people from Judaea and Jerusalem thronged to hear him. He urged them to repent of their sins and wash them away in baptism, so that they could begin a new life, for God's reign, he declared, was very near.

Among those who went to listen to him were some Pharisees and Sadducees. The Pharisees, a privileged group, studied the Law of Moses in great detail and were very religious. They thought themselves better than ordinary people who were poor and had to earn their living. The Sadducees, too, enjoyed a high standard of living and mixed only with powerful and wealthy people.

But their wealth and position did not impress John. 'You brood of vipers,' he rebuked them, 'who has warned you to flee from God's anger? Show that you are sorry for your sins by living good lives. You are not safe simply because you belong to God's Chosen People. God can make people for himself out of stones if he wants to. If you do not do good deeds, you are like trees which do not produce good fruit, fit only to be cut down for firewood.'

John baptized people and told them that those who had clothing and food should share with those who had none. Tax-gatherers who made themselves rich collecting duties imposed by the Romans and by taking more money than was required, were to take only the actual tax. Soldiers who made money by threatening to accuse people falsely of some offence against the government unless they gave them money, were told not to bully or threaten but to be satisfied with their pay.

John's preaching caused such excitement that many people thought he must be the Messiah, the great warrior descended from David. They expected him to lead the armies of God's People against their oppressors and to bring about everlasting peace, when the whole world would worship the one true God. But John said that he was not the Messiah. Neither was he Elijah, who was expected to return before the coming of the Messiah, nor a prophet.

'"I am the voice of one crying in the wilderness,"' he quoted from Isaiah, '"Prepare a way for the Lord." I baptize with water. But there is one among you coming after me, who is mightier than I. I am not fit to undo his sandals. He will baptize you with the Holy Spirit.'

The very next day Jesus came to him asking to be baptized. John, knowing he was the Messiah, said, 'I ought to be baptized by you – do you come to me?'

'We should do what God requires of each of us,' Jesus replied, whereupon John baptized him.

The moment Jesus was out of the water, he saw the heavens opening and the Spirit of God descending on him in the form of a dove, and a voice was heard saying, 'This is my beloved Son in whom I delight.' John also saw the vision, as God had earlier promised him he would, and knew that Jesus was indeed God's Chosen One.

Jesus had grown up into manhood just like any other boy, but he was always aware that God had special work for him to do. At the moment when the Holy Spirit descended upon him, he realized that he was the Messiah, and that he was to found a more than earthly empire – the Kingdom of God. How this was to be done, he had now to work out by thought and prayer.

Three animals that John might have seen in the wilderness: left to right, a vulture, which to this day is regarded in Israel as the king of birds, the caracal lynx and a carpet viper.

The Temptation in the Wilderness

Matthew 4, 1–11; Mark 1, 12–13;
Luke 4, 1–14

Jesus could only think out how he was to bring about the Kingdom of God in complete solitude. So the Spirit led him into the wilderness where he was alone, except for the wild animals. For many days and nights he wandered through the desert thinking, and when he was weak with hunger, the devil came to him in his thoughts.

'If you really are the Son of God,' said the devil, 'turn these stones into bread.' This was three temptations in one. It was, first, as if Jesus had said to himself, 'Let me see if I really am the Son of God by performing a miracle,' – it was a temptation to doubt God. Secondly, it was a temptation to Jesus not to trust God to look after him. The Holy Spirit had led him into the desert and God would feed him when it was time. Thirdly, it was a temptation to establish the Kingdom by the wrong means. 'If you can feed yourself by a miracle, how much more easily can you feed a hungry world? Give everybody everything they want – food, clothing, goods, houses – and you will have the Kingdom of Heaven upon earth.'

But Jesus was determined not to doubt God, for he had heard him say, 'You are my beloved Son.' He would trust God to feed him, just as when the Israelites had had no bread in the wilderness, God fed them with manna. He knew that if everyone in the world had everything they wanted, they would still not be happy – for men have a hunger and need for God and his love which has nothing to do with possessions. So Jesus could not be caught in that trap. He answered the devil with Moses' words to the Israelites in the

desert. 'Man cannot live on bread alone,' he said. 'He also lives by every word that comes from the mouth of God.'

The devil next took Jesus in his thoughts to a high platform overlooking the Temple courtyard, from which preachers addressed large crowds. Let Jesus tell a huge multitude of listeners that he was the Messiah and then prove it by hurling himself unharmed to the ground, and everyone would believe him. 'God will give his angels charge of you to protect you – they will bear you in their hands lest you so much as strike your foot against a stone,' said the devil. But Jesus knew that men must be attracted of their own free will to God by believing in his goodness and his love, not because they are driven to believe by witnessing a miracle. Nor must God's followers challenge him by running into unnecessary dangers. Therefore Jesus answered the devil, 'You shall not put the Lord your God to the test.'

Finally the devil made Jesus imagine that he was on top of a high mountain from which all the nations of the world and their glory could be seen. 'All this will I give you,' he said, 'if you will fall down and worship me.' But Jesus knew that to worship the devil meant to bring in the Kingdom by force of arms, intrigue and deceit. There could be only peace, honesty, goodness and love in God's Kingdom. This is what he meant when he replied, 'Away with you, Satan, for it is written, "You must worship the Lord your God and him only must you serve."'

So Jesus triumphed over all the temptations, though often when he was tired and depressed, he must have longed for a quick and easy way to the Kingdom. But from the time of his experience in the wilderness, he always knew that there was only one way possible to show the love of God to man – the way that led to the Cross. Only by dying for his people could he save them from their sins.

The Wedding at Cana

John 2, 1–11;

Two days after leaving Judaea, Jesus, and Mary his mother, together with his disciples, then numbering five or six, were invited to a wedding at Cana-in-Galilee, a village near Nazareth. During the wedding-feast the wine began to run out, perhaps because although Jesus had been asked to bring friends, not so many of them had been expected. It would have been very embarrassing for the host and hostess if the wine had run out before the feast was over, and the bride and bridegroom might well have felt that their wedding-day had been spoiled. So Mary said quietly to Jesus, 'They have no wine left.'

'Lady,' said Jesus, 'don't be concerned. The time for me to take action has not yet come.'

But Mary was confident that her son would do something to save his hosts from embarrassment, and said to the servants, 'Do whatever he tells you.'

There were six stone water-jars standing there, each holding between twenty and thirty gallons. Jesus told the servants to fill the jars with water, and they filled them to the brim. 'Now draw some out,' he said, 'and take it to the man presiding over the feast.'

When the man tasted the water, it had turned into good wine. He called the bridegroom and congratulated him. 'Everyone serves the best wine first and then the poorer after people have drunk freely; but you have kept the best wine until now.'

This was the first deed of Jesus which revealed his glory and strengthened the faith of his disciples in him.

The large Palestinian stone water-jar *c.*74 BC may well be the same sort as the one which contained the water that Jesus turned into wine. The glass drinking-cup dates from the first century AD. Glass-blowing had recently been invented and was practised mainly in the coastal cities of Palestine and Phoenicia.

The Story of the Wedding-Robe

Matthew 22, 1–14

When guests were invited to a wedding in Judaea, the hosts, usually the bride's parents, gave a present of a wedding-robe to each of them as he arrived. The king who gave a feast for his son in this story that Jesus told, would therefore have provided wedding-clothes for every guest, and it would have been the greatest insult a man could offer him not to put on those he had been given.

'The Kingdom of Heaven,' Jesus once said, 'is like a king who gave a feast for his son's wedding; but when he sent his servants to call the invited guests, they would not come. He then sent other servants with the following message from him: "See, here is the supper I have prepared for you. My bullocks and fatted beasts have been slaughtered. Everything is waiting. Come to the wedding-feast."'

'But the guests the king had asked to come ignored the invitation. One went off to his farm, another to his business, and the rest seized the servants, brutally ill-treated them and finally killed them. The king was enraged. He immediately sent soldiers to kill the murderers and to set their town on fire.

'Then he said to his servants, "The marriage-banquet is ready, but the guests I invited were not worthy of the honour. Go out therefore into the streets and invite anyone you meet to come to my son's feast." The servants went out as he had commanded and gathered together all they met, good and bad alike, so that the king's hall was packed with guests.

'When the king came in to welcome them, he saw a man among them who was not dressed in the robe he had been given. So he said to him, "My friend, how do you come to be here without wedding-clothes?" The man did not answer. Furious, the king ordered his servants to bind him hand and foot and to throw him into the darkness outside to wail and gnash his teeth. For many are invited, but few chosen.'

The Death of John the Baptist

Matthew 14, 1–12; 11, 2–6; Mark 6, 14–29;
Luke 7, 18–23; 9, 7–9

Before Herod Antipas imprisoned John the Baptist, he was married to an Arabian princess. Some time after his marriage, he visited his half-brother, Herod Philip, who lived at Rome, and he fell in love with Philip's wife, Herodias. He persuaded her to run away with him; and when he returned to Galilee, he divorced his own wife and married Herodias.

The marriage horrified the Jews. It broke the Law of Moses on two counts. First, the Law forbade a man to marry his brother's wife even when the brother had died, much less while he was still alive. Then Herodias was also Antipas's niece, and the Law of Moses did not allow uncle and niece to marry.

It was because John the Baptist had spoken out boldly against this marriage that Antipas imprisoned him. At first the king would have liked to kill him, but he was afraid of the people who thought John was a prophet. And while John was in prison, Antipas had summoned the wild-looking preacher before him several times. He discovered him to be a truly good and holy man and was awed and impressed by him. What John said made him think deeply, although much of it left him puzzled and disturbed.

Jesus did not reply to John's friend with a direct 'Yes'. But he healed many sick people in front of them and said, 'Tell John what you have seen and heard. The blind see, the deaf hear, lame men walk, lepers are cured, dead men are raised, and the poor have good news – the Gospel – preached to them. Happy is the man who is not turned away by what I am doing.'

Soon after this, Herod Antipas's birthday was celebrated at his palace by a grand feast. Herodias's daughter, who was called Salome, danced before Herod so gracefully that she delighted him and his guests; and in front of them all, he solemnly promised that he would reward her by giving her anything she wanted.

'O King,' said Salome, 'let me first consult my mother.' She left the banqueting-hall and went to the women's quarters, and when she returned and curtsied low before the King, the guests listened eagerly to hear what her request would be.

'What do you ask?' said Herod.

In the silence, Salome's answer rang out clearly. 'Give me here on a dish the head of John the Baptist.'

The king was greatly distressed. But he could not break the oath which he had given in front of so many witnesses, and he ordered a soldier of his guard to execute John immediately. The soldier did as he was told, beheading him in the prison. He brought John's head on a dish and gave it to Salome, and she handed it to her mother.

John's followers were allowed to take away their master's body. They buried it, and then went to tell Jesus.

A statue of the Roman emperor, Tiberius Caesar. John's appearance as a prophet can be dated from the fifteenth year of Tiberius Caesar's reign (AD 14–37).

Herodias had no such respect for John. She nursed a bitter grudge against him and would gladly have had him killed if she could. But she was unable to do anything as long as her husband continued to listen to and admire the eloquent preacher from the desert.

When John had been in prison probably for a year, he sent two friends to Jesus to ask him, 'Are you indeed the Messiah or are we to expect someone else?' Perhaps long imprisonment had shaken John's faith. He might have been wrong in thinking Jesus to be the Christ. After all, months had passed since his baptism and Jesus had made no such claim. Or perhaps it was his disciples that needed to be convinced, and John wanted Jesus to reassure them.

Jesus and the Fishers of Men

Matthew 4, 18–25; Mark 1, 14–20; 2, 13–14;
Luke 5, 1–11, 27–28; John 1, 35–44

Before Jesus went into the wilderness, he met for the first time a man called Andrew who was to be one of his twelve apostles, as his closest followers were called. Andrew was already a follower of John the Baptist. On one occasion, he went home with Jesus and talked to him for many hours; and the following morning, Andrew told his brother Simon that he had found the Messiah. He took him to meet Jesus, who said to him, 'You are Simon; but I shall call you Peter, which means the Rock.'

After the temptation in the desert, Jesus remained near John the Baptist, more of whose followers joined him, as Andrew had done. But John, afraid of no man, condemned the wicked things that Herod Antipas, ruler of Galilee, had done, and he was thrown into prison. When this happened Jesus returned to Galilee and began to preach himself, saying, 'The time has come. God's reign is near. Repent, and believe this good news.'

Walking by the Sea of Galilee one day, Jesus saw Peter and Andrew. He called them and said, 'Follow me, and I will make you fishers of men.' They obeyed him without hesitation, and a few moments later he called two more fishermen, James and John, the sons of Zebedee. These four, together with Philip, a former disciple of John the Baptist, were Jesus' first followers. Eventually he gathered round him an inner circle of twelve friends, one for each of Israel's tribes.

The sixth disciple was Matthew, a collector of taxes for the Romans, and therefore he was regarded as a traitor by patriotic Jews. Jesus, saw him in the tax-office, and said simply, 'Follow me,' whereupon Matthew left his work and followed him. Simon the Zealot was a very different man. The Zealots were patriotic Jews who hated the Roman rule and believed that one day they would throw it off by force of arms. No doubt Simon thought that Jesus, as the Messiah, would soon declare himself as a military leader who would march triumphantly to victory against the Romans. We are not told how the other apostles joined Jesus.

Some time later, when Jesus' fame as a preacher and healer had spread throughout Galilee, he was surrounded on the seashore by a vast crowd of people, all pushing and jostling to be near him. Two boats belonging to Peter, Andrew, James and John were drawn up on the beach and the four men were washing their nets. Jesus climbed into one of the boats and asked Peter to take it out a short distance from the land, and from there he taught the people. When he had finished, he told Peter to sail into deep water and lower his nets.

'Master, we worked all night and caught nothing,' Peter said, 'but I will try again.'

No sooner were the nets lowered than they enclosed a shoal of fish so huge that they began to break. James and John in the other boat hurried to help, but the weight of fish began to sink even the boats themselves. When Peter saw the miraculous catch, he was filled with a great sense of awe. He felt himself utterly unworthy to be in the presence of such a man as Jesus and begged him to leave him. But Jesus said again, 'Do not be afraid. From now on you will be fishers of men.'

As soon as they had brought the boats to land, the men gave up their everyday lives and followed Jesus. They worked with him until the end of his life gathering men for the Kingdom of Heaven.

The Healing of the Paralytic

Matthew 4, 23–24; 9, 1–8; Mark 2, 1–12;
Luke 5, 17–27

Jesus began his ministry by travelling through the whole of Galilee. He taught in the synagogues, preaching the good news that the Kingdom of God was near, and healed all kinds of pain, sickness and disease. His fame spread far and wide. Everywhere he went, crowds pressed upon him, eager to hear him, or to be cured of their ills.

On one occasion Jesus was in a private house, sitting under the verandah bordering the courtyard round which the house was built. He was teaching a crowd of listeners who thronged the courtyard, filling the passage leading to it from the street outside. Four men carrying a paralyzed friend of theirs on a mattress tried to force a way through to Jesus, but the crowd was so dense that it was impossible to get near. The men, convinced that if only they could bring their friend to Jesus he would cure him, were at first in despair. But one of them suddenly saw how it could be done.

'I'll run and get two lengths of rope,' he said to the other three. 'Carry our friend up to the roof, and I'll tell you my plan when I get back.'

The three men struggled up the stairs built on the outer wall of the house to its flat roof. By the time they had reached it, the first man had returned with the ropes. He explained his idea to the others and helped to carry the sick man to a spot just above where Jesus was teaching. Then he and his friends clambered on to the verandah roof and made a hole in it large enough for the mattress to go through.

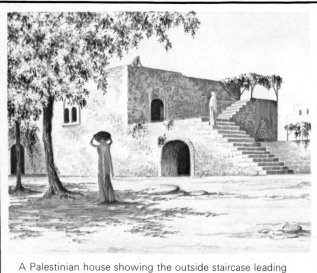

A Palestinian house showing the outside staircase leading to the flat roof. Most of the houses would have been small, four-walled, single-storey buildings made of soft-baked bricks.

Passing the ropes under the mattress, they lowered the man over the side of the roof and through the hole they had made. The people close to Jesus pressed back to make room for him, and Jesus looked down compassionately at the man. He saw how strong was the faith of the friends who had brought the patient to him and he was much moved.

But Jesus realized that the man needed healing of the mind before his body could be made whole. Indeed, it is possible that he was paralyzed because he felt so guilty about sins he had committed that his body could not move until his guilt had gone. So, instead of saying, 'Be cured,' Jesus said, 'My son, your sins are forgiven you.' His voice and his eyes had such power and authority that the man knew that his sins were indeed forgiven.

Among the crowd there were some religious men learned in the Law of Moses. They were shocked and affronted by what Jesus said.

'What does the fellow mean? It's blasphemy to talk like that. Only God can forgive sins.'

Jesus knew what they were thinking. 'Why do you have such thoughts?' he asked. 'Which is easier to say, "Your sins are forgiven" or, "Rise and walk"?'

Those listening to him knew that anyone could say, 'Your sins are forgiven,' for no one could tell whether they were forgiven or not; but everybody could see whether a man would rise and walk when he was told to.

Jesus continued, 'But let me prove to you that the Son of Man does have the power to forgive sins.' He looked at the paralyzed man and said, 'I say to you, stand up, roll up your mattress, and go home.' Immediately the man did so, in full view of them all. They were astonished, and praised God, saying, 'Never before have we seen anything as wonderful as this.'

Jesus and the Sabbath Day

Matthew 12, 1–15; Mark 2, 23–28; 3, 1–7; Luke 6, 1–11

One Sabbath day, Jesus was walking through cornfields with his disciples, accompanied by several Pharisees. His disciples were hungry because no Jew was allowed to eat anything on the Sabbath until after the morning service at the synagogue. So they began to pluck the ears of corn, rub them in their hands and eat them. The Pharisees were not concerned that the disciples might be hungry; they were determined to see that every single rule should be kept. Plucking was regarded as reaping, and rubbing as threshing, so, in their eyes, Jesus' friends were guilty of working on the Sabbath. This was a sin.

'Look at what your disciples are doing,' they cried. 'It is not allowed.'

Jesus replied, 'Do you not remember what David once did, when he was desperate for food? He went into the House of God, and he and his followers ate the consecrated loaves which only the priests are allowed to eat. You will remember, too, that the Law does not condemn the priests in the Temple when they do work on the Sabbath connected with the Temple services. There is someone here who is greater than the Temple, and his followers should not be condemned.

'If you had known,' Jesus continued, 'what the prophets meant when they said, "I will have mercy and not sacrifice," you would not condemn men who have done no wrong.'

By this he meant that God in his mercy had made the Sabbath that man might rest and have time to spend on things other than work. But the Pharisees had turned it into a sacrifice by imposing rules which oppressed men and took all the joy out of the Sabbath.

'The Sabbath was made for man,' Jesus concluded, 'not man for the Sabbath.' By this he meant that the Sabbath was instituted to meet man's needs. Men were not created just to observe the Sabbath.

Later that day, Jesus entered a synagogue where there was a man with a withered right arm. One of Jesus' enemies asked him, 'Is it lawful to heal on the Sabbath day?' while others watched him in silence to see what he would do. They wished to be able to accuse him of working on the Sabbath. Jesus replied to their question, as he often did, by asking others of his own. But first he called to the man with the withered hand, 'Stand up and come forward.'

When the man was standing in front of them all, Jesus looked round and asked, 'Is it right to help people on the Sabbath day or to hurt them, to save life or to kill? Is there a man among you who will not rescue a sheep of his if it falls into a pit on the Sabbath – and how much more is a man worth than a sheep?'

No one answered him a word. He looked round in anger and sorrow at their obstinacy and said, 'Therefore it is right to do a good deed on the Sabbath.'

He turned to the man standing before them all and said to him, 'Stretch out your right arm.' At once the man did so, and his arm was made sound again like the other.

After this, his enemies began to plot against Jesus to destroy him, but the time was not yet ripe for their plans to succeed. Jesus withdrew from the district with his disciples and returned to the country near Galilee.

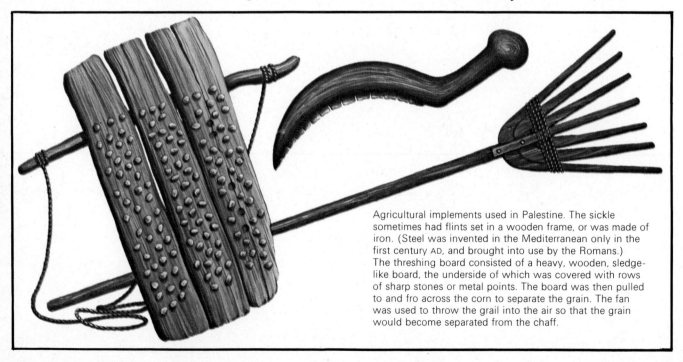

Agricultural implements used in Palestine. The sickle sometimes had flints set in a wooden frame, or was made of iron. (Steel was invented in the Mediterranean only in the first century AD, and brought into use by the Romans.) The threshing board consisted of a heavy, wooden, sledge-like board, the underside of which was covered with rows of sharp stones or metal points. The board was then pulled to and fro across the corn to separate the grain. The fan was used to throw the grail into the air so that the grain would become separated from the chaff.

The Teachings of Jesus

For three hundred years the Jews had eagerly looked forward to a time when a heavenly kingdom would be established on earth. God would rule his holy people through his servant, the Messiah, and all men would live righteously and in peace with one another. So when, after the arrest of John the Baptist, Jesus began proclaiming in Galilee, 'The time you have been waiting for has arrived. The Kingdom of God is here. Change direction – be sorry for your sins and turn to goodness. Believe this good news which is sent from God,' (*Mark 1, v 15*) there was a thrill of excitement among his hearers. No doubt some of them went home and sharpened their swords, ready to fight for the coming kingdom.

But not even Jesus' closest friends understood what he was trying to teach. He had come to bring the Kingdom to men, but a spiritual kingdom which would develop slowly until it reached perfection after the end of the world. In it good and bad would grow side by side until the time came for the harvest to be reaped, when the evil weeds would be separated from the good wheat and only righteousness left in the Kingdom.

In what Jesus said, he astonished all who heard him as one having great authority. He seemed to have first-hand knowledge of what he was saying, and did not rely on opinions from other teachers. This was because he knew God as his Father. Since he knew him, he was able to say that he was Love. So God, the Ruler of the Kingdom of Heaven, could be addressed by all men praying to him as 'Our Father'.

God is the Father of all men because he created them. But they can also become his children in a special way. To all those who received him and gave him their allegiance, he gave the right to become children of God (*John 1, v 12*). And because God is Love, the law of his Kingdom is Love. 'You must love God with all your heart, with all your soul, with all your mind, and with all your strength, and you must love your neighbour as yourself' (*Mark 12, vv 29–31*). But Jesus added something new. When asked, 'Who is my neighbour?' he told the story of the Good Samaritan, in which a man helped his enemy. For, Jesus taught, 'You know what men were taught in the old days – "You must love your neighbour and hate your enemy." But I tell you that you must love your enemies and pray for those who persecute you. This is the way to become children of your Heavenly Father who makes his sun rise on good and bad men alike and sends his rain on the honest and dishonest.' (*Matthew 5, vv 43–45*).

By loving one another, Jesus did not mean 'feeling affectionate towards'. Since God is the Father of us all, we are all brothers and sisters; and although there are times when brothers and sisters may not feel at all affectionate, they must behave properly if the family is not to break up. In God's family love must show itself in certain ways. The Christian must go on forgiving someone who has wronged him 'until seventy time seven' (*Matthew 18, v 22*), for he cannot receive forgiveness from God until he has himself forgiven others. He must not criticize others unkindly – 'Do not judge' (*Matthew 7, v 1*); that is, he must not accuse other people of doing things for wicked, selfish or other wrong reasons when he is not in a position to know

'Blessed are the poor in spirit: for theirs is the kingdom of heaven.

'Blessed are they that mourn: for they shall be comforted.

'Blessed are the meek: for they shall inherit the earth.

'Blessed are they which do hunger and thirst after righteousness: for they shall be filled.

'Blessed are the merciful: for they shall obtain mercy.

'Blessed are the pure in heart: for they shall see God.

'Blessed are the peacemakers: for they shall be called the children of God.

'Blessed are they which are persecuted for righteousness' sake: for theirs is the kingdom of heaven. Blessed are ye, when men shall revile you, and persecute you, and shall say all manner of evil against you falsely, for my sake.

Rejoice, and be exceeding glad: for great is your reward in heaven: for so persecuted they the prophets which were before you.'

the whole truth. He must be actively kind and live his life according to what is called the Golden Rule – 'Always treat other people as you would want them to treat you' (*Matthew 7, v 12*). He must not resent or resist injuries done to himself – 'Do not oppose yourself to the man who wrongs you' (*Matthew 5, v 39*) – because if wrong is exchanged for wrong, there is no end of revenge and injury; but if a wrong is forgiven; and the one who does it can accept forgiveness, it is ended.

In order to carry out God's Law of Love, a citizen of the Kingdom of God must try to train himself with God's help to become a certain kind of person. In St Matthew's Gospel, Chapter 5, verses 3 to 10, are the Beatitudes, as they are called, or Blessings. A man is blest – that is, he has an inward joy which comes from living a good life even if his outward existence is one of sadness, poverty or frustration. Some people believe the Beatitudes to be different sides of the perfect Christian character; others think that they represent different types of goodness. A man is blest if he knows his need of God, for this will drive him into the Kingdom of Heaven. If he is sorrowful, he will be comforted and strengthened; for if

sorrow comes to him, and he knows it to be sent by God, he can be ennobled by it, and if he sorrows on behalf of others, he will develop his gift of sympathy. If he is of a gentle spirit, a far more heroic quality than pride or aggressiveness, he will inherit the earth. Those who hunger and thirst for the triumph of good will have their desire fulfilled. They who show mercy will have God's mercy given to them. Those whose hearts are pure – that is, those who love goodness and long to be noble and true – will understand God better in this life and see him face to face in the next. Those who try to make peace between men and nations are blest because they are like God who sent Jesus to make peace between him and men. They are, therefore, in a very special sense the sons of God. Those who suffer insults, persecutions and false accusations for Jesus' sake and the cause of right are blest; for they are in the company of the great and good men of old who were also persecuted, and they will be compensated for their sufferings in heaven.

Since Love is the Law of the Kingdom of God, and love is shown in the ways people help and serve one another, the greatest men in the Kingdom are those who serve the others most. This is the opposite of the kingdoms of this world, where the men of highest rank have the largest numbers of others to serve them. Jesus' disciples found this very hard to understand and accept, and, indeed, the law that the greatest man is he who gives the most service to his fellow-men is still not believed nor observed by the world.

Since God's Kingdom is not of this world, it cannot appear in its perfection in this life, nor can it be confined to it. Jesus taught his disciples that life continued beyond death. Just before his own death he said, 'In my Father's house there are many dwelling-places. I am going to prepare a place for you. I would not have told you this if it were not true' (*John 14, v 2*). So it is our destiny that in the life to come we shall see God face to face in the perfection of his Kingdom.

These are some of the teachings of Jesus. There are many others, some which will be found in his stories retold in this book. He taught not only in what he said, but in everything he did and was. His whole life, and especially his death when he gave himself for the sins of men, was a living out of the love of God for man; and as he lives still and speaks to us by his Holy Spirit, we can yet learn more for ourselves of what his teaching means.

The Centurion's Servant

Matthew 8, 5–13; Luke 7, 2–10; John 4, 46–54

There was an army-officer who lived at Capernaum, a centurion in command of from fifty to a hundred soldiers. He was probably a native of Palestine, though not a Jew, serving in Herod Antipas's army. He knew that Jews did not like entering the house of a Gentile, because this made them ceremonially unclean, and they then had to undergo a tiresome purification ritual. But then his young servant, whom he valued very highly, fell ill.

Hearing about Jesus, the centurion asked some Jewish friends to persuade him to save the life of his servant, who was dying. The friends were glad to do this, because as they told Jesus, the centurion had shown himself to be a friend of the Jewish nation, and had built a synagogue for the Jews living at Capernaum. They urged Jesus to cure the servant, for his master, they told him, deserved this favour.

Jesus agreed to go with them. Someone must have run on and told the centurion that he was coming, for when he was not far from the man's house, he met other friends whom the centurion had sent with a message for him.

'Sir,' the message ran, 'do not trouble yourself further. I am not fit that you should come into my home, and that is why I did not come myself to ask you this favour in person. Just give the command, and I know that my servant will be cured. I know that this will be so, because, as an officer, I have to carry out orders given to me; and I have soldiers under me who,

in turn, have to obey me. I say to one, "Go," and he goes; to another, "Come here," and he comes, and to my servant, "Do this," and he does it.'

Jesus was filled with admiration for the centurion when he heard this. Turning to the crowd which was following him, he said, 'I tell you that nowhere, not even in Israel, have I come across faith as strong as this. Many strangers from other nations in the East and West will enter the Kingdom of Heaven, while those who were born to inherit it will be driven into the darkness outside to wail and gnash their teeth in frustration and disappointment.'

He turned to the centurion's friends and said, 'Go; as he has had faith, his prayer is granted.' When they returned to the house, they found that the servant had completely recovered.

There was yet another occasion when Jesus healed someone without seeing him. An official of Herod's household had a son who was dangerously ill at Capernaum. Hearing that Jesus was at Cana, the father galloped to meet him.

'I beg you, sir,' he pleaded, 'cure my son.'

Jesus tested his faith with a rough answer. 'Unless you see signs and wonders, you will not believe.'

The father did not argue. 'Come, sir. Come before my son is dead.'

Jesus said to him, 'Return home. Your son will live.'

Without hesitation the man believed him and started on his journey home. The next day he met his servants riding to greet him. Joyfully they shouted, 'Sir, your son is going to live!'

'When did he begin to improve?' asked the boy's father.

'At one o'clock yesterday afternoon the fever left him.'

The father realized that that was the exact time Jesus had said to him, 'Your son will live,' and he and all his household became believers.

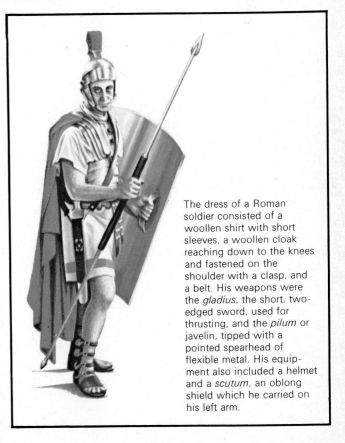

The dress of a Roman soldier consisted of a woollen shirt with short sleeves, a woollen cloak reaching down to the knees and fastened on the shoulder with a clasp, and a belt. His weapons were the *gladius*, the short, two-edged sword, used for thrusting, and the *pilum* or javelin, tipped with a pointed spearhead of flexible metal. His equipment also included a helmet and a *scutum*, an oblong shield which he carried on his left arm.

185

The Anointing of Jesus

Luke 7, 36–50 ; Matthew 26, 6–13; Mark 14, 3–9;
John 12, 1–8

A Pharisee named Simon once invited Jesus to dine with him, but he did not welcome him very warmly. While Jesus was at the table, a woman who lived in the town and who had heard that he was at Simon's house, went to see Jesus, carrying with her an alabaster flask of perfume. The woman had lived a sinful life, but she had repented and she sat behind Jesus weeping. Her tears fell on his feet. She wiped them with her hair, kissing them and pouring the perfume over them.

Simon, seeing what was happening, said to himself, 'If this fellow were really a prophet, he would know what kind of woman this is who is touching him.' But Jesus knew what he was thinking and said, 'Simon, I have something to say to you.'

'Say it, Master,' Simon replied.

'There was once a moneylender to whom two men owed money. One owed him five hundred pieces of silver, the other fifty. They were both quite unable to pay him back, so he freely forgave them their debts. Which debtor, do you think, loved the moneylender most?'

'I suppose the one who was forgiven most.'

'You are right,' said Jesus. He turned to the woman. 'You see this woman?' he continued. 'When I came into your house you did not even pay me the courtesies which are normally given to every guest. You gave me no water to wash my feet. This woman has washed my feet

with her tears and wiped them with her hair. You did not give me the kiss with which guests are usually welcomed; but ever since she came in she has been kissing my feet. You did not anoint my head with ordinary oil; but she has anointed my feet with precious perfume.

'So I tell you that her many sins have been forgiven her, and, as a result, her love is great. Where little has been forgiven, there is only little love shown.'

Jesus turned to the woman. 'Your sins are forgiven,' he said. The other guests muttered indignantly to each other, saying, 'Who is this, that he can even forgive sins?' But Jesus said

The most expensive unguents were prepared from vegetable oils to which spices were added from southern Arabia and India. Such precious unguents were kept in vessels with very narrow openings, from which they were decanted drop by drop. Our picture is from a Roman fresco of the first century AD.

to the woman, 'Your faith has saved you. Go in peace.'

There was another time, in the last week of his life, when Jesus was anointed with perfume. He was at the village of Bethany, near Jerusalem, at the home of another Simon, who had once been a leper. A supper was given in his honour, during which Mary, the sister of Lazarus, whom Jesus raised from the dead, brought a small bottle of pure nard, a very precious ointment, in an alabaster flask. She broke the flask and poured the perfume over his head so that the whole house was filled with the pungent scent of the ointment.

Some of those who were present were angry. 'What a waste!' they said. 'Why, this perfume could have been sold for thirty pounds and the money given to the poor.' They turned upon Mary, but Jesus defended her. 'Let her alone,' he said. 'Why do you have to upset her? It is an excellent thing she has done for me. You have the poor always among you and you can help them whenever you want to; but you will not always have me. She has in this way perfumed my body for burial. And I tell you this, that wherever the Gospel is preached, men will remember this deed of Mary's and will speak of her.'

The Parable of the Sower

Matthew 13, 1–23; Mark 4, 1–20; Luke 8, 4–15

One day when Jesus was teaching on the shore of the Sea of Galilee, he climbed into a boat to avoid the great throng of people. By pushing the boat away from the shore he could talk to the crowd more easily. Often he taught them by telling stories called parables. These were stories which had an inner, deeper meaning which the listeners had to try to understand for themselves.

As Jesus began his teaching he might have seen a man sowing seed in a field close by the sea. The man was probably walking along the furrows with a basket of seed under one arm, throwing handfuls of it with wide sweeps of the other. So Jesus told his parable.

'Watch that sower sowing his seed,' he said. 'As he sows, some of his seed falls on the footpath running along the field. See how the birds swoop down and eat it up because it is lying on top of the ground. What escapes the birds will be trampled on by people using the path.

'There's a patch of rocks with little pockets of soil among them. The seed that falls there will spring up quickly because the earth isn't deep or moist enough for the corn to take root properly; but when the hot summer sun comes, it will scorch and wither the young corn and it will die because it has no roots.

'Some seed will fall among those clusters of brambles and thistles. They will grow up with the corn and choke it.

'But watch the seed falling on the good soil. It will grow up to become a fine, fruitful crop. Some of it will produce a hundred times as much as is sown, some sixty times as much, some thirty times.

'Let those who hear this story try to understand it.'

Later, when they were alone, the disciples asked Jesus why he taught in parables and what the story meant. He replied, 'You have been given the privilege of understanding the secrets of the Kingdom of God, but they have to be given in parables to most people. The more imagination and understanding a man has, the more he will get out of these stories of mine, and he will be increasingly enriched by them; but if he has little or none, then he will forget even the little they meant to him when he first heard them.

'I speak to them in parables because although they look, they do not see, and although they hear, they do not understand. Isaiah's

prophecy is fulfilled in them, "You may hear and hear but never understand; you may look and look but never see. For this people's mind has become closed; their ears are dull of hearing and they have shut their eyes. Otherwise their eyes might see, their ears hear, and their minds understand, and they might turn again for me to heal them."

'But happy are you, because you both see and hear. Many prophets and good men have longed to see and hear what you do, and have not done so. But if you do not understand this parable, how are you to understand any other?

'This is what it means. The seed is the word of God. The footpath represents some who hear the word; but the moment they hear it, the evil one comes and takes it away. The stony ground stands for those listeners who receive the word joyfully, but they last only for a short time. The moment difficulties or persecutions arise, they give up. The thorns symbolize those who hear the word but are so concerned with the anxieties of everyday living, or making money, or the pleasures of life, that the word becomes unfruitful. But the good soil represents those who hear the word and make it part of themselves, and they bear good fruit according to their spiritual abilities.'

Thistle seeds are the favourite food of the goldfinch, a bird that is often seen in summer perched on dry thistles which abound in the countryside.

189

Stories that Jesus Told

Jesus told many stories when he preached. Here are some of them.

Matthew 13, 24–33, 36–43

The Kingdom of Heaven is like a man who sowed wheat in his field. But one night his enemy sowed weeds among the wheat. When the corn sprouted, the weeds appeared as well.

'The man's servants asked him, "Sir, did you not sow good seed in your field? Where have the weeds come from?" He replied, "An enemy must have sown them."

'"Would you like us to gather them up?"

'"No," he said. "You might root up the wheat too. Let both grow together until harvest. Then I will tell the reapers to separate the weeds and tie them in bundles to be burned, but to collect the wheat into my granary."'

Later, Jesus explained the story to his disciples. 'The sower of the good seed is the Son of Man' – a name he gave himself. 'The field is the world. The good seed represents the sons of the Kingdom, the weeds the sons of the evil one. The enemy is the devil, the harvest is the end of the world and the reapers are the angels. At the end of the world, the Son of Man's angels will gather out of the Kingdom everything and everybody evil and throw them into the fiery furnace, where men will wail and gnash their teeth. The righteous will then shine like the sun in their Father's Kingdom.'

Matthew 18, 21–35

Peter once asked Jesus how often he should forgive a man who wronged him. Would seven times be enough?

'No!' said Jesus. 'Forgive him seventy times seven! The Kingdom of God is like a king who decided to settle accounts with his servants. One owed him millions, and was unable to pay. The king therefore ordered him, his family and all his possessions to be sold to pay the debt. But the man begged for time, promising he would pay everything. The king was so moved with pity that he completely forgave him the debt.

'As the man was going away, he met a fellow-servant who owed him twenty pounds. He seized him by the throat, saying, "Pay what you owe me!" The man fell at his feet imploring him for time to pay. But he refused and had him imprisoned until he should pay.

'The other servants were very distressed, and told the king what had happened. He immediately summoned the first man and said, "Villain! I forgave you your debt because you begged me to do so. Could you not have shown your fellow-servant mercy as I showed you?" The king was so angry that he handed the man over to the torturers until he should pay the debt in full.

'My Heavenly Father,' ended Jesus, 'will forgive each of you only as you forgive your fellow-men from the heart.'

Matthew 19, 27–30; 20, 1–16

On another occasion Peter said to Jesus, 'We have given up everything to follow you. What reward shall we have?' Jesus replied, 'When the Son of Man is enthroned in glory, you also will have thrones from which you will judge the twelve tribes of Israel. Everyone who has sacrificed anything for my sake will get a hundred times as much as he has given up, and life eternal as well. But many who are first shall be last and those who are last, first.

'For the Kingdom of Heaven is like a landowner who went out early in the morning to hire labourers for his vineyard. Agreeing to pay the men the usual daily wage, he sent them to their work. Three hours later, he saw other labourers standing idle in the market-place. "Go into my vineyard," he said, "and I will pay you whatever is fair." At midday and in the afternoon, he did the same; and when only one hour of the working-day remained, he still found men standing about unhired. "Go into the vineyard, too," he said.

When evening came, the landowner told his steward to pay the labourers, beginning with those who had been hired last. They were each given a full day's wage. The labourers hired first thought they would get more, but they too received a day's wage. They grumbled at the landowner. "These fellows have only worked one hour," they complained, "and you have paid them as much as us, who have sweated all day in the heat!"

'But the landowner said to one of them, "My friend, I am not being unfair to you. We agreed on the usual day's wage. Take your money and go home. If I choose to give the last man the same as you, is it not my business to do what I like with my own money? Must you have a grudge because I am generous?"'

Matthew 25, 1–30

Jesus warned his disciples that only God knew when the Day of Judgment would be. He told them two stories to warn them that they should always be prepared, and that while waiting, they should use the talents they had been given in God's service.

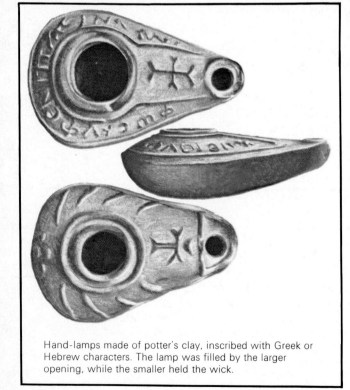

Hand-lamps made of potter's clay, inscribed with Greek or Hebrew characters. The lamp was filled by the larger opening, while the smaller held the wick.

'The Kingdom of Heaven is like ten girls, friends of a bride, awaiting the bridegroom. They took their lamps and went out to meet him at a point where the bridal procession would pass. Five of the girls were foolish and took no spare oil; the other five had the sense to bring flasks of oil with their lamps. As the bridegroom was a long time coming, they all fell asleep. But at midnight there was a shout, "The bridegroom is coming! Be ready to meet him!" The girls arose and trimmed their lamps. "Our lamps are going out," said the foolish girls to the thoughtful ones. "Give us some of your oil." "No," said the others, "there might not be enough for you and us. Go and buy some for yourselves."

'While they were away, the bridegroom arrived. The girls who were ready went with him into the wedding-feast. Soon after, the

others came, clamouring, "sir, oh, sir, open the door for us." But he answered, "I tell you, I do not know you." '

Jesus ended, 'Be watchful, for you do not know the day or hour of God's coming.'

'The Kingdom of Heaven is like a man going abroad who entrusted his money to his servants. To one he gave five hundred pounds, to another two hundred and to a third one hundred.

'The first man traded with his five hundred pounds and made another five hundred. The man with two hundred pounds made two hundred more. But the third man dug a hole in the ground and hid his master's money.

'Long afterwards, the master returned and called his servants to account. The first man came forward happily and said, "Sir, you gave me five hundred pounds. Look, I have made another five hundred."

'"Well done," said his master. "You have proved yourself trustworthy with a small sum. You will be given charge of a large one. Come and share your master's happiness."

'The second man handed over his two hundred pounds' profit equally happily and was greeted in the same way.

'But the third servant handed back only the one hundred pounds he had been given. "I knew, sir," he said, "that you were a hard man. You reap where you have not sown, and you gather where you have not scattered. So I was afraid and hid your money in the earth. There it is. I give you back what belongs to you."

'"You idle rascal," said the master. "So that's what you thought of me, is it? In that case, you should have deposited my money with the bankers, and when I came back, it would have been returned to me with interest. Take the hundred pounds away from him and give it to the man with five hundred – and throw the useless rascal out!"'

Jesus Calms the Storm

Matthew 8, 23–27; Mark 4, 35–41; Luke 8, 22–25

Frequently exhausted by all the teaching and healing that he did, Jesus liked to retreat with his friends to rest and pray in quiet and solitary places such as there were on the other side of the Sea of Galilee.

One evening, after working hard all day, he sent away the crowds and said to his disciples, 'Let us sail to the other side of the lake.' They set off accompanied by several other small ships, and Jesus, tired as he was, was soon lulled to sleep lying on a cushion in the stern.

Like many inland lakes, the Sea of Galilee is subject to ferocious storms of wind which sweep down the mountain ravines from the north. Without warning, the calm waters are churned into mountainous waves within minutes and small ships sink before their sails can be lowered.

Such a storm swept down on the sea when the boats bearing Jesus and his friends were on their way to the other side, and almost before they knew what was happening, the disciples realized that waves were pouring into their boat. In spite of all their efforts to bale out the water, they were in danger of being swamped.

Through it all, Jesus slept as trustingly as if he were in his own bed. In despair the disciples woke him. 'Master, Master, we are drowning!' they cried. 'Don't you care?'

'Why are you afraid?' he said. 'How little you trust God!' Then he stood and turned, facing the howling wind and lashing waves. 'Peace! Be still,' he commanded.

Immediately it was as if there had never been a storm. A great calm fell. The disciples were more afraid than ever, but for a different reason, and with a fear that was awe, not terror. 'What sort of man is this,' they asked themselves, 'that he can give orders to the winds and waters and even they obey him?'

Jesus Walks on the Water
Matthew 14, 22–33; Mark 6, 45–52

On another occasion when Jesus and his friends had been on the other side of the lake, Jesus urged them to sail home without him, and went up into the mountains to pray alone. When evening came, the boat was far out in the middle of the sea, buffeted by a strong wind, and the disciples had to strain at the oars to control their course. The struggle continued until nearly six o'clock the next morning, when Jesus approached them, walking on the water. He would have passed them by, but when they saw him, they shrieked aloud in terror, saying, 'It is a ghost!'

At once he reassured them. 'Courage!' he called. 'It is I. Do not be afraid.'

Peter shouted, 'Lord, if it is you, tell me to come to you on the water.'

'Come,' Jesus called.

Peter stepped out of the boat and began to walk towards Jesus. But when he realized how very strong the wind was, he was seized with panic and began to sink. 'Save me, Lord,' he cried.

Jesus at once stretched out his hand and caught him. 'How little you trust me!' he said. 'Why did you doubt?'

Jesus and Peter stepped into the boat, and immediately the wind dropped. The men in the boat fell at Jesus' feet and worshipped him, saying, 'Truly, you are the Son of God.'

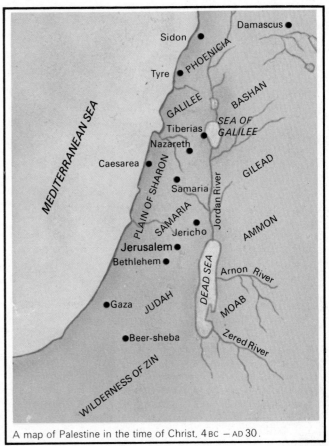

A map of Palestine in the time of Christ, 4 BC — AD 30.

A Maniac Cured

Matthew 8, 28–34; Mark 5, 1–20; Luke 8, 26–40

After calming the storm, Jesus and his disciples landed on the south-eastern shore of the Sea of Galilee, in the country of the Gadarenes. Suddenly, a ferocious madman who lived amongst the tombs there, rushed out barring the way ahead. He was a terrible sight, naked and filthy, and his flesh was covered with bleeding wounds where he had gashed himself with stones. Hanging from his wrists were broken chains, for people had often tried to bind him with fetters; but he was tremendously strong and had snapped them like string, fleeing from his would-be captors into the desert. Nobody had been able to tame him. Night and day he wandered among the tombs and nearby mountains, crying out and cutting himself. Those who knew of him believed he was devil-possessed.

When he saw Jesus, the maniac ran to him and flung himself down before him. The devils within him shrieked at Jesus, using the madman's voice, 'You Son of God Most High – what do you want with us?' for Jesus was already saying, 'Out, unclean spirit, come out of the man!' 'Have you come to torment us before our time?' the devils yelled. 'In God's name, don't. Don't send us out of the country. Don't send us to hell.'

'What is your name?' asked Jesus.

'Legion,' the madman babbled, a legion being a Roman regiment, 'for there are many of us inhabiting this body.'

Now there was a large herd of pigs feeding close by on ground sloping steeply to the sea. The devils begged Jesus to send them away into the swine.

Below: a bronze pig found at Pompeii. The Gadarenes, followers of a Hellenistic culture, ignored the Jewish law forbidding the eating of pigs' meat. Large herds of swine were bred as a highly profitable business, since the pork was not only bought locally, but was also salted and sold to the Roman army.

'Go, unclean spirits! Begone from the man!' Jesus commanded.

As he spoke, the disciples saw the herd of pigs, panic-stricken, rush down the slope into the sea. In a few minutes, they had all plunged into the water and been engulfed by the waves. Not a single animal survived.

The swineherds were terrified. They ran to the town and told everyone they met what had happened. In a short time great crowds could be seen hurrying towards the tombs where they knew Legion lived. There they found him clothed and in his right mind, sitting at the feet of Jesus.

Frightened by what they saw, their fear turned to terror when they were given an account of the madman's cure by those who had actually seen it. They implored Jesus to leave the district.

As Jesus was stepping into the boat, the cured man begged him to allow him to go with him. But Jesus said, 'Go instead to your own people and tell them all that God has done for you and how he took pity on you.' The man went off, proclaiming throughout the Gadarene district how Jesus had healed him. Everyone who heard him was astonished.

There are many who feel that Jesus would not have sent the devils into the herd of pigs to destroy them. Perhaps in the crisis of being cured the madman gave one last great shriek which frightened the pigs; and, seeing them stampede, the disciples thought that the devils had gone into them. Perhaps when Jesus ordered the devils to go, he threw up his hands in a gesture of command and seemed to the disciples to point towards the pigs, already panic-stricken by Legion's yells.

Whatever the truth, Jesus would never have done anything that was wrong.

Jairus' Daughter

Matthew 9, 18–26;
Mark 5, 22–43; Luke 8, 41–56

Shortly after Jesus had cured the Gadarene maniac, a man named Jairus, a president of the local synagogue who was both wealthy and respected, came to him in great distress. He fell at Jesus' feet and entreated him earnestly, 'Master, my little daughter is dying. She is only twelve. Please come and lay hands on her and she will live.'

Jesus went with him at once, followed by a great crowd which pressed so closely round him that he was almost crushed. He was wearing, as every Jew did, a robe with a tassel on each corner, to remind him of the Law of Moses. In the crowd was a woman who had suffered for twelve years from an illness which had made her life a misery. She had spent everything she had on doctors but, far from curing her, they had, if anything, made her worse. But she was convinced that if she could only touch Jesus' clothes, especially one of the tassels, she would be healed.

She had to fight hard to force her way through the crowd, which hustled her hither and thither, but for a moment she was within reach of Jesus. She thrust out her hand and just touched one of the tassels on his robe. But the touch was enough. Immediately she felt that she was cured.

She was not alone in feeling that something had happened. Jesus also knew that power

The great tallith, right, was the normal head-scarf worn to show a person's 'Jewishness'. It was compulsory to put it on in addition to one's other clothes, either over a skull-cap or draped over the shoulders. The small tallith, left, was worn by every male Jew, next to his shirt.

had been drained from him. He stopped and turned. 'Who touched me?' he asked.

Everybody denied touching him, and the disciples were astonished at the question. 'Master, you see the crowd pressing upon you on every side,' said Peter, 'and yet you ask who touched you?'

'Someone touched me,' Jesus replied, 'for I felt power go out of me,' and he continued to look searchingly at the crowd.

When the woman felt his eyes upon her and saw that she could not be hidden, she knelt before Jesus, trembling with fear, and in front of the crowd confessed that it had been she.

Jesus did not want her superstitiously to think that she could be cured without his willing it or because there was some magic in his clothes. He said to her, therefore, 'Have courage, daughter. It is your faith which has made you well. Be cured of your disease and go in peace.'

Although Jairus said nothing, he was growing more and more worried that the delay would cause Jesus to arrive too late to save his daughter. Indeed, his fears were justified; for, as Jesus was talking to the woman, a servant

came to him and said quietly, 'Sir, your daughter is dead. Trouble the Rabbi no further.' But Jesus overheard the message and said, 'Do not be afraid. Only believe. She will be well again.'

Jesus sent away the crowd and, taking Peter, James and John with him, arrived at Jairus' house. There he found the flute-players and mourning-women who were hired for funerals wailing and howling. Jesus said to them, 'Begone! Weep no more. The child is not dead. She is only asleep.' They jeered at him, knowing that she was dead.

But Jesus led his three friends and her parents into the girl's room. He took her hand and said gently, 'Little girl, I command you to get up!'

Instantly she opened her eyes, rose, and began to walk. Her parents were utterly amazed. Jesus told them to give their daughter something to eat, and not to say anything about the cure. But in spite of this, the story of the raising of Jairus' daughter from the dead soon spread all over the country.

Jesus the Healer

Throughout his life, Jesus taught and healed. He cured every kind of sickness, disease, plague and pain, and gave his disciples the same powers of healing when he sent them out by themselves to preach the good news of the Kingdom of God. He made the lame walk, the blind see, the dumb speak, the paralyzed move and the maimed whole. He made lunatics sane again and cast out unclean spirits from those possessed by the devil. There are many stories of his cures. Here are some of them.

Matthew 8, 14–15; Mark 1, 29–31; Luke 4, 38–39
After a synagogue service, Jesus visited Peter's mother-in-law. She was ill with a high fever, but the moment Jesus took her hand and rebuked the fever, it left her, and she rose and waited on him at table. Sufferers from fever are very weak for some time after it; but Jesus' touch gave the woman back her full strength immediately.

Mark 1, 23–28; Luke 4, 33–37
At the beginning of his ministry, Jesus went into the synagogue at Capernaum to teach. The people were astonished, for his teaching was original and fresh, unlike that of the lawyers who were chiefly concerned about interpreting details in the Law of Moses.

There was a man in the synagogue, possessed by a devil, who recognized Jesus as the Son of God. He suddenly yelled out, 'What do you want with us, Jesus of Nazareth? I know you – you are God's Holy One!' Jesus rebuked the

devil within the man. 'Silence! Come out of him!' he said. Immediately the man fell down, twisting and writhing on the ground. Then he gave a great cry. When he recovered, he was completely sane and well.

Everyone in the synagogue was astounded. 'What's happening?' they asked each other excitedly. 'This is certainly a new kind of teaching!' 'Yes, he knows what he's talking about!' 'Even devils obey his orders!' The news of the cure spread rapidly, and soon all Galilee was talking about Jesus.

Mark 1, 40–45; Luke 5, 12–15
Soon after, a leper knelt before Jesus, begging for help. 'If only you are willing,' the man said, 'you can heal me.' Jesus was sorry for him, but was also angry that the man doubted his willingness to cure him.

'Of course I am willing,' he said. 'Be well again!' At once the leprosy vanished. Sternly Jesus told the man, 'Be sure you say nothing to anyone. Show yourself to the priest and let him declare you free of leprosy. Then make the offering which the Law of Moses requires.'

But the man told everyone far and wide what had happened, with the result that Jesus could no longer visit any town without crowds of people thronging round him to be helped or cured. Even when he was in the open country, people came to him from every direction. It was only with difficulty that he managed to withdraw sometimes to lonely places to rest and refresh himself in prayer.

Luke 7, 11–17
Jesus was approaching a town called Nain when he met a funeral coming out of the city gate. The dead man was the only son of his mother, a widow. When Jesus saw the woman's sorrow, he was filled with compassion for her and said, 'Do not weep'. He stepped forward and laid his hand on the bier. Puzzled, the bearers stopped, wondering what he intended to do.

Then Jesus spoke. 'Young man, rise up!' he said.

Immediately the dead man sat up and began to talk, and Jesus helped him off the bier and restored him to his mother.

The crowd all round was silent for a time, deeply awed by what had happened. Then they burst into praise to God. 'A great prophet has risen up among us,' they cried, 'God has shown that he cares for his people.' And again the news of what Jesus had done spread far and wide throughout the district.

Matthew 15, 21–28; Mark 7, 24–30
Once, because his teaching so angered his enemies, Jesus went to the Gentile regions of Tyre and Sidon to rest. He would have liked to remain unknown, but even before he had left Jewish territory, a Canaanite woman from the district to which he was going, followed him. Between gasps for breath she cried out, as she tried to catch him up, 'Have pity on me, Son of David, my daughter is cruelly possessed by a devil.' Jesus answered her not a word.

His disciples were worried by the wails of the woman, and asked Jesus to grant her request and send her away. He answered, 'I was not sent except to those of Israel who need help.' But the woman caught them up and, running to Jesus, threw herself at his feet. 'Help me, sir,' she pleaded.

Jesus said, 'It is not fair to take the children's bread and throw it to the dogs.'

'True, sir,' she replied, 'but the dogs do get the scraps which fall from their master's table.'

When Jesus heard this, he said, 'What great

201

faith you have! Because you said that, your wish is granted.'

The woman returned home and found her daughter resting peacefully in bed with the devil gone out of her.

Mark 7, 31–37
From Tyre and Sidon Jesus returned to the district where he had cured the Gadarene maniac. A deaf man who could not speak clearly was brought to him. Jesus took the man away from the crowd and showed him by signs what he was going to do. He pushed his fingers into his own ears to show the man that he was going to break through his deafness. He touched his own tongue first as a sign that he would cure his speech. Then he spat and touched the man's tongue with the saliva, which was at that time thought to be a healing agent by both Jews and Gentiles. After this, he raised his face to heaven in prayer and groaned, moved with pity for the sorrows of mankind. Then he said, 'Be opened.'

Immediately the man heard and spoke clearly. Jesus told those who knew of the miracle to say nothing about it. But the more he forbade them, the more they reported it, for they found everything that Jesus did wonderful beyond description.

Luke 13, 11–17
One Sabbath, when Jesus was teaching in a synagogue, he saw a woman who had been bent double for eighteen years, and was quite unable to stand up straight. He called her to him and said, 'You are free from your illness,' and laid his hands upon her. At once she stood erect and began to praise God.

But the president of the synagogue angrily said to the congregation, 'Come and be cured on one of the six working-days, not on the Sabbath.' Jesus was indignant. 'What hypocrites you are!' he said. 'Is there a man among you who does not untie his ox or donkey from its stable on the Sabbath to give it water? Here is a woman, one of God's Chosen People, crippled for eighteen long years; was it wrong for her to be untied from her bonds on the Sabbath day?'

His enemies had no answer to these words of Jesus; and the ordinary people were delighted at all his wonderful deeds.

Luke 17, 11–19
Jesus was entering a village on his way to Jerusalem when a band of ten lepers, who were not allowed to go near other people, called to him from a distance, 'Master, have pity on us.' He called back, 'Go and show yourselves to the priests.' This was a way of telling them that they were cured, for it was the priests' duty to examine all men who had had leprosy, if they

claimed to be healed, and pronounce them free from the disease.

While the ten were on their way, they found themselves cured. One of them immediately ran back, shouting praises to God, and, throwing himself at Jesus' feet, thanked him. He was a Samaritan. Jesus said, 'Were not ten healed? Where are the other nine? Could only this one, and he a foreigner, come back and give praise to God?' To the man he said, 'Stand up and go your way. Your faith has cured you.'

John 5, 1–16
While at Jerusalem for one of the feasts, Jesus went to a place called Bethesda where five colonnades surrounded a pool of water. Beside it lay a crowd of people suffering from every kind of illness; for every now and again the pool was disturbed (it was thought by an angel) and people believed that the first sick person to plunge into it after each disturbance would be healed. Jesus saw there a man who had been crippled for thirty-eight years and asked him, 'Would you like to be cured?' The man replied, 'Sir, I have no one to help me into the water when it is disturbed, and while I am crawling towards it, someone always plunges in before I can reach it.'

Jesus answered, 'Stand up, pick up your mattress, and walk.' The man did so.

This was another cure which Jesus did on the Sabbath. It was chiefly because Jesus cured the sick on the Sabbath, that the Jews began to persecute him.

202

Matthew 20, 29–34; Mark 10, 46–52; Luke 18, 35–43
A blind beggar named Bar-Timaeus was sitting by a roadside near Jericho when he heard an excited crowd of people passing. He asked one of them what was happening. 'Jesus of Nazareth is passing by,' he was told. At once Bar-Timaeus began to shout as loudly as he could, 'Son of David, pity me!' The crowd told him to be quiet, but he shouted all the louder.

Jesus said, 'Call him,' and the people close by encouraged him to go to the Master. Bar-Timaeus threw away his cloak so that he could move quickly, sprang up and groped his way rapidly to Jesus.

'What do you want me to do?' asked Jesus.

'Oh, sir – I want to see!'

Jesus, deeply moved, touched his eyes and said, 'Go – your faith has cured you.' At once Bar-Timaeus' sight was restored and he followed Jesus, praising God.

The Feeding of the Five Thousand

Matthew 10, 1–10; 14, 13–21;
Mark 3, 14–19; 6, 7–13; 30, 35–44;
Luke 6, 12–16; 9, 1–6; 10, 12–17;
John 6, 5–13

Jesus one day called his twelve disciples to him and said, 'I am sending you to teach and heal the people of Israel. Tell them that the Kingdom of God is near. Heal the sick, raise the dead, cleanse lepers, and cast out devils. You have received freely – give freely in return.'

With these and other instructions, he sent them out by themselves. After several weeks they returned to him, full of the wonders they had been able to do in his name; and at about the same time, the news of John the Baptist's death was brought to Jesus. Partly because he knew that the disciples would be drained of energy after all their teaching and healing, and partly because of his sorrow at John's death, he sailed alone with his disciples to a deserted place on the north coast of the Sea of Galilee.

But it was never easy for Jesus to find solitude. Quickly the news spread that he had sailed northwards, and great crowds hastened round the coast and were waiting for him when he landed. As he looked at them, with all the sick and maimed longing for him to cure them, his heart went out to them. They seemed lost and in need – sheep without a shepherd. And so, in spite of his own great need for solitude and rest, he spent the remainder of the day healing the sick and teaching the healthy.

Evening drew on. His disciples said to Jesus, 'Master, send them away to the farms and villages round about to find food and lodging.'

Jesus thought he would test their faith.

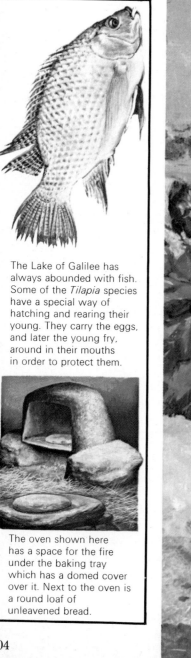

The Lake of Galilee has always abounded with fish. Some of the *Tilapia* species have a special way of hatching and rearing their young. They carry the eggs, and later the young fry, around in their mouths in order to protect them.

The oven shown here has a space for the fire under the baking tray which has a domed cover over it. Next to the oven is a round loaf of unleavened bread.

'Give them something to eat yourselves,' he said.

'Are we to spend twenty pounds on bread?' they asked. 'Even that would not be enough to give every one of them a little.'

Andrew, Peter's brother, said doubtfully, 'There's a boy here who has five loaves and two small fishes. But what use are they among so many?'

Jesus said, 'Tell the people to sit down on the grass in groups of fifty.'

When the people were seated on the spring-green grass, Jesus took the loaves and fishes from the boy, blessed them, broke them in pieces and gave them to the disciples to distribute to the crowd. The disciples expected all the food to have gone before they had finished giving it even to the first row of fifty; but the more they gave away, the more there seemed to be in their hands. Row after row were fed, and still the food lasted; and when every man in the crowd had received a portion, there was still enough to spare for Jesus and his disciples. Everyone was satisfied and, when the meal was over, the scraps left filled twelve large baskets. Five thousand men, besides women and children, were fed that day.

Seeing this miracle, the people were convinced the Jesus must be the Messiah. They were prepared even to use force to make him their King. But Jesus knew that their reasons for doing so were wrong. They wanted a King who could always give them bread, not one who required them to live good lives. So he escaped from them into the mountains to be alone and refresh himself in prayer.

On a later occasion, Jesus performed a similar wonder when, after teaching a crowd of four thousand for three days, he fed them with seven loaves and a few small fishes. Seven baskets-full of fragments were left over. Immediately after feeding the four thousand, Jesus sailed home with his disciples.

Peter the Rock

Matthew 16, 13–28; Mark 8, 27; 9, 1; Luke 9, 18–27

Walking with his disciples Jesus asked them, 'What do people think I mean when I call myself "Son of Man"? Who do they think I am?'

'John the Baptist, risen from the dead,' said one disciple. 'Elijah,' said another. 'If not Elijah,' said a third, 'perhaps Jeremiah or one of the other prophets come back to us.'

'Who do you say that I am?' Jesus asked.

'You are the Christ,' Peter replied, 'the Son of the living God.'

Jesus answered him with deep feeling, 'You are greatly blessed; for it was not mortal man that revealed this to you, but my heavenly Father. I named you Peter, the Rock. Upon the rock of what you have just said I will build my church; and nothing that evil or death can do will ever be able to conquer it. I will give you the keys of the Kingdom of Heaven. Whatever you forbid or allow on earth will be confirmed by God in Heaven.

'You must tell nobody that I am Christ. But since you know who I am, I must tell you what is going to happen to me. I shall have to suffer greatly. I must go to Jerusalem where I shall be rejected by the rulers. I shall be killed, and after three days I shall come alive again.

But the disciples did not understand him, or believe what he meant. Grasping Christ's arm, Peter spoke for them all. 'Such things can never happen to you, Master,' he cried. 'You must not say such dreadful things.'

Jesus turned abruptly and looked round sternly at his disciples and particularly at Peter. In what Peter had said he recognized the temptation he had faced in the desert after his baptism – the temptation to choose an easier way to win his kingdom than by suffering on the Cross. The devil was speaking through Peter.

'Away with you, you Satan!' he said to Peter. 'You are a rock, but now you are one lying in my path to trip me up. You think as men think, not as God thinks.'

Shortly after, he spoke both to his disciples and to a crowd which had gathered round him.

'If any man wants to follow me, he must forget himself. He must be ready every day of his life to follow me to the death, yes, even the shameful and agonizing death of a criminal upon a cross, if God requires it. For anyone who treasures his own safety, is lost; but whoever willingly gives up everything of his own for my sake, and for the sake of the Kingdom of God which I preach, shall find his true life. What is the use of winning everything in the world if you lose your own soul doing it? What can be more valuable to a man than to find his soul? What can a man give to buy it back if he should lose it?

'If any man, then, is ashamed of me and my words in these wicked times, then the Son of Man will be ashamed of him. When he is with God his father in his glory, then he will reward every man according to what he has done with his life. And I tell you, there are some standing here who shall not die until they have seen the Son of Man come to the Kingdom of God.'

A Vision of Glory
Matthew 17, 1–21; Mark 9, 2–29; Luke 9, 28–45

One night, a week after Peter's recognition that Jesus was indeed the Christ, Jesus took Peter, James and John to the top of a high mountain where they could be alone. He began to pray; and while he was praying, his appearance completely changed. It was as if he glowed from within with a light all his own. His face shone like the sun and his clothes became a dazzling white. At the same time, the three disciples saw two men standing and talking with him who also shone with glory. They were talking with Jesus of the fate he was to meet in Jerusalem and of the way in which he was to die there. The disciples knew that they were Moses and Elijah, representing the Law and the Prophets, the two great foundations of Judaism.

It seemed to Peter and his companions that they had passed through a deep sleep while Jesus was praying and had awoken to see the vision. As they watched, Moses and Elijah began to move away from Jesus; and Peter, scarcely realizing what he was saying, yet knowing that he wanted to make this wonderful experience last for ever, said, 'Lord, how wonderful it is for us to be here! If you want me to, I will make three huts in this place, one for you, one for Moses and one for Elijah.' He could not think what else to say.

He was still speaking when a bright cloud overshadowed them, and out of it a voice said, 'This is my beloved Son, my Chosen One, in whom I take delight. Listen to him.'

The sound of the voice struck terror into the disciples, and they fell on their faces. Jesus went to them, gently touched them and said, 'Stand up. Do not be afraid.' One by one they raised their heads. The bright cloud had gone. There was no one there but Jesus and themselves, and he was his familiar self.

The next day, as they went down the mountain, Jesus told them not to tell anyone about the vision until the Son of Man had risen from the dead. 'What can he mean by this "rising from the dead"?' they asked each other, 'and where does Scripture say that the Son of Man must suffer and be rejected? Since the teachers have taught us that Elijah must come before Christ, why will Jesus not allow us to tell them that we have seen Elijah, that he has come, and the way is now ready for the Messiah – the Christ. And here he is – Jesus of Nazareth!' So they asked Jesus, 'Why do the Pharisees and scribes say that Elijah has to come first?'

Jesus replied, 'Elijah does have to come first to prepare the way. He has, in fact, already come, and they did what they wanted to him.' He was speaking of John the Baptist who did not even himself know that he was Elijah born again, but Jesus knew.

When the little company rejoined the other disciples, they found them surrounded by a great crowd of people. Jesus asked what was the matter. A man replied, 'Master, my son is possessed by a spirit which makes him dumb. When it attacks him, it throws him violently to the ground. He foams at the mouth and gnashes his teeth. I asked your disciples to cast the spirit out, but they could not do it.'

Jesus cried out, 'O faithless generation, how long must I be with you? How long must I put up with you? Bring him to me.'

They brought the boy who was at once convulsed with a terrible fit.

'How long has he been like this?' asked Jesus.

'Since childhood,' the father answered. 'Often the devil has tried to destroy him by throwing him into fire or water. If you possibly can, please pity and help us.'

'If I possibly can!' said Jesus. 'Everything is possible to one who believes.'

'Oh, I believe,' cried the father. 'Help me where my faith is weak!'

Jesus rebuked the unclean spirit. 'Deaf and dumb spirit,' he said, 'out of him, I command you. Never enter him again!'

The boy gave a wild shriek, went into fit after fit and at last lay like one dead. Many thought he was dead. But Jesus took his hand, raised him, and he stood upright. Later, Jesus' disciples asked him privately, 'Why could we not cast the devil out?' 'Your faith is too weak,' said Jesus. 'If you only have faith no bigger than a mustard-seed you will be able to command mountains to move. Nothing will prove impossible for you.'

Jesus and the Children

Matthew 18, 1–7, 10; 19, 13–14; Mark 9, 33–37, 42; 10, 13–16; Luke 9, 46–48; 18, 15–17

Jesus' disciples did not understand until after the death of their Master that the Kingdom of Heaven about which he talked so much was not a kingdom like any they knew. They expected that one day, when he was ready, he would proclaim to the world that he was the King of the Jews. He would raise a great army and lead it triumphantly against the Romans. He would drive them headlong from Judaea, before going on to conquer the whole world. Then he would set up his throne in his capital city of Jerusalem, and would rule in majesty, surrounded by governors of provinces, chieftains of tribes, visiting kings and rulers in their royal purple, and lords and ladies of high degree. Among these grand people, they, his friends, once humble fishermen and ordinary folk, would hold high rank. One of them would be his Prime Minister, another his Treasurer, another his Lord Chief Justice. But which of them would be the greatest?

Journeying one day towards Capernaum, they discussed the question among themselves. Jesus was ahead of them, walking by himself, but he heard the argument behind him; and when they reached the city and were in the house together, he called his twelve disciples and asked them, 'What were you discussing on the way here?'

They were silent at first, as they were a little ashamed. Then they asked him directly, 'Master, who is to be the greatest among us in the Kingdom of Heaven?'

Jesus called a child who was playing near by

to come to him. He put his arms round him and then made him stand among the disciples in the place where he himself sat when he taught them, so that the child appeared to be their teacher. Then he said, 'Unless you stop arguing about which of you is to be the greatest, change your values and become like children, you will never even enter the Kingdom of Heaven. Whoever wants to be great among you must put himself in the humblest place and become like this child. He must be ready to become everybody else's servant. For the mark of greatness in my Kingdom is the willingness to help others, and the greatest will be he who is most prepared to serve.

'Whoever respects and honours someone who believes in me with a humble childlike faith, respects and honours me; and whoever honours me, honours God who sent me. But if anyone destroys a believer's childlike humility and trust, it would be better for that man if, before he had done such a terrible thing, he had had a great millstone hung around his neck and had been drowned in the sea. Never despise the humble believers. I tell you that their guardian angels look continually into the face of my Heavenly Father.'

On one occasion mothers brought their children to Jesus that he might lay his hands on them in blessing and pray over them. The disciples tried to prevent the people from troubling him but Jesus was indignant and said, 'Let the children come to me. Do not stop them. The Kingdom of Heaven belongs to such as these. I tell you truly that whoever will not submit to the Kingdom of Heaven like a child will never enter it at all.'

One by one, he put his arms around them all, laid his hands on them and blessed them, and went his way.

Mediterranean murex shells are the source of the dye which came to be known as the Royal Purple. The larger of the molluscs were cracked open and the gland extracted by hand; the remainder subjected to a mass crushing operation. It has been proved that 12,000 *Bolinus brandaris* yield about 1·5 grammes of crude dye—enough to colour the fringe on a woman's dress. The dye ranged in colour from red—black to violet.

Mary, Martha and Lazarus

Luke 10, 38–42; John 11, 1, 5–44

Jesus had three friends whom he dearly loved, and who lived at Bethany, a village not far from Jerusalem. They were two sisters and a brother – Martha, Mary and Lazarus.

Once, when Jesus was visiting their home, Martha set about making him and his disciples as welcome as possible. Busily she prepared and served dish after dish for them to eat, and found, as many cooks do, that one pair of hands was not enough. There was so much to prepare, so many mouths to feed, so little time in which to do it all. While she was serving one course in the main room, the next needed her attention in the kitchen. And all the time she was so busy, Mary, quiet, earnest and very different from her energetic, practical sister, sat behind Jesus, as he reclined at the table, listening to every word he uttered.

At last Martha, tired, hot and harassed, could bear it no longer. She went to Jesus. 'Lord,' she complained, 'do you not care that my sister has left me to do all the work by myself? Won't you ask her to come and help me?'

Jesus did not give her the answer she expected. 'Martha, Martha,' he said, 'there's no need to fret and fuss so over all this cooking and serving of yours. The simplest meal would have suited me, a couple of dishes or, indeed, just one. In listening to me, Mary has chosen the best dish of all, and it shall not be taken away from her.'

It was Mary who showed her love for Jesus a week before his death by anointing his feet with very precious ointment and wiping them with her hair.

Not long after the supper-party, at a time when Jesus was far away preaching and healing, Lazarus became very seriously ill. Terrified that their beloved brother would die, Martha and Mary sent a messenger to find Jesus and tell him the news. They were certain that, as soon as he heard it, their friend would hasten to them, lay his hands on Lazarus, and all would be well.

When he heard the message, Jesus said to his disciples, 'This illness will not end in death, but will show the glory of God and glorify the Son of God.' Because he then remained where he was for two days, his disciples thought that he was not worried about Lazarus' illness. They knew he could have healed him at a distance as he had cured the centurion's servant and the official's son. They were therefore surprised when he said,

at the end of the second day after the message had come, 'Let us go back to Judaea.'

'The Jews there wanted to stone you only a short time ago,' they said. 'It is dangerous to go back.'

'My life is like a day, which is not due to end yet,' said Jesus, 'so I shall be safe in Judaea for the present. But when my day is done and evening comes, then I shall be in danger. But now I have to go. Our friend Lazarus has gone to sleep, and I must go and wake him.'

The disciples said, 'If he has gone to sleep, he will recover.' Then Jesus said plainly, 'Lazarus is dead. I am glad I was not there, for your faith will come to be strengthened. Now, let us go to him.'

His disciple, Thomas, who, although he loved Jesus dearly, was a gloomy man, said, 'Let us go that we, too may die with him.'

When Jesus arrived at Bethany, he found that Lazarus had already been dead for four days. Martha met Jesus before he arrived at her home.

'Oh, Master,' she said, 'if only you had been here, Lazarus would not have died.' Then, because she knew that Jesus had raised men from the dead, and clutching at any hope, she added, 'Even now I know that God will grant you anything you ask him.'

'Your brother will rise again,' said Jesus.

'I know,' said Martha, 'that he will rise again at the resurrection on the last day.'

Jesus answered, 'I am the resurrection and I am life. If a man believes in me, he will live even though he dies. No one who is alive and has faith in me shall ever really die. Do you believe this?'

'Yes, Lord,' she said. 'I believe that you are the Christ, the Son of God, who was to come into the world.'

With these words, she went back to her sister Mary and said privately to her, 'The Master has come and would like to see you.' Mary rose quickly and went to the place where Jesus had met Martha, followed by her friends who thought that she was going to the tomb of her brother to weep.

As soon as she saw Jesus, Mary fell at his feet. 'If only you had been here, Master, Lazarus would not have died.'

When Jesus saw her and her friends all weeping, he was troubled and deeply moved. 'Where is he buried?' he asked.

They showed him the place. Jesus burst into tears.

'How he must have loved him,' they murmured.

Jesus went to the tomb, which was a cave with a stone placed against it. 'Take away the stone,' he said.

Martha exclaimed, 'Master, he has been

N. Dear

dead for four days. There will be a stench.'

Jesus answered, 'Did I not promise you that if you only believe you will see the glory of God?'

So they removed the stone, and Jesus, looking upwards said, 'Father, I thank you for having heard me. I know that you do always hear me, but I said it on behalf of all these round me, that they might believe that you sent me.'

He raised his voice in a great cry that echoed in the cave, 'Lazarus, come out!'

In the gloom of the cave something white stirred. Blindly, with short, stiff steps – legs, arms and body shrouded in linen bands, his face wrapped round with a cloth – Lazarus moved into the sunshine. A noise, a great sigh of awe and terror came from the onlookers. Lazarus stopped in front of Jesus, who said, 'Unbind him and let him go.'

Many of the Jews who saw Lazarus restored to life believed in Jesus; but some went to the Pharisees and told them what had happened. They and the high priests immediately called a meeting of the Sanhedrin, the supreme council of the Jews.

'Whatever shall we do?' they said. 'The man is performing miracle after miracle. If we leave him alone, everyone will believe that he is the Messiah, and he will lead a rebellion. The Romans will come and take away our position, blot out Jerusalem and the Temple and destroy our whole nation!'

Caiaphas, who was High Priest that year, replied, 'Do you not see what we must do? Do you not realize that this one man should be put to death for the people rather than that the whole nation shall perish?'

He spoke more truly than he knew. For his words were a prophecy that Jesus was to die for his people; and not only for them, for by his death he would gather into one all God's people throughout the world.

From that day on, the Jews plotted to bring about Christ's death. He appeared publicly no more among them for a time, but went to a town on the edge of the desert, where he stayed quietly with his disciples.

The Good Samaritan

Luke 10

On one occasion a man who had spent his life studying the Law of Moses tried to catch Jesus out with a very difficult question. He asked him, 'How can I gain eternal life?'

Jesus answered, 'What does the Law say?'

The man replied, 'First, you must love God with all your heart, soul, strength and mind. Then you must love your neighbour as much as you love yourself.'

'That is the right answer,' said Jesus. 'Do that, and you will have eternal life.'

'Ah,' replied the lawyer, 'but who is my neighbour?'

Jesus answered by telling him a story.

'A man travelling from Jerusalem to Jericho was attacked by robbers. They took everything he had, even his clothes, beat him senseless and then left him lying on the road, half-dead. A priest happened to go along the same road, but when he saw the wounded man he went past on the opposite side as quickly as he could. Then a Levite, one of those who praise God in the Temple services, came by. He glanced at the wounded man. Then he, too, passed by on the other side. Finally, a Samaritan traveller came to where the man was lying.'

At the word 'Samaritan' the lawyer's face became scornful. Like every Jew he hated the Samaritans. They were the descendants of foreigners whom the Jews had found living in their country when they had returned from exile in Babylon, five hundred and fifty years before. They were called Samaritans because they had been exiled to Samaria, part of the kingdom of Israel, by the Assyrians who had conquered them. These foreigners believed that there were many different gods, each one ruling his own country. If you lived in a country, you had to worship the god of that country. So, when they came to live in Samaria, the foreigners worshipped the Israelites' god, Jehovah.

When the Jews returned and began to rebuild God's temple at Jerusalem, the Samaritans wanted to help. But the Jews would not let them, for they thought that the Samaritans did not worship God in the right way. This led to bitter quarrelling which grew worse and worse as the years went by, until nobody could hate anyone more than a Samaritan a Jew.

So the lawyer was certain that the passing Samaritan would not help the robbed and wounded man from Jerusalem.

He was wrong, however.

'The Samaritan pitied the poor man lying by the road,' Jesus continued. 'He went to him, washed his wounds with wine to clean them, and oil to soothe them, then bound them up. He placed him on his own donkey, took him to an inn, where he looked to his every need himself.

'The next day, the Samaritan had to leave the inn, because he had business to attend to, but the Jew was still badly hurt and it was necessary to leave him at the inn until he was better. The Samaritan took out some money, gave it to the innkeeper and said, "Please look after my friend and give him all he needs. I think this will be enough to pay for everything, but if you are put to any extra expense, I will repay you when I come back this way."

'Now,' said Jesus to the lawyer, 'which of these three men proved to be a good neighbour to the man who was robbed and beaten?'

The lawyer did not want to answer at first, and even when he did, he could hardly bear to say, the Samaritan. Instead he mumbled, 'I suppose it was the man who took pity on the wounded traveller.'

'Yes,' said Jesus. 'Then go and do the same yourself.'

Coins current in the time of Christ. The coin on the left is a silver tetradrachm from the imperial mint, showing the head of Augustus. The thirty pieces of silver paid to Judas were probably tetradrachms. Right is a coin of the Roman emperor, Tiberius. Coins struck during his reign for use in Palestine did not include the emperor's head.

The Prodigal Son

Luke 15, 1–2, 10, 11–32

Jesus was often reproached by the Pharisees because he mixed with people whom they regarded as sinners. In answer, he said, 'Those who are well do not need a doctor; only those who are ill. I have not come to call good men, but sinners, to repent.' And he told this story.

'There was once a man who had two sons. The younger one said to him, "Father, give me now the share of the property you intend to leave me when you die." So the father divided up his estate and gave the younger son his share. A few days later, the young man sold everything he had been given, took the money and journeyed into a far distant land. There he wasted the money in a life of idleness and pleasure, with no thought of what he would do when his wealth was gone. When he had spent all he had, there came a terrible famine throughout the country where he was living, and he began to be in need. He was forced to hire himself out to one of the local farmers, who sent him into the fields to look after his pigs. He was so hungry that he was ready to eat the carob-tree pods which were given to the pigs, for nobody gave him any food at all.

'Then he came to his senses. "How many of my father's paid men have more than enough to eat," he thought, "and here am I dying of hunger. I will go to my father, and I will say to him, Father, I have sinned against Heaven and against you. I am no longer fit to be your son. Treat me as one of your hired servants."

Pods of the carob tree, which the prodigal son fed to swine. The carob grows in very dry soil, and the pods—which are green at first—turn brown when ripe. They are rich in sweet syrup, and are eaten by people as well as used for fattening cattle.

Footwear consisted of sandals fastened with straps or latchets. They were removed on entering a house or holy place. At all other times to be bare-footed was a sign of mourning.

'So he set off to go to his father. But while he was still far away, the father saw him and was filled with pity for the pathetic, ragged figure. He ran to him and threw his arms around him and kissed him. The son began to say, "Father, I have sinned against Heaven and you and do not deserve to be called a son of yours any longer." But before he could say more, the father called the servants.

"Bring the best robe I have and put it on him," he said. "Bring a ring for his finger and sandals for his feet. Fetch the fatted calf and kill it, and let us feast and make merry. For this son of mine was dead and is alive again. He was lost and is found." So they began to celebrate.

'Now the elder son was out working on the farm. When he was returning, he heard the sound of music and dancing. He called a servant and asked him what was happening.

"Your brother has returned," the man said, "and your father has killed the fatted calf because he is so glad to have him back safe and sound."

'The brother was angry and refused to go in. His father came out and pleaded with him, but he replied, "I have slaved for you all these years. Not once have I disobeyed any order you gave me. Yet you have never given me so much as a kid that I might enjoy myself with my friends. But as soon as this son of yours – who has wasted your money with evil companions – returns, you kill the fatted calf for him!"

'"My dear boy," said the father, "we are always together, you and I, and everything I have is yours. But this was a day when we had to rejoice, because this brother of yours was dead and has been restored to life. He was lost and has been found."'

Zaccheus

Luke 18, 10–14; 19, 1–10

After curing Bar-Timaeus, the blind beggar, Jesus entered Jericho and made his way through the town. There was a man living there whose name was Zacchaeus. Although he was a Jew, he was the chief of all the tax-gatherers in the district and a very wealthy man. But like all tax-gatherers, especially Jewish ones, he was detested by his fellow-countrymen, because he collected money from them to give to the hated Romans who ruled their country.

Zacchaeus had heard many wonderful stories about Jesus, but he had never seen him. When he knew that the prophet was making his way through the city, he ran to catch a glimpse of him, for he was eager to find out what kind of man he was. But Zacchaeus was a very short man, and he could not see over the heads of the crowd of people which immediately surrounded Jesus whenever he entered any village or town. So he ran on ahead of the throng and climbed a mulberry tree by the road along which Jesus would pass, and there he waited.

To his astonishment, Jesus stopped at the foot of the tree and looked up into its branches. Although Zacchaeus had never seen him before, Jesus spoke his name, 'Zacchaeus,' he said, 'come down at once, for I am going to stay at your house today.'

Zacchaeus clambered down as quickly as he could and led Jesus to his house where he welcomed him joyfully. But many in the crowd began to mutter disapprovingly that the Teacher had agreed to be a sinner's guest.

Perhaps because he heard what they were saying, perhaps because he had been moved by the expression on Jesus' face when he looked up into the tree, Zacchaeus stopped at the door of his house. He turned and faced the crowd. But it was to Jesus that he spoke.

'Here and now, Master, I promise to give half of everything I possess to the poor. If I have cheated anybody by taking more from him in taxation than he should have paid, I will give him out of the half that remains of my property four times as much as I took.'

Jesus said to those round him, 'Today salvation has come to this house. Zacchaeus is a son of Abraham, too, and the Son of Man has come to seek and save people like him who have lost their way.'

Jesus once told a story about a Pharisee and a tax-gatherer. Both went up to the Temple to pray. The Pharisee stood in the attitude of prayer where everyone could see and admire him and said, 'Thank you, God, that I am not like ordinary men who are greedy, dishonest and unfaithful. Thank you that I am not like that dreadful tax-gatherer over there. I fast every Monday and Thursday; and I give a tenth of everything I get to charity, far more than the Law of Moses requires me to give.'

But the tax-gatherer was so ashamed of himself that he stood a long way off from the Pharisee whom he thought far more righteous than himself. He would not so much as raise his eyes from the ground, but beat his breast and said, 'God be merciful to me; I am the worst of sinners.'

'I tell you,' said Jesus, 'that it was the tax-gatherer, not the Pharisee, who went home with his sins forgiven. For God will bring low those who think highly of their own goodness and look down on everyone else. But those who are humble will be raised high in the sight of God.'

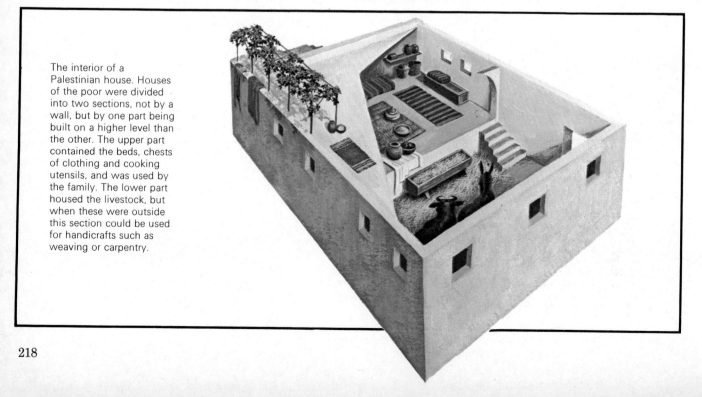

The interior of a Palestinian house. Houses of the poor were divided into two sections, not by a wall, but by one part being built on a higher level than the other. The upper part contained the beds, chests of clothing and cooking utensils, and was used by the family. The lower part housed the livestock, but when these were outside this section could be used for handicrafts such as weaving or carpentry.

The First Palm Sunday

Matthew 21, 1–13; Mark 11, 1–11; Luke 19, 28–48;
John 12, 12–19

On the first day of Jesus' last week on earth, he sent two disciples into a village a short way from Jerusalem. 'You will find an ass tethered there, which I have arranged to borrow,' he said. 'Untie it and bring it to me. If anyone asks you why you are taking it, say, "The Lord needs it," and he will let it go.'

The disciples brought the ass to Jesus. They put their cloaks on its back and Jesus prepared to ride into Jerusalem. The prophet Zechariah had written centuries before that the Messiah would ride into Jerusalem on an ass, and Jesus, by doing this, was for the first time claiming openly to be the Messiah. As the little band set out towards Jerusalem shouting and cheering, they were joined by others from the villages round about.

Running to Jerusalem, people spread the news that the Messiah was coming, and from the city, excited over the recent raising to life of Lazarus, enthusiastic crowds poured out to welcome Jesus. Some spread their garments on the road, others strewed palm-branches, leaves and flowers, and the crowd chanted, 'Hosannah to the Son of David! Blessed is he who comes in God's name!'

'They are calling you Messiah,' said some Pharisees in the crowd. 'Stop them!'

'If they were silent,' Jesus answered, 'the very stones would shout.'

There is a bend in the road to Jerusalem where the traveller sees the whole panorama of the city suddenly breaking gloriously into view. When Jesus reached the spot, he burst into tears. 'Oh, Jerusalem,' he mourned, 'if only you had known those things that would have given you peace. But the time will come when your enemies will besiege you and utterly destroy you – and all because you did not realize that God had come to you.'

So Jesus entered Jerusalem in triumph as the Messiah. As was the duty of every pious Jew, he went immediately to the Temple to pray. He looked round at all the activity there before leaving the city and returning to Bethany where he spent the night.

The following day he went back to the Temple. At the beginning of his ministry, he had driven the traders out of the Temple courtyards, but they had soon returned. Here the money-changers had established themselves, making handsome profits by changing foreign money into the Jewish half-shekel which had to be paid into the Temple treasury. There, too, were the men who sold sacrificial doves, charging enormously high prices to

pilgrims who had to buy their wares. Everywhere traders used the Temple courts as a short cut, carrying their merchandise through them as though they were a public road and giving no respect to the sacredness of the buildings.

It had been prophesied that the Messiah would cleanse the Temple, and Jesus did so, driving out all the traders. He overturned the money-changers' tables and the dove-

sellers' stalls. He forbade anyone to carry any merchandise through the Temple or to carry on business of any kind. 'It is written,' he cried, 'that God's house shall be called a house of prayer for all the nations of the world. You have made it a den of robbers.'

Every day during his last week, Jesus preached and healed in the Temple. Even the children shouted, 'Hosannah to the Son of David!' until the high priests and scribes seethed with indignation. 'Listen to what they are saying,' they cried. 'Yes,' replied Jesus. 'Have you never read what the prophets say, "God has caused children and babies to praise him perfectly"?'

Christ's enemies longed to kill him, but by day people surrounded him continuously, and he spent every night outside the city at Bethany. He was to die, but only at a time of his own choosing.

The Last Supper

Matthew 26, 14–35; Mark 14, 10–31; Luke 22, 1–39;
John 13, 1–35; 18

To the Jewish leaders, plotting the arrest and death of Jesus, came an unexpected visitor. 'How much will you pay me to betray my Master to you?' asked Judas.

Nobody knows why he did this terrible thing. It could have been greed for money, but the priests gave him only thirty pieces of silver, the price of a slave. Perhaps Judas thought that if Jesus found himself in real danger, he would use his powers to escape and become the expected all-conquering Messiah. Whatever the reason, from that moment he watched for an opportunity to hand Jesus over to the Jews.

The next day the disciples asked Jesus where they were to eat the Passover supper. He said to Peter and John, 'Go to a certain place in Jerusalem where you will see a man carrying a pitcher of water. He will lead you to a house where you will be shown a large room upstairs reserved for us. There you will find everything ready.' Jesus had made these secret arrangements to protect himself from his enemies.

That evening, the twelve disciples and their Master had barely sat down to the feast when the same old jealous quarrels broke out as to who should be greatest in Christ's coming kingdom. Perhaps the reason was that someone was needed to serve at table and nobody was willing. Jesus reminded them that in his kingdom the greatest man was he who most willingly served his fellow-men. Then he himself gave them an example. He took off his outer clothes and tied a towel round his waist. Taking a bowl of water, he began to wash his disciples' feet, work usually done by the meanest slave.

Peter tried to stop him, but Jesus said, 'You do not now understand what I am doing but later you will. If you do not let me wash your feet, you can have no fellowship with me.' 'Then wash my hands and head as well,' replied Peter. 'A man who has bathed needs

only to wash his feet,' Jesus replied, 'and all of you – except one – are clean.' He said this because he knew that Judas was planning to betray him.

When he had finished, Jesus said, 'Do you understand what I have been trying to teach you? You rightly call me, "Lord". If I, your Lord, have washed your feet, how much more ought you to serve one another, for servants are not greater than their master.'

Soon after Jesus became very sorrowful. 'One of you,' he said, 'is going to betray me.' His distressed disciples asked him in turn, 'Lord, is it I?' Peter signalled to John who was reclining next to Jesus to ask him whom he meant. John leaned back and asked Jesus, and he replied, 'The one to whom I give this bread when I have dipped it in the dish.' For the host to give a guest bread dipped in the dish was a mark of special favour, and by doing this Jesus tried to shame Judas from his disloyalty. But Judas rose to leave, and Jesus knew that this last appeal was in vain. 'Do what you have to do quickly,' Jesus

said, and Judas went out into the darkness. No one realized that he was going to betray Christ then. They thought he was about some business Jesus had given him to do.

Then Jesus took bread, broke it, blessed it and said, 'Take and eat. This is my body which is given for you.' Next he blessed a cup of wine. 'Drink this, all of you,' he said. 'This cup is my blood, by the shedding of which a new agreement is made between God and man, so that many may be saved from their sins.'

After the dinner they left the city to go to the Mount of Olives. On the way Jesus said, 'You will all be disloyal to me tonight.'

'Everyone else may be disloyal,' said Peter, 'but I shall never be.'

'This very night, before the cock crows twice,' Jesus answered, 'you will deny knowing me three times.'

Peter almost wept. 'Though I should die with you, I will never deny you,' he protested, and they all said the same. But sorrow overshadowed them as they entered a garden called Gethsemane to pray.

Gethsemane

Matthew 26, 36–58; Mark 14, 32–52; Luke 22, 39–54; John 18, 1–13

The garden of Gethsemane lay close outside the walls of Jerusalem. Jesus and his disciples often visited it, as Judas, busy collecting soldiers and Temple police with lights and weapons, knew well. When they arrived, Jesus left eight disciples by themselves and took Peter, James and John with him to a place a stone's throw away. As the four walked on together, the anguish of mind which had never been far away all that evening, burst over him in its full horror.

'My heart is almost broken with grief,' he said. 'Stay here while I pray over there, and pray with me.' He went on a little and throwing himself on the ground, prayed with all the strength of his mind, 'Father, if it be possible – and all things are possible with God – let me not have to face the horror ahead of me. But your will, not mine, be done.'

Before the mind of the lonely man praying, there appeared the angel of the love of God comforting and strengthening him to accept his fate. But he prayed the more urgently, with such desperation that the sweat poured off him on to the ground like blood pumping from an open wound. At last, exhausted, he returned to the disciples only to find them sleeping, worn out with grief.

'Could you not remain awake to support me one short hour?' he asked. 'Keep awake and pray that you yourselves may be spared testing. Your spirits are willing, but your bodies are weak.'

He left them again to pray, and when he returned he found them once more asleep and so ashamed when he woke them that they did not know what to say. A third time he left them to pray, yet knowing all the time that God had no other path for him but the way he had to follow. For all their shame, the heavy-eyed disciples could not keep themselves from sleeping.

When he returned to them for the last time, he said, 'Are you still sleeping? It is time. Let us go. My betrayer is here.'

While he was speaking, he and his disciples were surrounded by a great crowd of men armed with swords and cudgels, with Judas at their head. Jesus went to meet them.

'Whom do you want?' he asked.

'Jesus of Nazareth.'

'I am he.'

He spoke with such majesty that they drew back in awe, and some fell to the ground.

'Who is it you want?' Jesus asked again.

'Jesus of Nazareth.'

'I have told you that I am he,' said Jesus, 'but let these others go.'

Judas stepped forward from the crowd and embraced Jesus, for he had told them, 'This one I kiss is the man you want.' 'Greetings, Master,' he said.

Jesus said, 'Friend, you must do what you have to. But, oh, Judas, do you betray me with a kiss?'

The men seized Jesus. Peter drew his sword and struck out wildly, cutting off the right ear of Malchus, a servant of the high priest.

'Sheathe your sword and do not resist,' said Jesus, 'for those who use force die by force. I could this instant summon armies of angels to rescue me. But this is the only way in which the scriptures can be fulfilled.'

With a touch he healed Malchus' ear. Then he spoke to the crowd. 'Am I a criminal that you arrest me with swords and cudgels? Every day I taught in the Temple and you did not touch me. But all this fulfils prophecy. This is your moment, when evil is supreme.'

The men holding Jesus marched him away. Others tried half-heartedly to arrest the disciples, but they escaped in the darkness, one young man leaving his linen wrap in the hands of the soldiers and fleeing naked. Only when Peter and John had made sure of their own safety did they follow Jesus and his captors at a safe distance back to Jerusalem, fearful of what was to happen.

Jesus before the Sanhedrin

Matthew 27, 59–75; Mark 14, 53–72; Luke 22, 54–71; John 18, 12–27

Jesus was taken first to Annas, father-in-law of Caiaphas, the High Priest, and himself a former high priest. He questioned Jesus closely. 'I have always taught openly in synagogues and the Temple,' Jesus answered. 'Ask my hearers what I teach.'

One of the attendants struck Jesus on the face. 'Is that the way to talk to the High Priest?' he asked.

'If I have said anything wrong,' said Jesus, 'tell me what it is. If not, why do you hit me?' Annas ordered Jesus to be bound and taken to Caiaphas on the other side of the courtyard.

Meanwhile, John, who knew Caiaphas, had asked permission to bring Peter into the courtyard, where the attendants had made themselves a fire. One of the High Priest's serving-maids said to Peter, 'Aren't you one of the prisoner's followers?' 'No,' he said, and joined the others at the fire to warm himself. There, after they had noticed his Galilean accent during the general conversation, another maidservant looked hard at him and said, 'You were one of those with the Nazarene, weren't you?' Peter was taken aback. Confused, he stammered, 'I wasn't – what do you mean? No, I know nothing about the man.' He was so frightened that he withdrew for a time into an outer courtyard where, though he scarcely noticed it, he heard a cock crow.

After a while, finding the night air cold, Peter edged back into the circle round the fire. Gradually his self-confidence returned until the bystanders began to say, 'You must be a

to agree, as was required by Jewish law. At last two men said, 'This fellow declared, "I can destroy the Temple of God made with hands and in three days build another not made with hands."' This would have been sorcery. They had misunderstood a reference Jesus had made in speaking of the death and resurrection of his own body. But even their evidence did not agree.

Jesus said nothing, allowing the witnesses to contradict each other. At last, Caiaphas, losing patience, said, 'I put you on your oath. Answer. Are you the Messiah, the divine Son of God?'

'I am,' replied Jesus. 'One day you will see the Son of Man seated at God's right hand in heaven.'

Caiaphas tore his robe. 'Blasphemy!' he cried. 'What further evidence do we need now? How do you vote?'

'For death!' they yelled. In their fury they lost all dignity, blindfolding Jesus, spitting at him, mocking him and hitting him, shouting, 'Come on, prophet! Tell us who's hitting you, Messiah!'

But it was one thing to condemn Jesus to death, quite another to carry out the sentence. For the Romans ruled the land, and only they could execute a man. Pilate, the Roman governor, had first to be convinced that Jesus deserved to die.

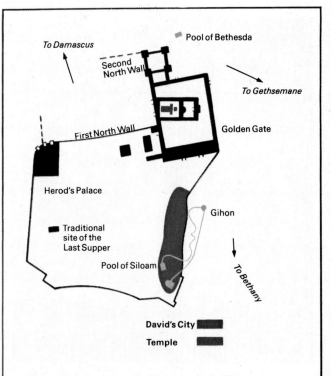

A plan of Jerusalem in the first century AD. The circumference of the town is not more than 4·5 kilometres, and it lies in a depression, surrounded on three sides by ridges of hills. The old city is situated between two valleys, and was originally divided by a third valley which has long been silted up. To the south-east there is a view towards the desert, and it is from this direction that the hot wind blows in during the summer.

follower of this Jesus fellow, with that Galilean accent of yours.' Terrified, Peter cursed and swore in his anxiety to escape arrest. 'I don't know the man, I tell you,' he shouted. At that moment the cock crowed for the second time.

At that moment, too, Jesus, his arms bound, was hustled across the courtyard from Annas' quarters to Caiaphas'. He passed within feet of Peter, turned his head and looked straight into his eyes. 'Do you remember?' his look said. 'Three denials before the cock crowed twice?' But there was also such love and understanding in it that Peter could not bear it. He stumbled from the courtyard into the street outside, weeping as no man has wept since the beginning of the world.

Waiting with Caiaphas to try Jesus were the members of the Sanhedrin, the highest court of the Jews. Witness after witness came forward against him, but no two could be found

The Trial before Pilate

Matthew 27, 1–31; Mark 15, 1–20; Luke 23, 1–25;
John 18, 28–40; 19, 1–15

Judas heard early that his master had been condemned and had made no effort to save himself. Aghast at what he had done, he snatched up the silver coins and ran with them to the Temple, hoping, perhaps, that if he returned the money, Jesus might be released.

But when he said to the priests, 'I have betrayed an innocent man,' they were contemptuous. 'What do we care?' they replied. 'That is your business.' Judas flung down the silver and, running off in black despair, hanged himself.

Meanwhile the Sanhedrin took Jesus to Pilate, the Roman governor. They accused him of plotting against Rome, of encouraging people not to pay taxes to Caesar and of claiming to be a king. Pilate at once recognized their spite and said, 'Judge him by your own law.' They replied, 'We cannot put anyone to death.'

Pilate questioned Jesus privately. 'Are you the King of the Jews?' he asked.

'I am certainly a king,' Jesus answered, 'but my kingdom is not a worldly one, or my men would fight for me. I came to be a witness to the truth.'

'Truth!' said Pilate. 'What is truth?'

He took Jesus out to the Sanhedrin. 'I find nothing criminal in this man,' he said.

Caiaphas replied, 'Beginning in Galilee and coming now to Judaea, he stirs up people everywhere by his teaching.'

'Oh,' said Pilate, 'are you a Galilean?' He told the Sanhedrin, 'This man must be judged by Herod, ruler of Galilee, who is in Jerusalem for the feast,' and he sent Jesus to him.

Herod had long been wanting to see Jesus and to test his miraculous powers. But Jesus replied not a word to his questions and the stream of accusations from the Jewish leaders who had followed him to Herod. Herod and his soldiers had to satisfy themselves by dressing Jesus in a brightly-coloured robe, jeering at him as a mock-king and sending him back to Pilate.

Pilate summoned the Sanhedrin again. 'Neither I nor Herod can find anything this man has done to deserve being put to death. I shall flog him and let him go.'

'No!' they shouted. 'Crucify him, crucify him!' Then Pilate delivered Jesus to be flogged. After his soldiers had scourged him with lashes of cord plaited with pieces of metal and bone knotted into each of their many thongs, they put a soldier's scarlet cloak on him in imitation of the royal purple, worn only by emperors, rammed a crown of thorns on his head, gave him a stick for a sceptre and knelt before him, crying, 'Hail, King of the Jews!' Then they spat at him and beat him about the head with his 'sceptre'.

It was the governor's custom at Passover to release a prisoner chosen by the crowd. There was in prison at that time a murderer named Bar-Abbas who had taken part in a recent revolt. Pilate thought that the contrast between the bloodthirsty Bar-Abbas and the innocent Jesus would result in the Jews selecting Jesus, if they were given a choice; so he brought Jesus out to them, a pitiable sight, his head and body streaming with blood from the thorns and the flogging. 'Look at this man,' he said. 'Shall I release him or Bar-Abbas?'

To his astonishment, they yelled, 'Bar-Abbas!'

At that moment a message from his wife was given to Pilate. 'Have nothing to do with Jesus,' the message ran. 'He is innocent. Last night I had terrible nightmares about him.'

Above the mob's yelling, Pilate shouted, 'What am I to do with this so-called king of yours?'

'Crucify him!'

'Crucify him yourselves,' Pilate retorted, knowing that, under Roman law, they could not. 'I find him innocent.'

'By our law he ought to die becaue he calls himself the Son of God,' the chief priests replied.

Pilate was terrified. There were many things about this man he did not understand.

'Where do you come from?' he asked. Jesus made no reply.

'Do you not realize that I have power to release or crucify you?'

'You would have no power unless God gave it to you.'

Pilate said resolutely to the people. 'I shall release this man.'

But his determination was destroyed by one sentence from the priests. 'If you let this rebel go, you are no friend of Caesar's.' Pilate had already been in deep trouble with the Roman emperor, and another accusation would mean his ruin, perhaps his death.

Pilate sent for water and washed his hands in front of them all. 'I am clean from this innocent man's blood. You are responsible.'

'His blood be upon us and our children!' the people cried together.

Bar-Abbas was released, and Jesus, dressed in his own clothes, was led out to be crucified.

229

The Crucifixion

Matthew 27, 32–66; Mark 15, 21–47; Luke 23, 26–56;
John 19, 16–42

After his terrible flogging, Jesus was too weak to carry the horizontal beam of his cross which those condemned to crucifixion had to bear. The Roman soldiers therefore forced Simon of Cyrene, whom they met on the way, to carry the heavy spar. Jesus was accompanied by women who mourned aloud for him. Knowing the cruel fate that was to come to Jerusalem in a few years when it would rebel against the Romans and be utterly destroyed, he said to them, 'Do not weep for me, but weep for yourselves and your children in the days to come.'

Outside Jerusalem there was a hill known as Golgotha, or Skull Hill, from its shape. On top of it were upright beams standing firmly in the ground. Criminals condemned to crucifixion were secured by large nails piercing their wrists between the bones of the forearm, to the spars they had carried, and these were lashed horizontally to the uprights already in position. Each upright had a piece of wood jutting from it to form a kind of saddle on which the victim was supported. His feet were sometimes fastened to the upright by a single nail driven through both ankle-bones, sometimes tied. It was not only a hideously painful death but an utterly shameful one, reserved only for slaves and the basest criminals.

Jesus was offered drugged wine to help dull the pain, but he refused it. He knew he had to face death with all his senses clear. He was stripped of his clothes for which the soldiers crucifying him drew lots, nailed to the crossbeam and raised on the upright. As they drove the nails home, he prayed, 'Father, forgive them. They do not know what they are doing.'

Over his head was a placard with his 'crime' on it, written in Hebrew, Greek and Latin: 'This is Jesus, the King of the Jews.' The Sanhedrin protested to Pilate. 'Write,' they demanded, '"He said he was King of the Jews."' But Pilate would not change what he had written.

On either side of him, two thieves were also crucified. One of them abused Jesus, crying, 'You Christ, why don't you save yourself and us?' But the other rebuked him. 'We deserve our punishment, but this man has done nothing wrong.' Then he said to Jesus, 'Lord, remember me when you come to reign.' 'This very day,' Jesus replied, 'you will be in Paradise with me.'

The Pharisees, priests and passers-by jeered at Jesus, 'He saved others, but he can't save himself.' 'Come down off the cross,' they shouted, 'then we'll believe you really are the Messiah.' But friends were there as well as enemies. His mother and his dearly loved disciple, John, stood close by the cross, and even in his agony Jesus thought of their future life. 'Mother,' he said to Mary, 'be a mother to John. John, look after her like a son.'

But at midday the scoffers were silenced, for darkness came down upon the whole country and lasted until Jesus died at three o'clock. Towards the end, he cried out in a loud voice, 'My God, my God, why hast thou forsaken me?' The cry was not a cry of despair but the first words of Psalm 22. The Psalm begins with an almost exact description of Christ's sufferings, but ends in a great burst of praise to God. The first sentence of the Psalm would have brought to Jesus' mind, as familiar with the Psalms as children are with Sunday school hymns, the triumphant close, in which a man's dreadful suffering brings about the glorification of God by people yet to be born.

After the cry, Jesus said, 'I am thirsty.' One of the people by the cross raised on a stick a sponge full of wine to his lips. Now he could drink because he had completed all he had come to the cross to do. Then he prayed, 'Father, I give up my spirit into your hands,' and, almost at once cried triumphantly, 'It is finished!' With those words he died.

At that very moment the veil separating the Holy Place from the Holy of Holies in the Temple split from top to bottom. The earth shook and rocks cracked. Stories were told of graves opening and spirits appearing. The centurion in charge of Jesus' execution said, 'This man was, beyond question, a son of God.'

The bodies had to be taken down before six in the evening, when the Jewish Sabbath began, in order that the holy day should not be made unclean. So the soldiers killed the two thieves by breaking their legs, which meant that, since they could no longer support the weight of their bodies, they soon died through suffocation. As Jesus was already dead, the soldiers did not break his legs. But one casually drove his spear into Jesus' side, piercing him almost to the heart, as the flow of blood and water from the wound showed.

Joseph of Arimathea, a wealthy member of the Sanhedrin, who had not voted for Jesus' death, bravely went to Pilate and begged to be given his body. Pilate, surprised to hear that Jesus was already dead, sent for the centurion who confirmed that it was indeed so. Pilate granted Joseph the body; with Nicodemus, another secret follower of Jesus, he took down the body, anointed it with hastily prepared spices, and wrapped it in a clean linen cloth. In a garden cemetery not far from the place of execution, he had had carved out of the rock for his own burial a tomb like a small cave. In this tomb, never before used, he reverently

laid the body of the Messiah, and, with the help of Nicodemus and his servants, rolled a heavy stone in front of the cave to close it. Several women who were followers of Jesus saw where the body was laid, and went home to prepare spices so that, when the Sabbath was over, they could come back and embalm it properly.

They were not the only ones to note where Christ was buried. Servants of the Sanhedrin had also been told to watch and to report back to their masters, who went at once to Pilate.

'That false Messiah stated he would rise from the dead,' they said. 'Will you, therefore, seal the tomb and set soldiers to guard it in case his disciples come by night and steal the body and say that he has risen? If this should happen, things could be worse than ever.'

'You have your guard,' said Pilate. He may have meant, 'You have the Jewish Temple guard which I allow you to use for this duty outside the Temple,' or 'I will let you have a guard of Roman soldiers.' Whatever he meant, by the time darkness fell on the evening of that first Good Friday, there were no longer tumults and angry crowds and the coming and going of leaders and governors and kings. Over the whole land the Sabbath peace had fallen. The streets were empty and the houses still. Only in the cemetery where the guard sat round the lonely tomb in the garden of graves where Jesus lay, was there any movement or flickering of fire.

The First Easter And After

Matthew 28; Mark 16; Luke 24; John 20, 21

All that weary night and the next day and the night following, the guard kept watch. According to Jewish reckoning, Sunday would be the third day from the crucifixion. Their long vigil was nearly over.

At about five o'clock, when the first light broke over the horizon, there was an earth tremor which shook the guards fully awake. Before their startled eyes a figure, dazzling as lightning, white as snow, rolled back the stone from the cave where Jesus lay. For a few moments they were paralyzed with fear. Then they fled and told the Sanhedrin what had happened. The high priests gave them money. 'Say, "His disciples stole his body while we were asleep," ' they said. 'If Pilate hears of it, we shall see that nothing happens to you.'

About an hour later, six or seven women, friends of Jesus, including Mary Magdalene, went to the cemetery carrying spices to embalm his body. On the way, they worried that they might not be strong enough to move the stone, but on approaching the cave they were surprised to see that the stone had al-

A plan of a garden tomb. Built into a hill, it was approached by stairs (a) which led to the low opening to the tomb. This was covered by a large stone rolled across the entrance in a groove sloping downwards. A small anteroom (b) opened into the last room (c) and the body was placed in a niche (d).

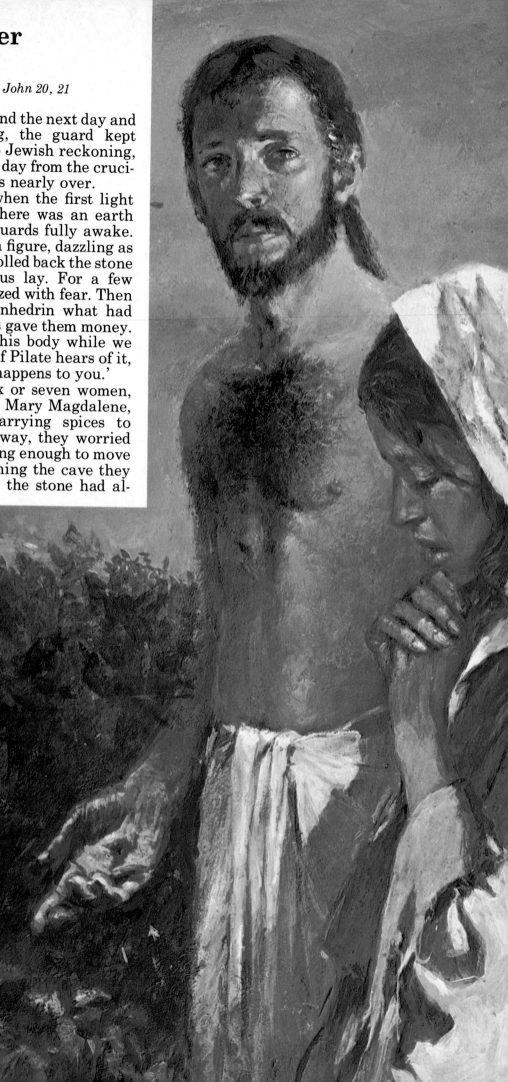

234

ready been rolled away. There was room for
only one or two of them at a time to enter the
tomb. Those who did were startled to find that
the body of Jesus had gone. While they were
puzzling over this, there suddenly flashed before their eyes two men clothed in dazzling
white. 'Do not be perplexed,' they said. 'Why
do you look for the living among the dead?
Jesus of Nazareth who was crucified is not
here. He has risen. Remember that he told you
when he was still in Galilee that the Son of
Man had to be betrayed and crucified and
would rise on the third day.'

Those at the back of the little crowd of
women, among them Mary Magdalene, saw
and heard little or nothing of the vision, but
when those in front turned in panic and
pushed their way out of the tomb in terror,
their fear infected the other women, and they
all fled.

Mary Magdalene gathered only that Christ's
body had disappeared. She ran to where Peter
and John were lodging. 'They have taken the
Lord out of his tomb and we do not know where
they have laid him!' she sobbed. The two men
ran to the garden.

Meanwhile, in the path of the other women,
hurrying home together, there appeared in
the still dim light of the very early morning,
the figure of a man. 'Greetings,' said the voice
they knew. Unable to believe their ears or
eyes, for they saw it was Jesus standing there,
they fell in worship to the ground. 'Do not be
afraid,' said Jesus. 'Go and tell my followers
we shall meet together soon.'

Joyfully the women told the remaining
disciples how they had met with Jesus. But the
story seemed nonsense to them, and they did
not believe it.

While this was happening, John and Peter
ran to the tomb. John, who was younger than
Peter, and able to run faster, arrived first.
But he was afraid to enter the cave and only
peered in. In the gloom he could make out the
linen cloths which had been wrapped round
the body.

While he was hesitating, Peter arrived and
shouldered his way past into the cave. He saw
that the body had indeed gone and that the
cloth which had been wrapped round Jesus'
head was rolled up in a place by itself.

John followed Peter into the cave. Neither
of them understood what had happened. They
knew only that Jesus was not there.

They left before Mary, following them with
the slowness of sorrow, arrived at the grave.
She stood outside the tomb weeping, and then
was suddenly aware of a man standing by her.
Her head was bowed in grief and her eyes filled
with tears so that she did not see his face.

'Why are you weeping?' he asked. 'Whom
are you looking for?'

Mary, thinking he was the gardener, said, 'Sir, if you have removed him, please tell me where you have put him and I will take him away.'

The man replied with one word, 'Mary'. But hearing her name and the way he said it, Mary knew at once who he was.

'Master!' she cried and sank to her knees. She wanted to embrace him, but gently he stopped her.

'Do not cling to me now,' he said. 'Go and tell my friends that I have risen and that I am going to return to my Father and your Father, my God and your God.'

She did not want to leave him, yet longed to show her love by doing all he asked. Full of joy, she ran back to Jerusalem. 'I have seen the Lord,' she told the disciples. 'He is alive!'

As the day wore on, the disciples' excitement grew. It seemed that the unbelievable was true. Peter, the broken-hearted coward who had denied his Lord three times, returned in the evening a new man, aflame with courage and confidence. Mary Magdalene and the

inn, until he had blessed and broken bread in the way they knew so well. He had then vanished from their sight.

They finished their story. And suddenly Jesus was there among the disciples, saying, 'Peace to you all,' and proving that he was not a ghost by eating before them and allowing them to touch him. No one could doubt any longer.

Thomas Didymus was not present. When the disciples told him they had seen the Lord, he said, 'Unless I see and feel the nail-marks in his hands and the wound in his side, I will not believe.' A week later, when Thomas was with the disciples, Jesus appeared, and, greeting them, stretched out his hands to Thomas. 'Look,' he said, 'put your finger into the nail-prints in my hands. Place your hand here in the wound in my side. Do not be unbelieving any longer.'

There was no need for Thomas to touch him. He knelt before him. 'My Lord and my God,' he said.

'You believe because you have seen me,' said Jesus. 'Blessed are those who believe without having seen.'

Besides these appearances, Jesus showed himself to his own brother James, who had not been his follower while he lived, and James became a believer. By the Sea of Galilee where he had spent so much of his life, he made almost his last appearance.

Peter and the other ex-fishermen had gone back to their old work of fishing. All one night they worked but caught nothing. In the early morning gloom they saw a man standing on the beach, but did not recognize him or realise that he was Jesus.

'Have you caught anything?' he called.

'No.'

'Try throwing the net to starboard.'

They did so, and immediately the net filled with fish. Peter remembered how, long ago, after a similar great haul, Jesus had told them they would catch men for him. 'It is the Lord!' he said.

After they had brought the net to land, they found a fire burning and breakfast already cooking. It was still too dark to see clearly. None of the disciples dared ask Jesus if it were he; but they knew it was, especially when he blessed and broke bread and gave it to them with fish to eat.

After breakfast, Jesus asked three times, 'Simon, do you love me?' Each time Peter answered, 'Lord, you know I do.' He was hurt at being asked three times, but each time wiped out one of the denials in the High Priest's courtyard. 'Shepherd my people,' said Jesus, 'and follow me.'

So Jesus showed himself to his friends for many days until it was time for him to ascend to his Father.

women were right. Jesus was alive. He had met him and talked to him. There was no doubt, no doubt at all.

He had barely finished talking when two disciples who had walked late that afternoon to Emmaus, a village outside Jerusalem, burst in panting. They had run all the way back because Jesus had joined them, showing them from the Scriptures why the Messiah had had to die. They had not recognized him in the twilight, though their hearts had flamed within them as he talked, nor in the dimly-lit

The Ascension
Acts 1

Jesus continued to appear to his disciples for some time after his resurrection. During this time he taught them more about the Kingdom of God although there was much that they did not understand until later. When the time drew near for him to leave the world and ascend to his Father, he told them not to leave Jerusalem until God's promise to them was fulfilled. He reminded them of what he had told them about this promise. 'You remember,' he said, 'that John baptized with water. But in a short time you will be baptized with the Holy Spirit.'

Yet right to the end, even on their last walk with Jesus to the Mount of Olives, the disciples showed that they still did not understand that Jesus' kingdom was not of this world. In spite of all that had happened, they still thought that he was going to set up an earthly kingdom with a court, an army, judges, ambassadors and other officials. And how certain he could be of success now! All he had to do was to reveal himself to the Sanhedrin and the Romans – the man who had died on a cross, lain in a tomb for nearly forty hours and had risen from the dead. They would have to accept him as King of the Jews.

So they asked, 'Are you now going to make Israel the ruling nation of the whole world?' But he told them, 'It is not for you to know the times when future events are to happen. This is God's business. But when the Holy Spirit comes upon you, you will receive power which will enable you to tell the world about me, beginning in Judaea and Samaria and then going on to every country in the world.'

He lifted up his hands and blessed them, and in the very act of blessing he was taken from them. Just as had happened at the Transfiguration a cloud overshadowed and hid him from their sight. Some people think that this was no ordinary cloud but the one which came down on the Tabernacle in Moses' time, showing the glory of the presence of God. When the cloud lifted from the place where Jesus had been standing, the disciples stood gazing up into heaven.

As they stood there, two men in white appeared and said to them, 'Galileans, why do you stand there looking up into the sky? Jesus, who has just gone from you into heaven, will one day return in his human shape, just as you have seen him go.'

The disciples knew then for certain that they would see Jesus no more until he returned in glory. They believed that this would be in a very short time, and returned to Jerusalem to wait for the promised baptism with the Holy Spirit, though they could not imagine how this would happen.

There was one thing that had to be done. Jesus had chosen twelve apostles, one for each of the tribes of Israel. By his betrayal of Jesus, Judas had forfeited his place among them, and this had to be filled. Peter suggested

that the number should be made up by someone who had been a disciple all the time Jesus had been with them on earth. There were not many men who had been faithful followers all that time, and two names were put forward, Joseph, who was surnamed Justus, and Matthias. They decided to pray to God and that he would show them which of the two he had chosen, then they cast lots. Matthias was selected; and the followers of Christ were happy to know that once again there were twelve apostles to represent the tribes of Israel in the kingdom that was to come.

The Coming of the Holy Spirit

Acts 2

Pentecost, a harvest festival and the anniversary of the giving of the Law to Moses, was celebrated fifty days after the Passover. Thousands of Jews from all over the world came to Jerusalem for the feast, and a babble of languages could be heard in the streets.

At Pentecost the disciples gathered together, probably in a room within the Temple courts. It was nine o'clock in the morning, the hour of public prayer. Suddenly there seemed to come from above the building a noise like a fierce wind rushing through the room. Above them, hovering under the ceiling, gleamed what looked like a mass of fire; and as they watched, it separated into individual flames which floated through the air and flickered over the head of every disciple present. They felt flowing through them a tremendous power and ecstasy unlike anything they had known in their lives before. One or two of them began to speak, but in languages they did not know. More and more joined in until all the disciples were shouting praises to God in foreign tongues at the tops of their voices; some laughing, some weeping with emotion and exaltation, as they felt themselves seized and uplifted by the power of the Holy Spirit sweeping through them.

Round the building where they had met, crowds quickly gathered, wondering what the commotion could be. The disciples poured out into the open air, still shouting praises to God

in foreign languages, so that they could be heard throughout the Temple courts. Quickly, little knots of people surrounded individual disciples. Here one talked Persian; there another spoke beautifully in Greek; a third praised God in Arabic; a fourth sang a Coptic psalm.

The crowd was dumbfounded. 'These are Galileans,' they said, 'who can barely speak their own language properly. How is it that every one of us hears them praising God so beautifully in our native tongues?' Some of the onlookers who heard the shouting and saw the disciples laughing and weeping with ecstasy, said contemptuously, 'They're drunk!'

But Peter heard them. When the noise had quietened a little, he called the other apostles to him and together they faced the crowds. The foreign tongues died away into silence. Peter's voice rang out clearly to the puzzled Jews. They stopped talking to each other and listened intently to his words.

'Fellow-Jews,' he said, 'we are not drunk, for it is still the hour of prayer; and no Jew eats or drinks on a feast-day until the hour has passed. No. What you have seen and heard is a fulfilment of the prophet Joel who prophesied a great outpouring of the Holy Spirit in the last days. Everyone then who calls upon God will be saved.

'Israelites, listen closely. You all know of Jesus of Nazareth who worked miracles and signs among you. It was you who gave him up to heathen men to crucify. But this was God's will, for he raised him from the dead, as David, who was his ancestor, prophesied he would. My friends and I know this to be true, for we have seen him alive with our own eyes. Raised from the dead, Jesus gave the Holy Spirit which he had received from God, as he promised. All you have heard and seen this morning is the work of the Spirit flowing from him. Let all Israel know for certain that God has made Jesus Lord and Messiah.'

The Jews were filled with remorse when they heard what Peter said, for they knew that Jesus had been crucified unjustly. 'What must we do?' they asked. 'Repent of your sins and be baptized in the name of Jesus,' replied Peter, 'and you will receive the Holy Spirit.' So successful was his preaching that that day three thousand of his hearers became followers of Christ.

241

The Martyrdom of Stephen

Acts 4–7

The time following Pentecost was almost as wonderful as the feast itself. Day by day new disciples were won over by the apostles' preaching; and they did many miracles so that there was a sense of lasting wonder at the power and goodness of God. Many even of the priests became Christians and members of the Church, as the community was later called. This is evidence that the Resurrection really did happen; for the priests could easily have proved it untrue by producing Jesus' body if it had still been in the tomb.

The first Christians believed that Jesus would return in glory in a very short time. There was little sense in keeping land or property if they were soon going to be with him, so they sold anything they possessed and used the money to provide food for all the Church members. They worshipped joyfully in the Temple every day and were held in great favour by the people.

There was opposition, too. The apostles were arrested by the Sanhedrin, imprisoned, forbidden to preach, released, imprisoned again, flogged and again imprisoned. But nothing could silence them, and a wise member of the Sanhedrin advised the others to take no further action against them. 'From time to time,' he said, 'movements like this begin and come to nothing. Their leaders perish and their followers are scattered. If this movement is not inspired by God, it will meet the same fate. But if God is with these men as they say, we may find ourselves fighting against him.'

A number of Greeks who had become Jews by religion and were called proselytes joined the followers of Jesus. The poor among them shared the food and goods which were divided among all the Church members; but the proselytes complained that they were given less than those who were born Jews. So the apostles chose seven men to see that the food was given fairly. One of them was called Stephen. He proved to be a man of great power, full of the Holy Spirit, who not only worked miracles but preached and argued successfully against learned men from the synagogues. They were no match for him; and they became so jealous of his success and felt so helpless against him that they found false witnesses to accuse him of blaspheming God and Moses. He was hauled before the Sanhedrin and charged with saying that Jesus of Nazareth would destroy the Temple and change the ancient customs handed down from Moses.

Stephen was allowed to speak in his own defence. He traced the history of Israel from Abraham down to Solomon, showing how the people had always rebelled against the good leaders who had tried to show them the way to God. 'You are just like your fathers,' he ended. 'Which prophet did they not persecute? They killed those who foretold the coming of the Messiah; you killed the Messiah himself.'

The Sanhedrin were beside themselves with rage. But Stephen, looking up, saw a vision of the skies parting. 'Look!' he said. 'I see the Son of Man at God's right hand.' This was more than his listeners could stand. With hands over their ears so that they should not hear such blasphemy, they rushed at Stephen, dragged him out of the city and stoned him to death. They took off their outer clothes to do this and laid them at the feet of a zealous young Pharisee called Saul, who approved of what they were doing. Stephen died crying out, 'Lord Jesus, receive my spirit. And do not hold this sin against them.' So died the first Christian martyr after Jesus himself.

N Dear

The Vision on the Damascus Road

Acts 9; 22, 1–21; 26, 4–21

Stephen's death marked the beginning of a great persecution of those who followed the Way, as Jesus' teaching came to be called. Since Pentecost, when even some priests became Christians, the followers of Jesus became numbered not in tens but in thousands; and their enemies felt that the movement had to be stamped out as quickly and thoroughly as possible. Many Christians fled from Jerusalem; but this was good, for everywhere they went they carried the good news of Jesus and the Kingdom.

Saul, who had guarded the clothes of those who had stoned Stephen, was a strict and zealous Pharisee and one of the most bitter opponents of Christianity. The high priest gave him letters to the synagogues at Damascus giving him authority to arrest all followers of Jesus and bring them bound, to Jerusalem. The high priest was delighted to help Saul. He would not have been so pleased, had he been able to foresee the future.

For when Saul was not far from Damascus, a light from the sky, more brilliant than the sun, flashed round him and his companions. They all fell to the ground. Saul heard a voice, and the men with him perhaps heard sounds but could not distinguish words. The voice called, 'Saul, Saul, why are you persecuting me? It is difficult for you to go on doing what you know deep down to be wrong.'

'Who are you, Master?' asked Saul, his eyes blinded by the light.

'I am Jesus of Nazareth whom you are persecuting.'

'What shall I do, Lord?'

'Get up and go into the city and you will be told. I am going to send you to take the gospel to the Gentiles, and I shall keep you safe in dangers both from them and your own

N. Dear

people. You will so influence the Gentiles that, by faith in me, they will have their sins forgiven and win a place with those whom God has made his own.'

The voice ceased. Slowly Saul's companions got to their feet. But he remained still huddled on the ground. Gently they raised him, but he was dazed with shock and completely blind. They took him to a house in Damascus where he stayed for three days neither eating nor drinking but thinking over what had happened and praying. On the third day, a disciple of Jesus in Damascus called Ananias had a vision. He heard the voice of God telling him to go to Saul whom he would find at prayer. Saul himself was told, also in a vision, that Ananias would come to him, lay hands upon him and restore his sight.

At first Ananias was afraid. 'Lord, I have heard of this man,' he said, 'and how he has persecuted your followers in Jerusalem. I know, too, that he has come to arrest your people here.'

'Go,' said God in the vision, 'I have chosen this man to carry the good news of Jesus both to the Gentiles and their rulers and to the Jews.'

Ananias obeyed. He sought out Saul and, laying his hands on his head, said, 'The Lord Jesus who appeared to you on the Damascus road has sent me so that your blindness may be healed and that you may be filled with the Holy Spirit.' At once there fell from Saul's eyes what looked like scales of skin, and he could see again clearly. He was immediately baptized; he ate and drank, and recovered his strength.

Soon, to the astonishment of all who knew him, he was in the synagogues proclaiming Jesus as the Son of God. Opponents of the Way could not defeat him in argument; for here was no ignorant Galilean peasant but a man of genius, deeply learned in the Scriptures. The Christian career of the man who did more than any other human being to spread the good news of Jesus had begun.

Peter and Cornelius
Acts 10; 11, 1–15

There was stationed at Caesarea a centurion called Cornelius. He was a Gentile and a God-fearer, as the Jews called those who admired their religion but were not prepared actually to be converted and become proselytes. He gave alms generously and prayed regularly to God.

One afternoon he had a vision. An angel appeared to him who said, 'Cornelius, God has heard your prayers and seen the good you do. Send to Joppa for a man called Simon Peter who is staying with Simon the tanner in his house by the sea.' The angel vanished without more explanation. Cornelius called two servants and a soldier who was also a God-fearer. He told them of the vision and sent them to Joppa, a day's journey away.

About noon the following day, Peter was on the house-top praying. He grew hungry; and while a meal was being prepared downstairs, he had a kind of waking dream. He saw the sky part and, descending from the rift in it, a great sail let down by ropes tied to its corners. In the sail were all kinds of creatures, four-legged animals, crawling reptiles and birds of every sort. As Peter looked at them, a voice said, 'Rise, Peter. Kill and eat.' 'No, Lord, no,' Peter answered, 'I have never eaten unclean food in my life.' The voice replied, 'You must not consider unclean anything that God has made clean.' Three times the words were repeated; then the sail was hauled up again into the sky.

Peter was still wondering what the dream could mean when Cornelius' messengers arrived. When he met them and heard the story of the centurion's vision, he knew that he must go with them and could do so without fear. The next day they set out together for Caesarea.

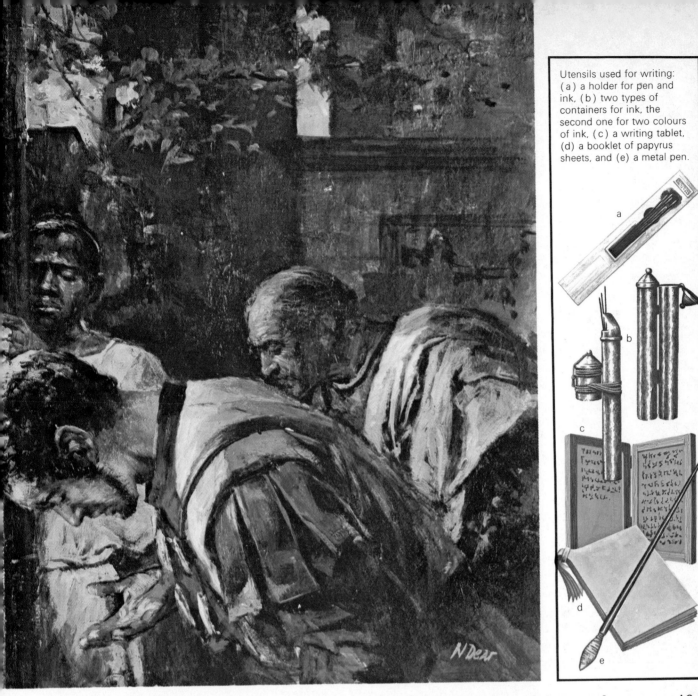

Utensils used for writing: (a) a holder for pen and ink, (b) two types of containers for ink, the second one for two colours of ink, (c) a writing tablet, (d) a booklet of papyrus sheets, and (e) a metal pen.

Peter found Cornelius eagerly awaiting him with his house full of relatives and close friends. As the apostle approached, the centurion bowed to him almost as if he had been a god, but Peter raised him to his feet. 'Stand up,' he said. 'I am an ordinary man, like any other.'

When he saw the crowd Cornelius had invited to meet him, Peter suddenly realized the meaning of his vision of the sail. 'You know,' he said, 'that a Jew is not allowed to visit a man of a different race. But God has shown me in a waking dream that I must not consider any man unclean. Why have you sent for me?'

Cornelius repeated the story of his vision, ending, 'We have all met here before God to hear what he has ordered you to say.'

Peter replied, 'I understand now that God has no favourites, but welcomes from every nation any man who fears him and does what is right.' He went on to tell them about Jesus, how he went about doing good, was crucified and rose from the dead. He ended, 'All the prophets speak of him and say that those who believe in him will have their sins forgiven.'

While Peter was still speaking, the Holy Spirit fell on the whole gathering. Everyone was seized with ecstasy and began speaking in different tongues. Peter and his Jewish companions were astounded that Gentiles should receive the Spirit; but he realized that he could not refuse baptism to Spirit-filled believers, whatever their race. In the name of Jesus Christ he baptized Cornelius, his family and friends.

When news spread to the church throughout Judaea that Peter had baptized Gentiles, many Jewish Christians objected. But once Peter had described his vision and how Cornelius had been guided to send for him, their complaints ceased. Realizing that God had given Gentiles the chance of repentance and eternal life, they were full of praise to him.

247

The Philippian Jailer
Acts 16

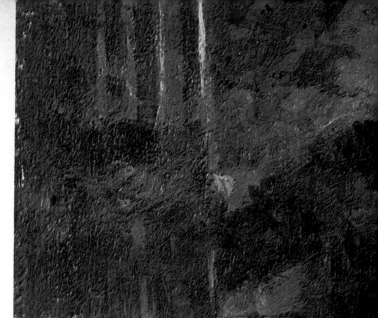

After his conversion Saul, given the Christian name of Paul, travelled round the countries of the eastern Mediterranean preaching the good news of Jesus Christ to both Jews and Gentiles. He did this in three great missionary journeys. The first took him to Cyprus and then through what is today called Asia Minor. On the second, after revisiting his Christian friends in Asia Minor, he crossed into Greece to the city of Philippi.

There, while Paul and his companion Silas were walking on the Sabbath day to a Jewish place of prayer outside the city, they were followed by a slave-girl who had strange gifts of fortune-telling. By these, she brought much money to her owners from people who paid her to tell their fortunes. She shouted after Paul and Silas, 'These men are servants of God most high. They can tell you how to be saved.' Day after day she cried after them until Paul, losing patience, turned and said, 'Spirit, come out of the girl.' Immediately she lost her gift and could tell fortunes no more.

Realizing that they would make no more money out of her, her owners were furious. Supported by a yelling mob, they violently dragged Paul and Silas off to the city magistrates. 'These rascally Jews,' they cried, 'are disturbing the city, telling us Romans to follow illegal customs.' The noise was so great that the Christians were unable to make themselves heard. Without giving them a chance to defend themselves, the magistrates ordered them to be stripped, flogged and thrown into prison, ordering the jailer to keep them under close guard. He put them in the innermost prison and locked their feet in the stocks.

Paul and Silas were undismayed, passing the hours in singing praises to God. Suddenly, at midnight, an earthquake shook the prison to its foundations. The doors sprang open. The chains holding the prisoners fell from the walls. The jailer, startled from his sleep, was dismayed to see the open doors. Thinking that the prisoners had fled, he drew his sword to kill himself; for not only would their escape have meant that he had failed in his duty, a terrible disgrace, but he would have been executed himself. But Paul shouted, 'Don't harm yourself. We are all here.'

The jailer ordered lights to be brought and the other prisoners to be secured. But believing that the earthquake was due in some strange way to Paul and Silas, he bowed in terror before them and escorted them from the prison into his own home.

'Sirs,' he asked them, 'what must I do to be saved?'

'Believe in the Lord Jesus Christ,' they replied, 'and you and your whole household will be saved.' And they explained to him who Jesus was and what faith in him meant.

He washed their hurts and gave them food. Then he was at once baptized with everyone in his family, and all of them found great joy in their new-found belief in God.

The next morning the magistrates ordered the jailer to let the men go. He was delighted to give Paul and Silas the message, but Paul said, 'No. We are free-born Roman citizens. We have the right to be tried for any wrong we are supposed to have done. But the magistrates had the insolence to flog us publicly without a trial, Roman citizens though we are. They imprisoned us, and now they're trying to get rid of us on the sly. No, indeed. They won't get away with that. We will not go unless they escort us out themselves.'

The magistrates were alarmed, for flogging Roman citizens without a trial could bring them into serious trouble. They came to Paul and Silas, apologized to them, led them from the jail and begged them to leave Philippi. So, after saying goodbye to their friends, the two men went their way in peace.

The kind of ship that Paul might have sailed in, which carried as many as 276 passengers. Ships were sailed usually by one big sail on a single mast. Navigation was entirely by the stars or the sun, as the compass did not exist.

Paul at Jerusalem

Acts 20–23

After his third missionary journey Paul went to Jerusalem to attend the feast of Pentecost. There were moments of sadness on the way, for everywhere the Spirit had revealed to his friends that they would not see him again and that troubles and imprisonment awaited him in the city.

When he arrived, Paul told James, Jesus' brother, all that God had done among the Gentiles. James was delighted with the report but said, 'Hundreds of Jewish believers here have heard untrue stories that you teach the Jews living among the Gentiles not to follow the law of Moses. Now there are four men among us who have made special promises to God and are purifying themselves very carefully in the Temple. They have to make expensive sacrifices. Prove to everyone in Jerusalem that you honour the law of Moses by purifying yourself with them and by paying their expenses.'

Paul agreed and visited the Temple every day to purify himself. Outside the Temple he saw his Gentile friends as usual; and certain hostile Jews, seeing him in the city with an Ephesian called Trophimus, assumed, when they later saw him in the Temple, that he had smuggled Trophimus into the holy building. They seized Paul, screaming, 'Israelites, help us! This is the wretch who attacks our religion and law and this Temple all over the world. And now he has profaned this holy place by bringing Gentiles into it.' A shrieking mob dragged Paul from the Temple, and soon the city was in such an uproar that a company of Roman soldiers came running to restore order. They arrested Paul, but when their commander tried to discover what he had done, there were so many different accusations that he could make no sense of what was said. He ordered Paul to be taken into the barracks, and so violent was the crowd that he had to be carried through it by the soldiers.

The apostle asked permission to address the crowd from the steps of the barracks. They listened quietly while he told them of his experience on the Damascus road, but when he said that God had sent him to the Gentiles, uproar broke out again. The Roman commander, not understanding the reason for the riot, prepared to flog Paul into confessing what he had done: but when he told him he was a free-born Roman citizen who could not be flogged unless convicted of a crime, the officer hastily released him.

The next day he took Paul before the Sanhedrin to discover what accusation the Jews where bringing against him. The council consisted partly of Sadducees, who did not believe in life after death, and partly of Pharisees, who did; and Paul cleverly won half the Sanhedrin to his side by saying, 'I am a Pharisee, and this trial is really about life after death.' The Sadducees and Pharisees began to quarrel so fiercely that the commander was afraid they would tear Paul to pieces. He hauled him from among them back to the barracks.

The day following, about forty Jews who hated Paul, plotted to murder him. 'Ask the commander to bring him to you for further questioning,' they told the Sanhedrin, 'and we will ambush him on the way.' Fortunately, Paul's nephew heard of the conspiracy and informed the commander. That night, accompanied by a strong escort of soldiers, Paul was hurried away secretly to Felix, the governor of the province. Although he did not know it at the time, this was his first stage on the journey to Rome, where God had promised him that he would preach the Gospel in the very capital of the Empire.

The Road to Rome

Acts 24–28

Paul did not go immediately to Rome. For two years he stayed in Caesarea, defending himself against the Jews in three court hearings, once before Felix, the governor, then before Festus, the next governor, and finally before King Agrippa, the last of the Herods. At the second hearing he claimed his right as a Roman citizen to be judged by the emperor himself. This was perhaps unfortunate as Agrippa affirmed that Paul was innocent and could have been freed if he had not appealed to Caesar.

As he had done so, he eventually set sail for Rome as a prisoner. He was handed over to a centurion called Julius who treated him with great kindness. They sailed first to Asia Minor where Paul visited his old friends; there they changed ships and after many days of difficult sailing reached Crete. Paul, an experienced traveller, knowing that the stormy season was about to begin, warned Julius not to sail, and advised him to winter in the island; but the centurion took the advice of the sailing-master and captain, who wanted to hurry on. When a favourable breeze sprang up, they put out to sea.

But soon the breeze turned into a howling north-easter, driving them away from the land. The ship ran before it under the shelter of a small island where the sailors managed to strengthen her by passing ropes under her and lashing their ends together to prevent the planks from bursting apart. Afraid of striking quicksands nearby, they lowered sail and ran before the wind. Next day, they lightened the ship by throwing its furniture overboard, and on the third day they threw overboard spare sails, rigging and everything else they could to prevent her sinking.

Day after day the storm raged. They saw no sun by day nor stars at night. The crew began to despair of ever reaching land.

But Paul gave them hope. 'Only the ship will be lost,' he said. 'Last night I saw in a vision an angel of God who told me that I must appear before Caesar and that not a single one of you would lose his life.'

During the fourteenth night of the storm, the sailors sensed they were near land. Taking soundings, they found the water getting steadily shallower; and, when daylight came, they saw a bay with a sandy beach on to which they tried to run the ship. The bow stuck fast while the stern was pounded by the waves. The soldiers wanted to kill the prisoners in case any should escape, but Julius forbade this and ordered everyone to get to land as best he could. Some swam, some floated on bits of the ship, and all of the two hundred and seventy-six on board came safely to shore.

They found they were on the island of Malta. The inhabitants were kind to them, making a bonfire to warm them against the cold and wet. Paul picked up some sticks to throw on the fire and a viper, driven out by the heat, fastened on his hand. The islanders, expecting him to drop dead, muttered to each other, 'This must be a murderer whom God will not allow to live even though he has escaped drowning.' But when nothing happened to Paul, they said, 'He must be a god!'

They remained three months in Malta, during which Paul healed many people, including the chief magistrate's father. When he and his companions finally sailed for Rome, they were greatly honoured by the Maltese.

At last Paul reached Rome where he was welcomed by his fellow-Christians. There he lived for two years awaiting trial, teaching the truth about Jesus Christ first to the Jews, then to anyone who would listen. The Bible tells us no more of him than this; but when Nero became emperor, he persecuted the Christians, and Paul is said to have been crucified by him like the Master he had so faithfully served.

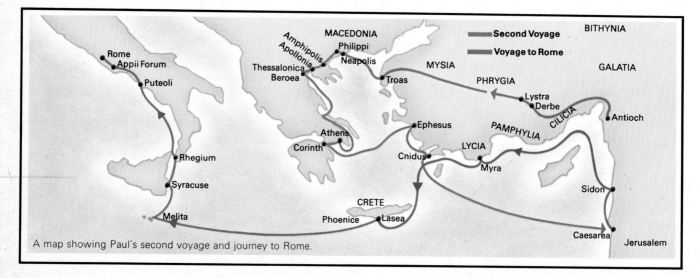

A map showing Paul's second voyage and journey to Rome.

The New Jerusalem

Revelation 21–22

The Bible begins with the creation of the world. It closes with a vision of the end of all things, which is at the same time the beginning of God's creation of the New Jerusalem. There, all who love him from every nation will live and be happy with him for evermore. John, who wrote Revelation, the last book in the Bible, had a vision in which he saw the perfect city that would one day be. He could express what he saw only in terms of the most beautiful things known to men; but Heaven is not Heaven because it is made of gold and precious stones, but because it is the place where those who love him live in the presence of God.

'I saw a new heaven and new earth,' wrote

John, where there was no longer any restless sea to separate men from each other and those they love. I saw new Jerusalem coming down from heaven and heard a voice proclaiming, "At last God will live with men and they with him, and there shall be no more death nor weeping nor pain." The city needed no sun nor moon, for it shone with the glory of God within it, like the brilliance of a diamond. It had a high wall made of diamond with twelve gates, three on each side, each gate guarded by an angel; in the wall were twelve foundation stones, and on them the names of the twelve apostles. The foundation stones were made of twelve different precious stones, like those in the High Priest's breastplate, showing the holiness of the city; and the buildings within the walls were made of gold, pure and clear as glass. Each gate was made of a single pearl and bore the name of a tribe of Israel, the Chosen People of God.

'The city was as high as it was broad as it was long. This also showed its holiness, because the Holy of Holies in both the Tabernacle and the Temple had been a perfect cube. There was no Temple in the city, because God himself was its Temple. There was no night, for the light of God shone always, and the gates of the city were ever open to receive everything rich and splendid, provided that it was also good, honest and free from any stain of evil.

'Down the centre of the city ran a wide street and in the middle of the street there flowed from the throne of God the river of the water of life sparkling like crystal. On either side was a grove of the tree of life bearing a different crop of fruit every month of the year. The leaves were used to heal all the nations of the world.

Those who dwelt within the city came not only from the Chosen People of Israel, but consisted of all those inscribed in God's book of life, a vast throng beyond counting, drawn from all tribes, peoples and languages. In that city they shall see God face to face, and they shall live with him for ever.'

John's vision ended with words of Christ himself. 'I am coming soon to reward everybody according to his deeds. Happy are those who live good lives; for they will have the right to enter the New Jerusalem and eat of the tree of life. Come all of you who are thirsty. Drink the water of life which I give freely to all who desire it.'

John echoed the words of the promise of Christ, 'Oh, yes, Lord Jesus – come quickly!' and ended with a blessing to all readers of his book, 'The grace of the Lord Jesus be with all God's people. Amen.'